Understanding the Business of Global Media in the Digital Age

This new introductory textbook provides students with the tools they need to understand the way digital technologies have transformed the global media business of the 21st century. Focusing on three main approaches—media economics, critical political economy, and production studies—the authors provide an empirically rich analysis of ownership, organizational structures and culture, business strategies, markets, networks of strategic alliances, and state policies as they relate to global media. Examples throughout involve both traditional and digital media and are taken from different regions and countries to illustrate how the media business is influenced by interconnected historical, political, economic, and social factors. In addition to introducing today's convergent world of global media, the book gives readers a greater understanding of their own potential roles within the global media industries.

Micky Lee is an Associate Professor of Media Studies at Suffolk University, Boston, USA. She has published in feminist political economy, information and communication technologies, and finance, information, and the media.

Dal Yong Jin is Professor in the School of Communication at Simon Fraser University, Canada. His major research and teaching interests are in social media and platform technologies, mobile technologies and game studies, media (de-)convergence, globalization and media, transnational cultural studies, and the political economy of media.

Understanding the Business of Global Media in the Digital Age

Micky Lee and
Dal Yong Jin

Routledge
Taylor & Francis Group

NEW YORK AND LONDON

First published 2018
by Routledge
711 Third Avenue, New York, NY 10017

and by Routledge
2 Park Square, Milton Park, Abingdon, Oxon OX14 4RN

Routledge is an imprint of the Taylor & Francis Group, an informa business

Library of Congress Cataloging-in-Publication Data
A catalog record for this book has been requested

ISBN: 978-1-138-68896-4 (hbk)
ISBN: 978-1-138-68898-8 (pbk)
ISBN: 978-1-315-53796-2 (ebk)

Typeset in Berling and Futura
by Apex CoVantage, LLC

eResources are available for this title at: www.routledge.com/9781138688988

Printed and bound by CPI Group (UK) Ltd, Croydon, CR0 4YY

Contents

Illustrations

Tables

Figures

Introduction and Overview

At the end of the chapter, students will be able to:

- list economic decisions that consumers make;
- differentiate economic from business decisions in the media industry;
- suggest how an approach would lead to different sets of questions asked about the media industry;
- state how the five objectives relate to students' career goals;
- explain why an economy lens is inadequate to understand the media business.

We want you to think about the last film that you watched or the last song that you listened to. We want you to think about what *economic* decisions you made to watch the film or listen to the song. For example, how much did you pay to watch the film or listen to the song? If you did not pay for it but got it for "free," who paid on your behalf? What were other ways that you could watch the same film or listen to the same song? If there were alternatives, why did you choose one way over others?

We asked ourselves the same questions, and one of us wrote:

I watched a documentary film directed by an Asian American based in San Francisco. The filmmaker uploaded the film on Vimeo—a video-sharing website developed in the U.S.—and provided me with the password. I watched it for "free," but only because I was deciding whether the college library should purchase a copy. If I did not watch it on Vimeo, I could purchase a copy of the film for personal use. I did not choose the alternative because I watched it for work and I knew the personal copy cannot be used for classroom screening. I knew the filmmaker would allow me to preview it for "free" if I would eventually ask the library to buy a "public screening" copy that costs fifteen times more than a personal copy. I made a series of *economic* decisions to watch the film: I have limited money to spend so I have to decide how I should spend it; I also have limited time to find out the alternatives so I have to balance how much I want to spend with how much time I want to spend to find out about the alternative means.

Now we want you to think from the point of view of the producers: what kinds of *business* decisions did they make so that their products can be delivered to the consumers? For example, how did the producers price their products? How much profit did they make from your purchase? How did they decide the platforms on which their products are delivered? Do you think they are aware that their products are available "for free"? If they are aware of the fact, what decisions were made to provide a "free" copy or to control the circulation of "free" copies?

For the Asian American filmmaker, her markets are mainly educational institutions, community centers, and public television. Film screening for students and community members requires a "public screening license" even if the audience does not pay to see the film. Therefore, a public viewing copy is priced much higher than a personal copy. The filmmaker probably takes in almost every dollar paid by the library. Because she owns the copyrights of her film, she does not need to pay another party when she sells a copy of the film. Her film can only be viewed from three platforms: DVD, Vimeo, and online streaming. She distributes her own work so it is not available on any rental service. However, the film is available on an online educational streaming service that is subscribed to by university libraries. Anyone with access to the database can watch the film. Because she provided me with the password to preview the film on Vimeo, many others must have watched the film this way. Why would she trust that

I do not show the Vimeo copy in class? First, both she and I know that the video quality is low; the image does not look good enough for a big screen. Second, both she and I know that libraries usually have a budget to acquire educational films, so instructors rarely pay out of their own pocket for a public viewing copy. The above shows that the filmmaker has made a series of *business* decisions so that her products can be delivered to the audience and that she can make enough money to cover the cost of producing, distributing, and marketing the film.

After answering the sets of questions on economic and business decisions, which set was easier to answer? We believe the set about *economic* choices is probably easier than the set about *business* decisions. As a media consumer, you are presented with choices: whether you should pay for the products or not; which platform you choose to enjoy the products; what alternative products and platforms there are. You have probably consciously asked yourselves this set of questions as a consumer. However, a media consumer rarely thinks from a business perspective; that's why the second set of questions may be more difficult to answer. This book is written to help you answer the second set of questions. One way to do this is to switch from thinking from a media consumer perspective to a media producer one. This book guides you through questions that media producers ask when they engage in the business.

Objectives of the Book

To guide readers to ask questions about business decisions, this book has five objectives. In the following, we will explain each of them by drawing on the exercise that we did at the beginning of the chapter.

Objective 1: We Aim to Provide an Overview of the Transformation of the Business of Media as a Result of Digital Technologies

In the exercise, we ask readers to think about what alternatives there are to watching a film or listening to a song. You could watch a film on a DVD, but you could also go to a movie theater or stream it online. If you live stream a movie, you could watch it on your computer, through your game console, or on your handheld device. The same goes for how you listen to a song: you could download it online, but you could also live stream it from a service or satellite radio. If you ask someone from an older generation how they used to watch a film or listen to a song, they would probably think it is a strange question, because there were hardly any choices: to watch a film, they would go to a movie theater; to listen to a song, they would buy a vinyl record.

Digital technologies allow users to have more choices to consume media products. Media producers make conscious business decisions about how their products can be distributed through an array of digital means. Because of the expansion of distribution options, "traditional" media companies such as broadcasting stations and film studios have been exploring different ways to deliver content. As a result, you may not even go to the theater to watch films anymore, because you exclusively rely on online streaming.

At the same time, you may find that some content is only available from an online streaming service. The reason is that "new" media companies are entering the content production market. These companies make shows that are only available on their own platform. Because of the blurred boundary between who produces the content, who invents the technologies, and who distributes the content, this book does not present the industry as a collective of individual entities (such as film, television, music, newspaper, magazine, and so on). Instead, we present the industry as something always in flux, something that keeps on changing because of the rapid change in digital technologies.

Objective 2: We Aim to Provide Examples From Different Regions and/or Countries to Illustrate How the Media Business Is Influenced by Historical, Political, Economic, and Social Factors

Both authors were born and educated in East Asia. They also worked there before moving to North America for graduate studies. Coming from one region to another allows us to understand there is neither a *given* nor a best way to how media industries should be run. In the 1960s, the American media industry was already powerful enough to export Hollywood films and American popular music to East Asia. Many Hollywood studios set up local branches in East Asian countries so that US films would be subtitled/dubbed and marketed locally. On the other hand, some American products remain unpopular in East Asian markets: US magazines may be bought in very specialized bookstores, but they are not readily available on regular newspaper stands.

Therefore, it is wrong to assume that the US industry overwhelmingly dominates industries of other countries.

Also, some media technologies were more advanced in East Asia before iPhone was launched. When we travel to East Asia from North America, it is always amazing to see how advanced mobile technologies are in Asia. Unlike the laissez-faire market system in North America, governments such as South Korea and Japan often intervene in markets. For example, after WWII, the Japanese government designated that the audiovisual equipment industry be bolstered. As a result, brands such as Sony and Panasonic became well known outside East Asia.

The above examples show that power relations between global media and information technologies are ambiguous at local, regional, and international levels. There is no universal rule stipulating how much a state should let the market alone. As a result, what media goods and technologies the audiences get are results of the interplay between international and national politics, between the state and the market. We illustrate these power relations by giving examples from North America, Europe, Latin America,[1] the Middle East, Africa, and Asia.

Objective 3: To Introduce Three Approaches—Media Economics, Critical Political Economy, and Production Studies—to Study the Media and Communication Industries by Discussing the Merits and Shortcomings of Each Approach

We asked you to consider two sets of questions at the very beginning of the chapter: one set is economic decision-making from a consumer's perspective; the other set is business decision-making from a producer's perspective. Both sets of questions are asked from a specific theoretical standpoint: namely, a media economic perspective. From this perspective, both the consumers and producers ask how limited resources should be allocated. If there is unlimited money and time, then there is not much of an economic decision to be made. From the other two approaches (critical political economy and production studies), we ask different sets of questions.

Although we asked questions from a media economic perspective at the beginning of the chapter, your answers may draw on both critical political economic and production studies approaches. For example, you may have watched a film by downloading the file on an online sharing site. Despite the fact that the film industry calls piracy a criminal activity, you probably did not do it to break the law. Some users download media files online because the products are not available in their region or because they feel the studios are making enough money already. Political economists discuss issues such as copyrights and profits.

A production studies perspective may have also informed your answers. For example, you may have uploaded your work on Vimeo, so you know why media producers allow the audience to watch their work without paying. You know that Vimeo is a vehicle for you to promote your work and establish your brand. If you believe media producers are not only employees, but also professionals who need to develop their identities in the industry, you are already thinking about the industry from a production studies approach.

As illustrated from the above, each of the three different approaches (media economics, critical political economy, and production studies) guides us to ask a different set of questions in the book. None of them is privileged over the other two because no one single approach asks *all* the questions there are to ask about the media industry. We need to emphasize, however, that the three approaches come from different traditions. Therefore, advanced students in media studies may need to differentiate between them and explain the merits and shortcomings of each of the approaches.

Objective 4: To Understand the Media Business Through the Lenses of Economies, Politics, Technologies, Civil Societies, Cultures, and Labor

We introduce six lenses to understand the business of media: economies, politics, technologies, civil societies, cultures, and labor. Each of the six lenses will be discussed in a single chapter; the six chapters on lenses will form the bulk of the book. In the next section, we will explain what the lenses are and why they shed new light on the business.

You may wonder whether the business of media is all about money; if yes, then why readers need to know anything other than economics. While business is commonly assumed to be all about money, the example that begins the chapter shows that economic and business decisions are about *more than money*. If money were the only consideration that you have when you watch a film or listen to a song, then you probably would consume the media very differently. In fact, you may not even consume the media at all, because it is not a basic necessity to sustain life.

There may be other considerations that influence how you consume media. For example, the piracy laws in your country may warn you against watching a pirated film (such as one downloaded from file sharing sites). As a good citizen, you decide that you will only watch films legally: buy a ticket at the theater, subscribe to an online streaming service, or buy a copy of the DVD. In another example, your choice may be constrained by technologies. The older generation is less comfortable with downloading media files, so they will watch a film or listen to a song in the most familiar ways, such as in a movie theater or on the radio. In yet another example, your economic decisions are based on who produces the media. While some consumers may not be willing to pay full price to see a film made by a major studio, they may be more willing to pay full price to see an alternative film because they understand that independent artists make very little money. In the last example, media consumption is a cultural activity: your family and friends influence your cultural taste. Seeing the latest *Star Wars* film in a movie theater is unlike seeing other films; it can be a cultural event where fans show off their homemade costumes. In short, economic and business decisions are informed by political ideology, technological competency, and cultural taste.

Objective 5: To Help Students Envision Their Careers in the Communication Industries

Last but not least, this book helps students envision themselves as entry-level workers. Some readers may wonder how this book helps them become better practitioners in the field. Although this is not a book that gives insider tips on how to succeed in the industry, we believe students can better position themselves in the job market by understanding how their future employment is contingent upon a number of factors, such as politics, technologies, and so on. While the news media like to see the economy as the only factor that matters in the job market, issues related to politics, technologies, civil societies, cultures, and labor all affect the labor market and working conditions. That's why we will spend most of the time talking about the six lenses.

In addition to the fourth objective, "to understand the media business through the lenses of economies, politics, technologies, civil societies, cultures, and labor," the first three objectives also position students as future practitioners in the field. The first objective asks readers to look at the media, telecommunications, and technology industries as an interlocking system. While students may assume a particular title (such as video producer) in a particular branch in a media company, the company itself may have business interests in other media industries or business sectors. A broad scope of knowledge enables workers to know how the company runs as a whole. Moreover, the digitization of production also asks practitioners to pick up more roles; job responsibilities are less defined than they used to be. For example, newscasters very often write, edit, and report their own stories. Independent filmmakers direct, film, edit, and market their own films.

The second objective asks readers to pay attention to examples of the media business from different regions of the world. Even though students may plan to work in a specific region as an entry-level worker, there will be more opportunities for them to work overseas as they advance in their career; this is particularly the case if they work for a transnational media corporation. Even if students are determined to stay in one region, media practices in other regions would influence how media are locally produced.

The third objective asks readers to approach the business from three perspectives. While students may prefer one approach to the other two, multiple perspectives enable them to make better economic and business decisions. For example, students who are doing freelance work may want to know how much they should price their labor, how they should establish a professional identity, and how freelancers could negotiate a power relationship with clients. Obviously, it is insufficient to see freelance work as *only* an economic or a cultural activity. Last, multiple perspectives would help students become critical content creators, because there is nothing absolute about how a media business should be understood and—in fact—run. If students are to accept that they can transform the industry by being critical content creators, the industry can indeed be transformed.

Organization of the Book

In this chapter, we provide a roadmap to illustrate how we organize the information in the book. The book is written so that the chapters do not need to be read in order. For example, readers may be more interested in reading about the six lenses before learning about the three approaches. Alternatively, they can start with any of the lenses. We provide indications throughout the book to show where relevant topics can be found.

Chapter 2, "The History of the Study of the Business of Media," begins with the thesis that even though humans have done international trading for a long time, they only began to study business as a discipline in the late 1800s. The earliest business schools did not enjoy the same prestige as they do nowadays. At the beginning, business schools were seen as trade schools. Even though an MBA is seen as a golden ticket to succeed in the business world, few CEOs of the largest media and telecommunications corporations actually studied for one. This may reinforce a myth that talents and passion are the only two factors that matter to success. This myth is also reinforced by books written about the industry: most of them are biographies of pioneers and moguls; few look at the industry comprehensively and critically.

Chapter 3, "Theories and Approaches to Study the Business of Media," introduces the three approaches: media economics, critical political economy of communication, and production studies. We will first lay out the tenets of each of them, and then we compare how they hold different views of a study of communication. Most of the chapter will be devoted to explaining the key theories and concepts in each of the approaches. We argue that the approaches may complement rather than compete with each other.

The next six chapters (Chapters 4–9) introduce and discuss the lenses (economies, politics, technologies, civil societies, cultures, and labor) that we will apply to understand the business of media. The six chapters have an identical structure: first, we use an example to raise questions about the specific lens. Then we will list the broad questions that will be answered in the chapter. Afterwards, we discuss how the three approaches see the lenses. The bulk of the chapter will be devoted to answering the broad questions by drawing on keywords and concepts of the three approaches. Finally, we will present a case study so as to apply the concepts and terms introduced throughout the chapter. We try to incorporate examples outside the United States and Europe, because we believe students learn best when they draw on their knowledge in the local context.

Chapter 4 discusses the first lens: economies. An economy is usually defined as wealth and resources resulting from production and consumption activities. We problematize the singularity of the term "economy" by arguing that the plural form "economies" better captures how economies are viewed and measured. Next, we examine the economy as both a singular and objective concept (such as "the economy is projected to grow by 3% next year") as well as a plural and subjective concept (such as "I feel the country's economy is going downhill"). If the economy is not always singular and objective, then how can it be studied? We conclude the chapter with a case study of an information economy. We show how an information economy can be estimated by comparing the economies of a public company (Google) and a private one (Bloomberg).

Chapter 5 discusses the second lens: politics. Politics is about the governance of people. On the surface, governing people does not seem to relate to resource allocation. But in many ways, politics and economies intertwine in the business of media. For example, how can we punish those who infringe on the private property of others? How can we reward those who develop an industry in accordance to state direction? We argue that the state and economies do not belong to two separate spheres, because the state plays a role in the business of media. The role becomes more complicated when we take into account regional and international political entities. We discuss how political organizations (international, transnational, regional, and national) influence the business of media through strategies (such as multinational production and distribution), media policies (such as the regulation of ownership and content), and regional/international policies (such as intellectual property, technological compatibilities, and standards). We use two case studies (Japanese Cool and the Korean Wave) to show how the Japanese and Korean governments export their popular cultures overseas.

The third lens, technologies, is discussed in Chapter 6. Technologies are the hardware, software, and knowledge through which media products are made and consumed. As the book's title implies, the business of media in the digital age is very different from that in an analog age. In an analog era, software was embedded in hardware. In a digital era, software is separated from hardware. For example, the earliest handheld computer game console had preinstalled games. Players could not buy new games and install them into the console. Once players were bored with the games, they could only buy a new console with other games. Now, the console is a standalone machine; different or new games can be played on the console. In fact, the console can also be used to watch television. Because digitization has brought a radical transformation to the media industry, we can say technologies underscore the discussion of the five other lenses (economies, politics, civil societies, cultures, and labor). In this chapter, we specifically look at how digitization has blurred the boundaries between the industries of media, technology, and telecommunications by discussing how technology and platform companies (such as Apple and Netflix) have expanded into the business of content production and distribution. We use cell phones in Africa as a case study to show that there is no predetermined way to perceive and use a piece of technology.

In Chapter 7, we introduce the civil societies lens. The concepts of civil societies and business seem to be antagonistic, but we argue that making money does not have to be the sole or even primary purpose of a media business. We first problematize the concepts of "public," "civil society," and "community." Then we discuss different business models of nonprofit media organizations, such as public media, state-owned media, and religious media. Next, we look at alternative media that have an anticorporation and anticapitalism stance. We use crowdfunding as a case study to ask if it is for the public and by the public.

Cultures, another antagonistic concept to business, is introduced in Chapter 8. We argue that "culture" is neither a static nor a noneconomic entity. In fact, culture is seen as a kind of wealth and resource; that's why some countries would invest in a "cultural economy" and "cultural capital." Next, we ask how culture is related to the concepts of "audience" and "media participants." Why would the media industry keep on saying that audience taste is "elusive" even though it spends so much on audience research? Also, why would the industry need to do research when media participants spend extra effort to ensure that they are visible online and in the public? Next, we will talk about two types of "cultures": the first type is production culture; the second type is work culture. How do media professionals learn about the practices and norms of the industry? Also, how does the US work culture influence local employees in global offices? We use a case study of marketing a Hollywood film in China to show how a commercialized global culture is made relevant to the Chinese audience.

In the last chapter on lenses (Chapter 9), we turn to the lens of labor. As we stated at the beginning of this chapter, the labor lens is introduced last not because it is the least important, but because the previous five lenses shed light on this one. We want readers to think of themselves as future media employees; therefore, we want them to ask two broad sets of questions: first, whether media workers are professionals; second, whether labor is objective or subjective. If media workers are professionals, what makes them different from doctors and lawyers? At what point in history were media workers seen as professionals? If labor were only objective, then most media workers would be dismayed to know their pay per hour is lower than most manual laborers. The "low pay, long hours" work conditions have not discouraged many aspiring young (or some not-so-young) people from joining the industry—why? Will the concept of "affective labor" be a plausible explanation? That media work is something that people "love" to do instead of something that they have to do because of the money? Affective labor is called flexible labor—what are other kinds of flexible labor? The case study to conclude this chapter is women's work conditions in the industry. It is not a secret that women fare worse than men do in the media industry—in what ways are they discriminated against? How can prospective women workers learn about the work conditions of the industry? What organizations help women to advance in the industry?

Chapter 10 concludes the book by summarizing the key points. We cannot emphasize enough that an understanding of the media business requires a shift in thinking from the perspective of a consumer to that of a producer. To make the shift happen, readers will learn how to ask questions about economic and business decisions. To understand how these decisions are being made, we will provide the necessary tools: three approaches to think about the business, as well as six different lenses through which the business can be critiqued. Digital technologies are the backdrop of the discussion: while we do not believe that technologies have directly changed the business, they have definitely transformed the industry structure and business practices. For one thing, it is impossible to talk about media without taking into consideration platform companies (such as Netflix) or social networking sites (such as Facebook). Finally, we give examples outside North America and Europe to show how the industry and practices are similar but different in Asia, Africa, and South America.

Note

1   Latin American examples are provided by Alexa Miguel of Suffolk University.

The History of the Study of the Business of Media

At the end of the chapter, students will be able to:

- state the value of studying the history of business of media;
- explain why some believe that the best way to learn about business is by doing it;
- briefly state some pioneer work in the media economic, political economic, and production studies approaches;
- explain why scholars are more interested in studying the media industry because of neoliberalism, globalization, and media convergence;
- explain how neoliberalism, globalization, and media convergence have impacted the teaching and learning of media studies in academia.

The titles of some best-selling business books on Amazon.com in 2016 were *The Personal MBA: Master the Art of Business* (Kaufman, 2012), *Grit: The Power of Passion and Perseverance* (Duckworth, 2016), and *Good to Great: Why Some Companies Make the Leap and Others Don't* (Collins, 2001). All these titles promise to reveal secrets to succeed in the business world. These three titles are not limited to specific types of business and professions; the tips are said to be applicable to all kinds of occupations. For example, the authors of *Personal MBA* promise to deliver to readers more wisdom than do the world's most competitive business schools; they believe leaders are self-made, not taught by others. The author of *Grit* suggests that passion and perseverance will lead individuals to great achievement. *Good to Great* examines how good management would lift a company up from mediocre to great.

If popular business books could provide readers with insights into how to succeed in the business world and if readers would become better leaders by heeding the advice, then what is the value—to media studies students in particular—of learning the history of business? We suggest a few reasons why an examination of media business history would shed light on current media business practices. First, the study of business is a very young discipline, even though human beings have traded for a long time. Trading used to be seen as an activity that did not merit study. It was believed that people learn to trade by doing it, not by reading about it. Moreover, in countries influenced by Confucian thought, government officials and scholars have a higher social status than merchants do. Traditionally, those who were not properly educated would become merchants. Clearly, this belief is no longer held as true, as business is one of the most popular subjects in East Asian universities.

The second reason why it is valuable for media studies students to read about the history of media business is that it is neglected in many media studies curricula. Even though communication history is a required class in many curricula, history textbooks tend to downplay the business aspect of the media. On the other hand, textbooks on the business of media tend not to mention the history.

The third reason is that there is little systematic understanding of the media business from a historical perspective, even though many books have been written about media titans, well-known companies, and tips to break into the industry. Popular business books tend to assume that what works in one industry and profession would work in others; they foster the wisdom that all business problems can be solved in the same ways. Therefore, someone who could manage a food and beverage company may as well manage a hi-tech company. The history of Apple Computer illustrates just that: John Sculley, who was once the president of PepsiCo, was tapped to be the CEO after the board pushed out founder Steve Jobs. The decision was later revealed to be unwise: Apple products invented under Sculley's helm were critiqued to be pedestrian; Mac computers had very little market share in the PC market. Many believe that if Steve Jobs had not returned to the company, revolutionary products such as iPod, iPad, and iPhone would not have existed. As we will explore in Chapter 4, "Economies," some aspects of the media business are different from other businesses because consumers' preferences are taste-driven more than price-driven; the cost to reproduce the products is very low. Media business is also different from other businesses because the income gap among workers is extreme: while there are a few top earners, most are not earning enough to make a living. Because the business of media can be idiosyncratic, advice from general business books may not apply to the media industry.

The fourth and last reason why studying the history of media business is important is because aspiring media workers can position themselves better in the industry if they understand the historical socioeconomic background of the media business. While popular business titles strive to make readers successful in both their professional and personal lives, they tend not to ask readers to conceptualize themselves as historical beings. In other words, they rarely point out that social and economic beings are structured by historical outcome. A critical viewpoint points out that the dominant class oppresses the subordinate class by presenting an ideology as the truth, thus making the subordinate class less likely to revolt against the dominant class. For example, a commonly held ideology in the media industry is that talent and hard work are all it takes to succeed. This ideology can be critiqued from a historical perspective: the commonly accepted notion of success narrowly defines what success means. In a capitalist society, success is usually seen as material success: having a good job and owning big-ticket items, such as a house, a car, and a comfortable retirement account. In the media industry in such a society, success means lucrative business deals and widespread fame. A producer who makes socially meaningful and transformative products is not considered successful if the products are not profitable. Arthouse film directors such as Woody Allen, Spike Lee, and Jean-Luc Godard are very often seen as failures even though they created a new way to tell stories. Reading about the history of the business of media would raise one's consciousness of *who* defines success in the business and *why* success is defined in a narrow way. To conclude, a historical perspective asks us to go deeper under the surface. For example, by seeing the

17

relationship between television stations and actors as employer and employee, media studies students will learn that media work is not all about magic.

Trading Before the Establishment of the Business School

Business is a very young academic discipline, unlike philosophy and mathematics that have been studied in higher education institutions for centuries. Business has not always been seen as a science, even though humans have been trading for a long time. Ancient clay tokens and wood carved with tallies in the prehistoric era show how humans used tools to keep track of livestock. Recently, archaeologists unearthed trade tokens in Turkey that are believed to have been used for bookkeeping purposes by prehistoric humans before writing was invented ("Tokens of trade", 2014). The different token shapes show that prehistoric humans were able to use them as abstract representations to represent commodities: not only did tokens help humans to record stocks, but they also enabled traders to exchange one kind of commodity with another.

The Silk Road also testifies to the long history of cross-boundary trading. The earliest route began in the Han Dynasty (206 BC). Various routes had since connected merchants from China to (what today are known as) India, the Middle East, Northern Africa, and Europe. As the name suggested, Chinese silk and other inventions, such as gunpowder and paper, were sought-after goods. Spices, such as cinnamon and pepper, from Asia and the Middle East were brought to the West, adding flavors to the bland European palate. The significance of the Silk Road was economic as much as cultural: the routes played a significant role in developing ancient civilizations, because merchants exchanged ideas about arts, religions, languages, and sciences.

Literature such as Shakespeare's *The Merchant of Venice* captures international trade in the early Renaissance era. The wealthy merchant Antonio of Venice engaged in the import/export business, because his ships and merchandise were said to be at sea. Antonio was similar to the Silk Road merchants, who brought goods from (presumably) the present-day Middle East and Asia to sell to Europeans. Moneylending activity was also described in the story. The moneylender was the villain, because he resented Antonio for lending money without charging interest. The villain had to lower his interest rate to keep the business afloat. Marriage was also said to be an economic exchange: suitors from Europe and North Africa brought expensive gifts to seek the hand of a wealthy heiress. Upon marriage, the bride was expected to consolidate the wealth of the husband's family.

In modern history, intercontinental trading was both a cause and an outcome of the British Empire expansion during the reign of Queen Victoria. The diplomatic and military costs for the expansion were financed by profits made from intercontinental trading, which in turn expanded the empire's influence to the Americas, Africa, and Asia. For example, the East India Company was founded as a royal charter to establish cotton, silk, tea, and opium trades in the areas now known as India and China. Another royal charter, the Hudson Bay Company, was incorporated in 1670 and dominated fur trade in what is now Canada.

The expansion of the British Empire, the glut of wealth, and technological advancement brought a long-lasting and irreversible social and cultural impact on human history. For example, slave trade brought Africans to Europe and the Americas and forever changed the populations in the Western Hemisphere. The abolition of slavery still has racial and economic implications on the Commonwealth, the Americas, and the Caribbean. The industrial revolution that began in the late 19th century ushered in industrial cities, where capitalists commodified labor power as something that can be bought and sold in the market.

The extremely abbreviated history of trading shows that humans have done business for a much longer time than we have studied business as an academic discipline. The above examples show that many modern-day business practices (such as accounting, moneylending, international trade, and human resources) are not new; they have been practiced for centuries, if not millennia, in human history. Humans were only serious about studying business practices as an academic discipline, however, in the past two centuries.

The first business school, Ecole Spéciale de Commerce et d'Industrie (now named ESCP), was established in 1819 in Paris by economists and business leaders (ESCP Europe, n/a). The first business school in the United States was the Wharton School at the University of Pennsylvania. It was founded by entrepreneur and industrialist Joseph Wharton (The Wharton School, n/a). The earliest business schools did not have much prestige when compared to medical and law schools. According to Bennis and O'Toole (2005), business schools were more like trade schools until the Ford and Carnegie Foundations poured money into making business a more respectable discipline. Van Fleet and Wren (1982) suggested that the earliest Wharton faculty members were hauled in from a liberal arts tradition; they looked down upon "practical" subjects taught at the business school. Nowadays, a business school education (in particular, an MBA) is seen as a route to lucrative job offerings in the private sector. The most selective business schools like to boast about their low acceptance rates and their graduates' high starting salaries.

The earliest dismissive attitude towards teaching practical skills at business school has not completely disappeared, even though business schools are now seen as prestigious. There is still a debate concerning whether business schools should teach practical skills or business theories. For example, a *Harvard Business Review* article (Bennis & O'Toole, 2005) stated that business schools are undermining practical skills:

> [Business schools] have adopted a model of science that uses abstract financial and economic analysis, statistical multiple regressions, and laboratory psychology. Some of the research produced is excellent, but because so little of it is grounded in actual business practices, the focus of graduate business education has become increasingly circumscribed—and less and less relevant to practitioners.
>
> (para. 2)

The *Harvard Business Review* authors believe business is a profession, not an academic discipline. To them, the best way to learn business is to do it.

Given the fact that an MBA from an elite business school is seen as a route to success and given the criticism that business schools do not teach practical skills, the question then is whether a business school education would be necessary for future leaders in the media industry. Further, if most leaders in the media industry do *not* have a business degree and if the media industry is *not* a specialized area in the most selective business schools, then we may ask *whether a business education is required for one to be a leader in the media industry*.

To answer this question, we first look at the education of the CEOs heading the largest media companies in the world in terms of revenue (O'Reilly, 2016). The top ten companies are Alphabet, the Walt Disney Co., Comcast, 21st Century Fox, Facebook, Bertelsmann, Viacom, CBS Corporation, Baidu, and News Corporation. Very few CEOs of the largest media corporations received a formal business education apart from the current CEOs of Comcast (Brian Roberts) and Bertelsmann (Thomas Rabe), who studied business in school. In fact, more CEOs studied computer sciences than business (Larry Page and Sergey Brin of Alphabet, Robin Li of Baidu). Among the CEOs, two are college dropouts (Mark Zuckerberg of Facebook and James Murdoch of 21st Century Fox) and some do not have a graduate degree. A few became CEOs by working their way up the ladder. For example, Robert Iger of Walt Disney began his career as a weatherman in a local television station; Robert Thomson of News Corporation started his career as a journalist then newspaper editor; Leslie Moonves of CBS began his career as an actor. Some entered the media business because their family owns it: media titans Rupert Murdoch (of News Corporation) and Sumner Redstone (of Viacom) have been passing their thrones to their children, who headed different branches of the empire.

Next, let us look at how much focus four MBA programs give to the media industry. We chose four programs from respectable universities in global media centers (New York, Los Angeles, London, and Tokyo). The two in the United States highlight their specialty in the media industry. Stern School of New York University has an Entertainment, Media and Technology program that:

> provides a broad understanding of the strategy and operating principles that drive the individual sectors of the entertainment industry, while exploring new industry concepts and analyzing leading companies. . . . Courses are offered in a variety of disciplines, including marketing, finance, economics, accounting, management, law, and information systems. Topics covered include movies, network television, production, theater, music, sports, cable, syndication, radio, telecommunications, new media, and publishing.
>
> (Entertainment, Media and Technology, n/a)

The Anderson School of Management at the University of California-Los Angeles has a Center for Media, Entertainment, and Sport. Students learn about the business models, marketing, finance, and business law of the entertainment industries. On the other hand, the MBA program at the University of London has only one course specifically related to the business of media: "Social Media and Internet Marketing." The University of Tokyo does not have any business program at the undergraduate or graduate levels. It offers undergraduate and graduate classes in economics, but it is not clear whether any media economics class is offered. An MBA program offered by a private university, GLOBIS, in Tokyo does not offer any courses related to the media industry.

Because of the tiny scale of the sample size (CEOs of the ten largest media companies and four MBA programs), we cannot make any empirical claim whether a business education touches upon the media industry. However, the MBA curricula in four universities located in global media cities inform us that the curricula differ widely: from a specialized area in New York University and UCLA to little inclusion in the University of London or the University of Tokyo.

A quick review of the CEOs' educational background of the largest media companies and the different MBA curricula seem to imply that *a business education may not be necessary for one to succeed in the media industry*. In fact, a fancy college degree may not even be needed, given that some CEOs are college dropouts and some began their careers at the bottom of the ladder. The quick survey seems to confirm an assumption that success in the media industry is more about "street smarts" than "book smarts" and that the only way to learn to do business is by doing it. Unsurprisingly, most of the popular titles on the business of media confirm this assumption as well.

How Has the Business of Media Been Studied in the Past?

Scholars have only begun to study the business of media in a more systematic way since the 1980s. A systematic way means a holistic examination of business structures and practices in the communication sectors. Many books that had been published on the history of media tended to look at one single media mogul, company, or industry. Some of these books cover the history of specific media (such as television); some lay out the history of a company or media mogul.

The following table shows books whose titles have specific keywords that indicate the focus of the subject matter: the media as a whole, a specific medium, company, or person.

Table 2.1 *Media industry books catalogued in the Library of Congress*

Keywords	Number of titles	The earliest published title and year
"history" and "media business"/"media industry"	5	*Youth and Media* (2013)
"media history"	55	*Mass Media History* (1984)
"television history"	29	*Life and Times of Lord Mountbatten: An Illustrated Biography Based on the Television History* (1968)
"radio history"	6	*Roy Rogers: A Biography, Radio History, Television Career Chronicle, Discography, Filmography, Comicography, Merchandising and Advertising History* (1995)
"newspaper history"	29	*American Tour [of] H. R. H. Prince Henry of Prussia* (1902)
"New York Times" in the title and "history" as a subject	216	*Great American Writers as Reported in the* New York Times (1983)
"RCA" in the title and "history" as a subject	15	*First 25 Years of RCA, a Quarter-Century of Radio Progress* (1944)
"William Randolph Hearst" in the title and "biography" as a subject	19	*Citizen Hearst, a Biography of William Randolph Hearst* (1961)
"Walt Disney" in the title and "biography" as a subject	80	*Walt Disney, Magician of the Movies* (1966)
"Bill Gates" in the title and "biography" as a subject	50	*Hard Drive: Bill Gates and the Making of the Microsoft Empire* (1992)
"Steve Jobs" in the title and "biography" as a subject	53	*Accidental Millionaire: The Rise and Fall of Steve Jobs at Apple* (1988)

A search of media history books from the Library of Congress catalogue shows that there are more titles written on individual companies and media moguls than the history of media as a whole. This is unsurprising, because well-known companies are seen as role models for aspiring business leaders. These books also have a larger readership than do academic books. The popular book market has more titles and it published on the histories of individual industries (such as television and radio) rather than on the media industry as a whole. The implication is that media used to be seen more as discrete entities (i.e., film, television, radio) than as a converged industry.

Pioneer Books and Journals That Study the Media Industry

Only in recent times did scholars pay attention to the study of media business. In this section, we review some pioneering books and journals that reflect the three approaches: media economics, political economy of communication, and production studies. Although each of the three approaches has metamorphosed since its inception, reviewing the rationales of some of the earliest work would inform why such research was deemed necessary at that time. A more detailed comparison of the three approaches will be the topic of the next chapter.

Media economics: The first book that systematically looked at the media industry as a whole is *Concentration of Ownership in the Media* (Compaine, Galey, LeGates, McLaughlin, & Oettinger, 1980). The preface of the third edition, titled *Who Owns the Media?* (Compaine & Gomery, 2000), states why the first edition was commissioned: a mid-level manager of the CBS corporation wanted to know the trends of merging in the industry and requested Compaine to compile a report. Because the book was conceived as a report, the goal was to collect hard data about the industry that informs policy-making. The report intended to have a nonideological stance on media ownership: it did not state whether merging is a good or bad thing for the public. The first edition achieved the purpose, because both proponents and opponents of a concentrated media industry used the data to argue for their cause. In the third edition of *Who Owns the Media?*, the authors believe that what was true about the US media industry in the early 1980s was still true in 2000: that few people actually care about who owns the media. Compaine and Gomery believe, however, that it is essential to know who owns the media because this knowledge will shed light on the varieties of media content.

In hindsight, the first edition of *Who Owns the Media?* might not advocate more for a media economic perspective than for other perspectives. The editor was more interested in gathering empirical data about circulation, audience, advertising, titles, subjects, and ownership than in advocating for any perspective. However, not taking a stance on what the data showed can also be criticized as privileging an objectivist way of seeing the issue of media ownership. In other words, the presentation of hard data is assumed to be neutral even though some data are not included, such as the remuneration of the CEOs and the salary of an average worker. The exclusion of such data may actually be ideological.

The Journal of Media Economics was inaugurated in 1988. The editors stated that the journal was necessary in the communication field because traditional journals have not shown enough interest in the economic issues of media and their operations ("Introduction", 1988). The journal then serves as an outlet for scholars from the disciplines of communication, economics, and public policy to share their research findings. The first issue published papers on a range of media, such as television, magazines, newspaper, and satellites.

Political economy: The studies of communication from a political economic perspective did not come from one single person or group. Instead, there were parallel developments in North America, Europe, and Latin America (Mosco, 2009). Writings of key figures, such as Dallas Smythe, Herbert Schiller, Armard Mattelart, James Halloran, Graham Murdock, and Peter Golding, have influenced the next generations of political economists. Winseck (2011) pointed out that there are four schools of the political economy of communication: conservative, radical, institutional, and cultural. Readers of this book do not need to know the fine distinctions between them. However, it has to be noted that the limited space devoted to the history of the political economic approach does not do justice to the complex development of this approach.

The International Association of Media and Communication Research (IACMR) has served as a forum for political economists. According to Wasko (2013), the political economy section was created in 1978 for scholars who were interested in a materialist approach to communication. The mandate of the section sums up what the approach entails:

> The Political Economy Section examines the role of power in the production, distribution and exchange of mediated communication. Drawing from the rich history of political economic theory, Section members study social relations in their totality, consider how they have developed historically, evaluate them according to standards of social justice, and intervene to bring about a more just and democratic world.
>
> (Political Economy Section, n/a, para. 1)

A few journals have published many groundbreaking pieces on political economy; titles include the *Canadian Journal of Communication*; *Critical Studies in Media Communication*; *Media, Culture, and Society*; and *TripleC: Communication, Capitalism & Critique*. The *Journal of Political Economy* (affiliated with the IAMCR section) was inaugurated in 2013. The editors wrote that political economy responds to the geopolitical environments of decolonization, the Cold War, and new leftist movements. They recognize that many political economists have branched out and engaged in questions about geography, culture, and a philosophy of technology. To this end, they ask:

> How should we reconcile particular genealogies of Marxism with the critical political economy of communication? Can this field be singularly defined or is there simply a plurality of approaches within it? Is the prospect of political praxis necessary for scholarly inquiry? Are cross-fertilizations with those subfields which eschew normative commitment possible or desirable?
>
> (Hope, Thompson, & Hirst, 2013)

Production studies: As we will explain in Chapter 3, production studies is a more recent approach for studying the media industry. However, it does not mean that scholars have never considered the media industry from a cultural studies perspective. Raymond Williams, a leftist intellectual who has influenced the development of the communication field in the United Kingdom, has considered the ideological aspect of the cultural industries. However, the cultural studies of communication (particularly in the US) has focused on the consumption of media rather than the production and distribution. Nonetheless, some scholars have begun to use cultural studies theories to understand the production side of media since the 2000s. The first volume that exemplifies this approach is *Production Studies: Cultural Studies of Media Industries* (Mayer, Banks, & Caldwell, 2009). As a collection of essays that look at the culture of production, the book focuses on three aspects that have been ignored by media economists and political economists: (1) self-identities of producers; (2) production spaces; and (3) production as lived experience. The editors acknowledge in the introductory essay that each of the contributing authors has their own approach and academic/professional experience. Some of the founding scholars of production studies draw on "forgotten" academics inside and outside the discipline and revitalize the forgotten work with contemporary examples.

The studies of media industries have gained much traction in the communication field in recent years. Not only was a media industry studies interest group established in the field's largest professional group, the International Communication Association (ICA), the journal *Media Industries* was also launched. We do not think the interest group and the journal, however, should be defined narrowly as production studies. The description of both outlets is broad enough to include the two approaches of media economics and political economy. For example, the media industry studies interest group stated that it

> promote[s] research and teaching practice on the history, organization, structure, economics, management, production processes and cultural forms, and the societal impact of media industries from a variety of theoretical, empirical, and cultural perspectives.
>
> (*Media Industries*, n/a, para. 1)

Issues that members study may concern "the relationship between government and industry; the intersection of audience and industry; audiences as consumers; the business of media; production and creative labor; ownership structure; and content diversity from a range of micro and macro-levels" (ibid.). The *Media Industries* journal invites articles that:

> explore a range of industry-related processes, such as production, distribution, infrastructure, policy, exhibition, and retailing. Contemporary or historical studies may explore industries individually or examine inter-medial relations between industrial sectors employing qualitative, quantitative, or mixed methodologies; of primary importance is that submissions adopt a critical perspective.
>
> (*Media Industries*, n/a, para. 1)

The editorial board is composed of scholars who self-identify as political economists, cultural studies scholars, and industry studies scholars.

Even though scholars who study the business of media will not agree that there is one best way to study the media industry, the establishment of the ICA media industry studies interest group and the publications the *Journal of Political Economy* and *Media Industries* show that there is a growing interest in understanding the political, economic, and cultural conditions under which media goods are produced and distributed. Scholars who study the business of media are no longer doing it in isolation, but they can turn to their communities to share work and exchange ideas.

Why Have Scholars Been More Interested in Studying the Business of Media Since 2000?

The above abbreviated history shows that communication scholars have started to pay more attention to the industry since 2000. Why has there been a surge in interest? Whereas the descriptions of some newer journals and professional groups may hint at how the industry may be studied, they do not explicate the broader political economic contexts that transform the media industries, as well as academia. The three interrelated changes discussed here are neoliberalism, globalization, and media convergence.

Neoliberalism

The "neo" in "neoliberalism" implies it is a new kind of liberalism. Liberalism is a political philosophy that concerns the role of the state in relation to its citizens. Many modern, democratic nation-states were founded with liberalism as a guiding principle. Unlike feudal states, democratic nation-states emphasize the rights and responsibilities of those who govern and those who are governed; the independence of executive, legislative, and judicial branches; and the individual as a political entity.

Neoliberalism, according to Harvey (2005), promotes political economic practices that advance "entrepreneurial freedoms and skills within an institutional framework characterized by strong private property rights, free markets, and free trade" (p. 2). In order for individuals to enjoy maximum economic freedom, the state needs to withdraw its involvement in many facets of public life. While liberalism emphasizes political well-being, neoliberalism emphasizes economic well-being. Under neoliberalism, any political actions that limit economic freedom are sanctioned. While this may sound like a good idea to *individuals* because the state cannot interfere with the kinds of jobs they do and the amount of money they make, neoliberalism may be harmful to *citizens* because of two reasons. First, equality among citizens is threatened because there is a differentiation of power among individuals. While the average individual does not have much political, economic, and cultural influence, a few individuals that have an enormous amount of influence could decide how the majority lives. For example, political and business leaders can make decisions that impact many lives; the wealthiest can exert control to make themselves wealthier; celebrities can change cultural tastes overnight. The concept of an individual then does not guarantee equality as much as that of a citizen. The second reason why the concept of an individual is harmful to that of a citizen is that the most powerful individuals can ask for minimal state intervention so as to privatize many public services. For example, most democratic countries provide public services such as military, law enforcement, and infrastructure. However, not all democratic countries provide free education and healthcare. A neoliberal state—even if it is democratic—can offer limited public services. What if prisons are run by private organizations? Will more people go to prison because private prisons need their "clients"? What if roads are run by private firms? Will people who are willing to pay more get into faster lanes? Broadly speaking, will the economically disadvantaged enjoy the same level of services as the advantaged? At which point will citizens of democratic states be unable to afford the minimum daily necessities, such as clean water and safe roads?

How has neoliberalism sparked scholars' interests in studying media industry? First, a concentration of media ownership has drawn criticism from scholars. Because a neoliberal state privileges individuals' economic freedom, those who already have a lot of economic and political influence have been given more freedom to own more media companies. Few will dispute the fact that the global media industries have become more integrated since the 1990s. Family-owned media companies—newspapers in particular—have become a thing of the past; many media companies are now public companies whose stocks are traded. A concentrated media has implications on media content. Therefore, even scholars who primarily examine media content cannot ignore the institutional structure that produces the content.

Neoliberalism also changed the nature of academia. For cash-strapped countries, higher education has been seen as a private good, a luxury consumer product. Students and their parents see higher education as an investment. What students learn in universities is believed to lead to employment with a good entry salary. Communication scholars often have to justify to prospective students and administration why studying the media leads to a viable career path. Learning about the business of media, ironically, is more essential to media students, because a media industry class is supposed to teach them how the industry runs; therefore, students can better position themselves as entry-level workers.

Globalization

Globalization was a heated topic among academics, journalists, and politicians in the 2000s. Some approach globalization from a political economic approach, others a cultural approach. Some scholars wonder how a more economically integrated world would impact the economies of individual countries and transnational corporations. Others wonder what a more integrated world would mean to the sovereignty of nation-states: would nation-states—especially the smaller ones—be able to govern without intervention from the more powerful countries and corporations? Some scholars focus on the cultural aspect of globalization: how would global culture impact local culture? Will local norms and customs be eroded by global culture brought by transnational corporations?

Globalization has led scholars to examine the structure and strategies of transnational corporations. As previously mentioned, the book *Who Owns the Media?* provides data on how each of the US media markets is structured. Media scholars gradually find it impossible to ignore the global operation of the largest media corporations that have branches and subsidies outside the country of origin. In the same vein, non-US media corporations, such as Bertelsmann, Vivendi, and Sony, also have branches in the US. In addition, gigantic information and platform companies can easily broaden their markets because they do not provide culturally specific content. Companies such as Google and Facebook provide services that can be customized for local needs. The recently published book *Global Media Giants* (Birkinbine, Gomez, & Wasko, 2017) illustrates how global media corporations operate. The volume covers some truly global corporations (such as The Walt Disney Co., Time Warner, Comcast, News Corporation), regional giants (such as Televisa, América Móvil, Bertelsmann, Viacom, Mediaset, Telefónica, and Sony), and information and platform companies (such as Apple, Microsoft, Google, Amazon.com, and Facebook).

Academia has become more globalized as well. Universities in the US, UK, Canada, Australia, and New Zealand admit a large number of international students. According to the Institute of International Education, more than one million international students were enrolled in US universities in 2015–2016 (The Institute of International Education, n/a). The four countries that send the most students to the United States are China, India, Saudi Arabia, and South Korea. The rise of international students impacts the teaching of most subjects, but particularly those that draw on cultural examples. While international students may be foreign to local examples given in class, they usually have no problem with understanding global media corporations and cultures. Global companies (such as Disney) and cultures (such as Hollywood blockbuster movies) are classroom examples that are readily understood by both domestic and international students.

The globalization of academia may also be explained by political economic reasons. As we mentioned in the previous section, neoliberal states may diminish funding for public services. Higher education in some countries has to drastically increase tuition because the states have decreased their funding to universities. Cash-strapped public institutions need to recruit more "full-fee-paying" students (such as international students, students from the upper middle class) to survive. On the other hand, international students also understand that a foreign education is attractive to employers who value workers' English competency and global knowledge.

Media Convergence

Digitization also sparked scholars' interest in studying the media industry. As shown in Table 2.1, media industry books used to focus on one single entity, such as a medium (film, radio, newspaper), a company, or an industry leader. Focusing on one single entity does not capture the blurred boundaries between the industries. As we will cover in Chapter 6, "Technologies," digital technology—with the help of neoliberal states—has demanded media companies rethink their business model. For one thing, digital technologies lower the cost to produce and distribute content, effectively lowering the cost of entry for companies. Newsrooms used to require a high entry cost, because a large physical space is needed for the expensive and bulky typesetting equipment. Nowadays, the cost of desktop computer and publishing software is so low that a publication can be launched in one's home.

The lower entry cost and the elimination of ownership regulation in some countries benefit large media companies as well. They can easily expand to other industries with fewer state regulations and less technological restriction: a newspaper company could also own a television station, a film studio could own a radio station, and so on. Cross-ownership lowers production and distribution costs, because they can feed on the content and technologies of each other. In the name of "synergy," media companies can expand one idea into different platforms. For example, Disney bought Marvel comics not only because it was one of the two major comic publishing companies in the US, but also because of its ownership of licenses to superhero characters such as Ironman. Disney could exploit the "concept" of Ironman and produce television shows, films, amusement park rides, entertainment shows, and so on.

Digitization not only made major media companies larger in terms of revenue size, but it also made telecommunications and technology companies invest in media production. Before the advancement of digital technologies, few communication scholars worried about who invented and manufactured the analog technologies that produced and distributed media content. In the analog era, scholars were certainly aware of the structure of large telecommunications companies such as AT&T, but they did not discuss how a monopoly of a telecommunications company would—or rather, could—influence content diversity. However, in the digital age, when a telecommunications company such as Comcast buys the television station NBC and the film studio Universal, scholars worry that a vertical integration would limit the choices that the audience has.

Digitization has transformed the teaching of media studies in many ways: first, the lower price tag of technology has enabled students to produce and distribute media content before taking their first media class. Second, students also have more choices of when, where, and how to consume the media. The apparent ease to produce, distribute, and consume materials may lead students to believe that anyone with passion and talents can make a name in the industry. While this belief had always been held among aspiring media workers, digital technology reinforces the "everyone can make it" mentality. Teaching and learning about the structure of the media industry is then more imperative than ever, because students will learn that passion and talents are just two of many required qualities to succeed in the media business.

Conclusion

In this chapter, we learned that although humans have traded for millennia, business studies is a very young discipline. Popular books about business tend to perpetuate a myth that business knowledge is universal: what is useful for one type of industry is useful for another. The education of the CEOs of the world's largest media and telecommunications companies shows that not only is an MBA unnecessary to succeed in the business world, but few CEOs have studied the media in school. Nonetheless, scholars have been studying the media and hi-tech industries more systematically since the 1990s due to three trends: globalization, neoliberalism, and media convergence. In addition, the three trends have implications on the teaching and learning of media in higher education institutions. In the next chapter, we show three approaches from which the media and hi-tech industries can be systematically examined.

References

Bennis, W., & O'Toole, J. (2005, May). How business schools lost their way. *Harvard Business Review*. Retrieved from https://hbr.org/2005/05/how-business-schools-lost-their-way

Birkinbine, B., Gomez, R., & Wasko, J. (2017). *Global media giants*. New York: Routledge.

Burrelle's Press Clipping Bureau. (1902). *American tour [of] H.R.H. Prince Henry of Prussia*. New York: Burrelle's Press Clipping Bureau.

Butcher, L. (1988). *Accidental millionaire: The rise and fall of Steve Jobs at Apple Computer*. New York: Paragon House.

Collins, J. (2001). *Good to great: Why some companies make the leap and others don't*. New York: HarperBusiness.

Compaine, B. M., Galey, O. H., LeGates, J. C., McLaughlin, J. F., & Oettinger, A. G. (1980, March 3). *Concentration of ownership in the media*. Hearings before the Subcommittee on Small Business and Minority Enterprise, 96th Congress.

Compaine, B. M., & Gomery, D. (2000). *Who owns the media?* (3rd ed.). Mahwah, NJ: Lawrence Erlbaum.

Duckworth, A. (2016). *Grit: The power of passion and perseverance*. New York: Scribner.

ESCP Europe. (n/a). *The world's first business school*. Retrieved from www.escpeurope.eu/escp-europe/history-of-escp-europe-business-school/

Great American writers as reported in New York Times. (1983). Sanford, NC: Microfilming Corp. of America.

Harvey, D. (2005). *A brief history of neoliberalism*. Oxford: Oxford University Press.

Hope, W., Thompson, P., & Hirst, M. (2013). Editorial. *The Political Economy of Communication, 1*(1), 1–3.

The Institute of International Education. (n/a). *Atlas project*. Retrieved from www.iie.org/Services/Project-Atlas/United-States/International-Students-In-US#.WEblufMcZVc

Introduction. (1988). *Journal of Media Economics, 1*(1), 3.

Kaufman, J. (2012). *The personal MBA: Master the art of business*. New York: Portfolio.

Mayer, V., Banks, M. J., & Caldwell, J. T. (Eds.). (2009). *Production studies: Cultural studies of media industries*. New York: Routledge.

Media Industries. (n/a). About the Journal. Retrieved from www.mediaindus
triesjournal.org/index.php/mij/about#edcol

Media Industry Studies. (n/a). *International Communication Association*. Retrieved from www.icahdq.org/group/mediaindustry

Mosco, V. (2009). *The political economy of communication* (2nd ed.). London: Sage.

NYU Stern School of Business. (n/a). *Entertainment, media and technology*. Retrieved from www.stern.nyu.edu/experience-stern/about/departments-centers-initiatives/interdisciplinary-initiatives/entertainment-media-and-technology-program

O'Reilly, L. (2016, May 31). The 30 biggest media companies in the world. *Business Insider*. Retrieved from www.businessinsider.com/the-30-biggest-media-owners-in-the-world-2016-5/#28-prosiebensat1–291-billion-in-media-revenue-3

Pember, D. (1984). *Mass media history*. Chicago: Science Research Associates.

Phillips, R. W. (1995). *Roy Rogers: A biography, radio history, television career chronicle*. Jefferson, NC: McFarland.

Political Economy Section. (n/a). *International Association for Media and Communication Research*. Retrieved from: http://iamcr.org/s-wg/section/political-economy-section

Radio Corporation of America. (1944). *First 25 years of RCA, a quarter-century of radio progress*. New York: RCA.

Ruddock, A. (2013). *Youth and media*. New York: Sage.

Swanberg, W. A. (1961). *Citizen Hearst: A biography of William Randolph Hearst*. Norwalk, CT: Easton Press.

Terraine, J. (1968). *The life and times of Lord Mountbatten: An illustrated biography based on television history*. London: Hutchinson.

Thomas, B. (1966). *Walt Disney, Magician of the movies*. New York: Grosset and Dunlap.

Tokens of trade: Prehistoric bookkeeping lasted long after the invention of writing. (2014, July 13). *Science 2.0*. Retrieved from www.science20.com/news_articles/tokens_of_trade_prehistoric_bookkeeping_lasted_long_after_the_invention_of_writing-140468

Van Fleet, D. D., & Wren, D. (1982). History in today's business school. *The Accounting Historians Journal, 9*(1), 111–118.

Wallace, J. (1993). *Hard drive: Bill Gates and the making of the Microsoft empire*. New York: HarperBusiness.

Wasko, J. (2013). The IAMCR political economy section: A retrospective. *The Political Economy of Communication, 1*(1), 4–8.

The Wharton School. (n/a). *The world's first business school*. Retrieved from www.wharton.upenn.edu/about-wharton/

Winseck, D. (2011). The political economies of media and the transformation of the global media industries. In D. Y. Jin & D. Winseck (Eds.), *The political economies of media: The transformation of the global media industries* (pp. 3–48). London: Bloomsbury.

Theories and Approaches to Study the Business of Media

3

At the end of the chapter, students will be able to:

- define an approach and a theoretical framework;
- explain the relation between an approach and a theoretical framework;
- define the three approaches in terms of how they view the media business: media economics, political economy of communication, and production studies;
- suggest how a media economic approach is influenced by neoclassical economic thought;
- suggest what some criticism of a media economic approach is;
- name the four goals of political economists;
- suggest how production studies scholars see an economy;
- explain why different approaches use the same keywords but understand them differently;
- name keywords and concepts in the approaches and explain how they relate to each other.

In this chapter, we introduce three approaches to study the business of media: media economics, critical political economy of communication, and production studies. In Chapter 2, we briefly stated some pioneering work in the approaches, and we continue the discussion in this chapter by introducing theoretical frameworks associated with each approach.

What are an approach and a theoretical framework? If an approach is a window that allows you to see the outside world, then a theoretical framework explains what you see. Because any window limits a view, a single approach can only offer a few explanations of the view outside the window. Therefore, we emphasize the use of multiple approaches because the more windows you open, the more of the outside world you will see and the better the explanations will be.

An approach is defined as a specific way to understand the object of study. The object of study here is "the business of media." In other books, the objects of study can be "television texts" or "audiences." An approach "assess[es] how useful [its] explanations are in terms of an understanding of the processes involved" (Thussu, 2006, p. 40). Although this definition of "approach" may imply that every theorist who writes with a certain approach would use the same theoretical framework, this is not the case. There are multiple theoretical frameworks in a single approach; it is typical that theorists who write in a single approach disagree with each other. Nonetheless, theorists who use a certain approach tend to agree more with each other than with others who use another approach. Scholars who follow a certain approach usually publish in the same journals and go to the same conferences so that they can advance the approach by fine-tuning the theoretical frameworks. Among the three approaches introduced in this book, the media economic approach and the critical political economy of communication approach are the most explicit at describing and explaining media economies, whereas the production studies approach is the least explicit.

"Theoretical framework" can be understood as the overarching structure that guides questions about why the media are the way they are. A theoretical framework seeks to provide a deeper understanding of things that are not readily obvious. For example, why do consumers spend money on media products that do not satisfy the basic needs and wants of human beings? Different approaches provide different theoretical frameworks to explain why this is the case. A critical political economic approach would argue that capitalists have created false needs and wants for consumers. Cultural studies scholars would argue that consumption is a way to make sense of modern life.

After learning what an approach and a theoretical framework are, we ask three broad questions in this chapter:

- What are the main thrusts of each of the approaches? How does each of them view the subject of the business of media?
- What are the strengths and weaknesses of each of the approaches? How are the weaknesses of each approach remedied in the other two approaches?
- What are some keywords and concepts used in the three approaches? How do these keywords and concepts shed light on the six lenses that we will introduce from Chapter 3 to Chapter 9: economies, politics, technologies, civil societies, cultures, and labor?

Media Economics

Media economics can be defined as "the study of how media industries use scarce resources to produce content that is distributed among customers in a society to satisfy various wants and needs" (Albarran, 2002, p. 5). More specifically, media economics refers to "the business operations and financial activities of firms producing and selling output into the various media industries" (Owers, Carveth, & Alexander, 2004, p. 3). In Chapter 1, we asked you to recall how you made economic decisions to watch a film or listen to a song. You need to choose the best possible option, because you have limited money and time. Similarly, firms need to decide how to invest limited resources so that they can maximize profits. If there is an endless supply of money and time, then it is unnecessary for either consumers or producers to make decisions.

Human beings deal with economic issues day in and day out. People make decisions about what to buy on a daily basis, from basic necessities such as food and housing to luxury goods such as vacations and designer goods. People also decide how they should make money to pay for basic necessities in order to survive. While making a living and buying things seem to be personal choices, economic ideology actually conditions what we buy, how we buy, and why we buy. According to Stilwell (2002, p. 2), [economic activities] . . . beset us collectively, generating political choices about how to balance economic growth against environmental concerns, how to redistribute income through taxes and government spending, and how to deal with national and global imbalances in international trade and economic development.

Like many others, Stilwell suggested that neoclassical economics, which emerged in the late 19th century, has been and still is the dominant economic thought of contemporary time. Neoclassical economists are interested in knowing "how people and society end up choosing—to employ scarce productive resources that could have alternative uses, to produce various commodities and distribute them—among various persons and groups in society" (Samuelson, 1976, p. 3, cited in Cunningham, Flew, & Swift, 2015, pp. 12–13).

The "neo" in neoclassical economics indicates that this school of thought is different from classical economics of the 18th century. Classical economics is interested in questions such as human rights and social justice. Economists of the neoclassical school rarely ask these questions; instead, they focus on how individuals' needs and wants can be satisfied. To determine how resources can be the most efficiently allocated, economists developed tools such as statistical analysis and econometric modeling. For example, we often hear in the news that economists use past data to predict the future by using economic models. If past data show that a fast-growing economy may lead to inflation, then a fast-growing economy at present may mean consumers need to prepare to pay more for the same goods.

In neoclassical thought, the market is seen to provide information about individuals' needs and wants. We often hear comments such as "there is no market for serious films" or "there is a market demand for production skills." The market is believed to send information to producers about supply and demand. In neoclassical thought, the market is an autonomous being that determines economic needs. The assumption of the market being autonomous can be traced to the "invisible hand" concept coined by Adam Smith in *The Wealth of Nations* (1776). Smith states that behaviors of self-interested individuals will benefit the society at large. The concept of a market being made up of individuals has gained much traction in recent decades. In mainstream economic thought, a market is conceived as a collection of decisions made by individuals. Because individuals are making choices, economists believe the market is rational. The market is believed to simply reflect the needs and wants of a group of people; "information flows freely to consumers who register their wants in the marketplace" (Mosco, 2009, p. 62). Therefore, market-based decisions are deemed the most efficient to allocate resources, because market relations are believed to "permit mutually advantageous exchanges and ensure the efficient allocation of resources" (Stilwell, 2002, p. 147, cited in Cunningham, Flew, & Swift, 2015, pp. 12–13).

Media economics is heavily influenced by neoclassical thought. To media economists, the production and consumption of media and telecommunications are not radically different from those of basic necessities and luxury goods. For example, consumers choose retailers and brands based on price, convenience, and quality. Consumers are believed to use the same criteria to choose television programs, media services, and technological gadgets. Similarly, all producers are believed to produce goods and services based on price, profits, and consumer taste. Because media economists assume that the production and consumption of media is similar to those of other goods, they employ the same economic concepts to analyze both the media industries and media goods. Nevertheless, media economists are also aware that taste plays a more significant role than prices in the media market. To give an example, media consumers will not choose to buy a song just because it is cheap.

Media economists study economies at a micro level; they are interested in understanding issues such as:

- Corporate behaviors: how do the media—as economic institutions—produce and distribute media content to consumers? Why do they use certain strategies to ensure maximum efficiency? (Albarran, 2002)
- Characteristics of media markets: how large is the market? How many firms are there in a market? What are the characteristics of the goods produced in the market?
- Consumers' behaviors: how do people choose the products? What factors determine their choices?
- Market demand and supply: how many jobs are unfilled in the media markets? What kinds of products are needed in the market to satisfy needs?

A media economic approach has received some criticism. The first one is that a media economic analysis of the media is not as value free as it sounds. Neoclassical economic thought appears to embrace a value-free economic system, because the market is believed to *merely* objectively reflect individual needs and wants. However, at the macro level, decision-makers need to decide what economic system works best; as such, a nation's choice of an economic system is a political choice. For example, because media and cultural activities significantly contribute to a nation's economy, the state may design policies to develop the media and cultural sectors. In this case, the decisions are not based on individuals' needs and wants, but on how decision-makers believe the economy could benefit the greater good.

Neoclassical economists also assume that perfect competition leads to market efficiency. In a perfect competition, the many sellers and buyers sell homogeneous goods in a single market. Because the buyers have perfect information about the goods, the market achieves an efficient allocation of resources. As a result, media economies in some countries rely on a free market system, which asks the government to work as the regulator with minimal power (Doyle, 2002, p. 32). However, the free market is mostly a myth. Almost no government allows for the import and export of illegal goods such as drugs. Few governments allow for the import and export of any goods; most will constrain the flows of goods based on a few reasons: avoiding competition between foreign and local goods; withholding trade as a political strategy; and controlling harmful goods. Some respective examples are prescription drugs in Canada not being allowed for export to the United States; countries not trading with socialist countries such as North Korea and Cuba; and the prohibition on trading endangered animals.

A Political Economy of Communication

The school of political economy introduced here is called critical political economy, which is grounded in Marxist thought, in particular how capitalism organizes social life and social relations. This approach critiques capitalism as a specific way to organize resources. Simply put, capitalists invest their money in machinery and labor to create commodities for the market. Profits gained from selling the commodities to consumers is reinvested in the production process. Capitalism relies on the constant transformation of resources (including raw resources and human power) into commodities.

This particular way of organizing resources creates a specific social relation between the owners of the means of production and workers. The workers have to continue selling their labor to capitalists in order to sustain their lives. However, they rarely save enough money to acquire capital to become capitalists. On the other hand, capitalists accumulate more wealth through making profits. This social relation is deemed unnatural because throughout history, humans had organized resources in different ways. However, in contemporary time, capitalism is seen as the *only* possible way to allocate wealth.

Political economists and media economists may examine the same market features (such as market structures, firm behaviors, competition, and consumer behaviors), but the fundamental assumptions and motivations are different (Wasko, Murdock, & Sousa, 2011, p. 3). Here, we name four goals of political economists: first, critical political economists grapple with larger political economic problems and policy issues. They address macro-level concerns, such as the causes and implications of global financial crises; the power of multinational corporations on nation-states and their citizens; the tension between economic growth and ecological sustainability; and economic insecurity and inequality, particularly among the poorest populations (Stilwell, 2002).

Second, political economists prefer to see things in totality rather than in isolation (Mosco, 2009). They examine the social whole that makes up the economic, political, social, and cultural areas of life. As such, they prefer a holistic approach, because the economy is believed to interrelate with other spheres (Golding & Murdock, 2005). For example, because political economists believe the sphere of economy interacts with that of nation-states, they study the role of the nation-state in relation to the media industries.

Third, political economists place much greater emphasis on ethical and normative questions than on media economics (McChesney, 1999a; Mosco, 2009; Winseck & Jin, 2011). Mosco (2009) notes that political economists are committed to moral philosophy; they care about the values that help to create social behavior. Thus, they explicitly write about basic moral questions such as justice, equity, fairness, and the public good (Golding & Murdock, 2005). Critical political economists believe in social change and historical transformation (Mosco, 2009), because no political economic system is predetermined and everlasting.

Therefore, political economists employ a political and historical analysis to show the neoclassical economic way to study an economy is not the *only* way (Wasko et al., 2011). In order to transform existing social relations, critical political economists believe the oppressed should gain a sense of consciousness so that they will understand their situations are not inevitable. Social consciousness is crucial for the oppressed to challenge an unjust and inequitable system of power.

Fourth, political economists believe in social praxis (Mosco, 2009): social transformation relies on unifying thinking and doing. Research is seen as a form of social intervention, an act of activism. Intellectual life is not seen as something confined within the wall of an ivory tower, but a means to effect social change.

As we mentioned earlier, political economists may agree with the big picture of the approach, but they disagree with the finer points. Therefore, they examine media issues from a specific angle. For example, McChesney (1999b) focuses on media ownership, in particular how corporations, advertising, and government policies influence media behavior and content. In contrast, Nicholas Garnham (2000) prefers to see the structures and processes of communication being deeply embedded within the wider structures and processes of a given social formation. In his words, "who can say what, in what form, to whom, for what purposes, and with what effect are determined by and in part determine the structure of economic, political, and cultural power in a society" (p. 4). Vincent Mosco (2009) emphasizes the role of power plays in the production, distribution, and consumption of communication resources. He asks political economists to pay attention to a specific set of social relations organized around power (p. 24).

Production Studies

In contrast to media economists and critical political economists of communication, production studies scholars are the least explicit at analyzing the economy. It does not mean that they ignore the economy of media production, but they see the economy as a condition under which media practitioners negotiate their sense of identity and agency in the industry. Production studies is relatively new to the wider field of media studies. Its visible emergence in the field may be explained by the fact that digital media production is becoming more integrated into the media and telecommunication industries.

Production studies can be defined as: "the study of . . . the people (producers) and processes (production) that cause media to take the forms they do. Crucially this involves a question of power" (Hesmondhalgh, 2014, p. 146). Power determines who makes a lot of money and who makes little. Power also determines a partial picture of the industry. Media moguls and celebrities obscure the impoverished living conditions of most media workers. The casualization of labor means more media workers are freelancers; thus, it becomes harder for media workers to have a middle-class lifestyle. The ultra rich and famous are confined to a "specialized cadre," thus raising questions about "how that group is chosen and trained, why it acts as it does, and how it relates to other social groups" (Garnham, 2000, p. 82).

As a scholarly approach, production studies examines specific sites and fabrics of media production as distinct interpretative communities, each with its own organizational structures, professional practices, and power dynamics. One of the founders of production studies, Vicki Mayer (2016), pointed out that this approach aims to study those populations who had been formally excluded in industrial hierarchies of cultural and economic value. As we showed in Chapter 2, many books have been written on media moguls and stars, but there are few titles on behind-the-screen workers, including most above-the-line workers (such as scriptwriters) and almost all below-the-line workers (such as cinematographers, carpenters). Production studies not only make these workers' activities and interpretative practices visible, but they also illuminate workers' precarious economic positions in the industry. Political economists and production studies share a similar concern of livelihoods of workers, but production studies offer insights into the lived experience of workers.

We mentioned in Chapter 2 that neoliberalism has ignited media scholars' interest in studying media as an industry. In a post-Fordist economy (referring to modern industrial production that has moved away from mass production towards specialized markets based on flexible manufacturing units) and a neoliberal capitalist society, media workers are asked to see themselves as empowered individuals and active economic beings. They are asked to not see themselves as passive workers in an organization or waged labor in a service industry. Workers' sense of agency is supposed to help them figure out their economic worth. From a production studies approach, an economy is not objective and thus cannot be solely analyzed with concepts such as market structure. From this approach, an economy is also subjective; therefore, it is important to know how participants negotiate their identities, roles, and functions in a media economy. While political economists focus on macroeconomic issues and media economists focus on microeconomic issues, production studies scholars tend to look at working conditions in a situated context: how workers feel about their identities depends on a number of factors, from gender, age, and educational level to economic status.

From this approach, media producers make cultures. In the process of making culture, they morph themselves into particular kinds of workers in modern, mediated societies. They work through professional organizations and informal networks to form communities of shared practices, languages, and cultural understanding of the world (Mayer et al., 2009). This contrasts with a Marxist assumption of workers, whose identities are rarely discussed. Critical political economists say little about the contributions of labor as determinants of cultural meaning and value (Davies, 2006, 21).

Production studies scholars prefer to study media by using grounded analyses of workers' experiences, observations, conversations, and interactions. Observational, on-the-ground research allows scholars better access to determining the nuances of language, behavior, ritual, and subjectivities. Grounded data shed light on an understanding of production communities in the larger contexts of policy shifts, economic imperatives, industrial organizations, national politics, globalization, and local or regional dynamics (Bank, Corner, & Mayer, 2016). Keane and Sanson (2016) suggest that production studies scholars employ methods such as ethnography and discourse analysis to analyze broader trends and relations of power; therefore, studies from this approach shows a nuanced and richly textured approach (an example is Caldwell, 2008).

Because of their approach, work done from a production studies approach is critiqued to be blind to macro-level issues. Keane and Sanson (2016) critique production studies for not connecting a situational analysis of work conditions to a global economy. Production studies scholars seem to be "suspicious of totalizing frameworks, preferring to see power as multivalent and capillary rather than centrally anchored by the logic of capital" (p. 9).

We have so far presented the thrusts of the three approaches: media economics, critical political economy, and production studies. Despite the fact that the summary is extremely condensed, readers may already see that there are significant differences between them in understanding media and culture in relation to an economy. We have also pointed out how they complement each other by addressing the weaknesses of each other. While students are certainly welcome to subscribe to one approach, the rapidly changing media environment demands an innovative way to conceptualize and solve problems through understanding, appreciating, and critiquing all approaches. We summarize the differences of the three approaches in Table 3.1:

Table 3.1 *Comparison of the three approaches*

	Market Economics	**Political Economy**	**Production Studies**
How an economy is understood	Autonomous; objective; devoid of political and cultural interests.	Integrated with political and cultural interests; interrelated with other spheres.	An intersubjective understanding.
How the market is understood	As the unit of study.	As a site of power struggle.	As an intersubjective construct.
Overarching question	Market allocation of resources.	Critique of capitalism.	Specific sites and fabrics of media production.
Goal	To describe, explain, and predict the markets.	To transform social relations; to prod social changes; to raise consciousness.	To provide a grounded analysis to understand the fluid meanings of media production.
Keywords	Corporate behaviors; characteristics of media markets; consumers' activities; supply and demand; market efficiency.	Ownership and control; power; capital; social relations.	Interpretations; shared meanings; identities; production as processes.
Methodology	Objective methods such as economic models and mathematical formulae.	Critical realism: document analysis; interviewing.	Interpretative methods such as interviewing; ethnography; participant observation.

Keywords and Concepts in the Three Approaches

In this section, we discuss some common keywords and concepts in the three approaches. Keywords such as industries, markets, and consumers are used in all three approaches even though they are understood and interpreted differently. One reason to explain the differences is that each of the approaches has a specific ontological stance. Ontology can be defined as a sense of reality. Media economists accept that media industries, markets, and consumers exist in a reality that can be understood and studied if the correct method is chosen. Political economists believe that media industries, markets, and consumers are sites of struggles. As a result, owners of media corporations have a different reality from that of the workers. Political economists view a reality through the eye of "capital": where it comes from and to where it flows. Production studies scholars believe that media industries, markets, and consumers are constructs. To them, realities are intersubjective; they become real when participants experience them and make meanings of them.

In this section, we select a few major keywords and concepts associated with the three approaches. Keywords and concepts will be in bold type and are organized under the following headings:

- Media economic approach: "supply and demand" and "business organization, industry, and sector";
- Critical political economic approach: "capitalism, class, social relations," "labor, value, commodity," "ownership and control," "market," and "regulation";
- Production studies approach: "media work" and "authorship/ creativity."

Keywords in Media Economics

Media economics draws upon the **neoclassical economic approach** to study the business of media. The individual is singled out as the primary object of analysis. Individuals are assumed to engage in **rational behavior** to maximize their own interests. **Perfect information** about the market enables rational behavior. Information is generated in a **market** where buyers and sellers meet. A market is supposed to be fair and just, because competition enables a rational allocation of goods and services. Buyers and sellers voluntarily engage in economic transactions in a market.

Supply and Demand

The theory of **supply and demand** marks a cornerstone of neoclassical economics (Cunningham et al., 2015). This theory describes the **market mechanism**. **Demand** can be calculated based on the **wants and needs** of consumers that are determined by commodity price, income, taste, population size and composition, and government policies (Low, 2000). In this market mechanism, there should be no **government intervention**. The state should not use price controls to make commodity prices higher or lower. However, the reality is that most governments use price controls. For example, they impose taxes on foreign imports in order to stimulate local production or they subsidize domestic production so that they can compete in foreign markets. In the absence of government intervention, supply and demand will come into an **equilibrium** that determines the market price of a good and the total quantity that should be produced.

Figure 3.1 shows how the theory of supply and demand works. The spot in the center of the graph shows that when demand equals supply, the state of market equilibrium will be attained. **Price** and **quantity** are two factors that determine supply and demand (Pindyck & Rubinfeld,

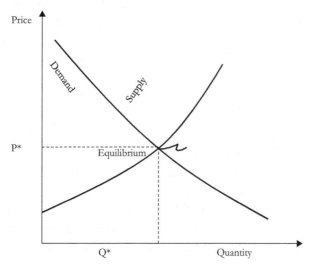

Figure 3.1 *Market equilibrium in the supply and demand curve. The theory of supply and demand assumes that individual consumers are* **rational** *and* **calculative;** *they demand more goods and services when the price is low. In contrast, individuals demand less when the price is high. Likewise, firms who supply such goods and services aim for* **profit** **maximization**: *the higher the price of a good is, the more the firms will supply the goods.*

1998). For all normal goods, the law of demand stipulates an inverse relationship between the price and the quantity. In other words, when goods are produced in small quantity, there will be a huge demand. On the other hand, when goods are produced in large quantity, the demand will drop. Because of this inverse relationship, any shifts in either demand or supply will upset the equilibrium. For example, when supplies fall but demand cannot be met, prices will rise. Consumers will then either cut back on demand or wait for normal supplies to be restored (Low, 2000). This scenario happened when Apple Computer first introduced the iPhone to the market. The demand was so high that eager consumers had to wait for months for the shipment.

The theory of supply and demand may not completely apply to media goods because of two reasons. First, taste plays a more significant role in consumers' demand than price does. As a result, media products are usually priced the same: most songs on iTunes cost the same; all movie tickets cost the same in a theater. A cheaper song will not drive consumers to buy it, let alone buy more. Second, the production of media goods is unlike that of other goods, because the first copy is significantly more expensive than the subsequent copies are. For goods like food, the cost to produce the first gallon of milk is the same as the cost to produce the second gallon. However, the cost to produce the *first* copy of a movie is significantly higher than the production of the *second* copy. Therefore, the theory of supply and demand may not easily apply to media markets.

Business Organization, Industry, and Sector

A **business organization** is a private entity whose chief goal is to make money. Like most organizations, a business entity is an organized group of people who share the same goal. In addition to making a profit, business organizations may have other goals as well. For example, some companies will highlight the social goods they provide. A business organization is made up of people who have specific roles. It also has a structure and hierarchy that governs who does what at what time.

While a media market is a place where buyers and sellers meet, a **media industry** refers to a collection of **business organizations** that produce the same goods. For example, all newspaper companies belong to the newspaper industry and all television stations belong to the television industry. Organizations in an industry operate in a similar way. For example, all newspapers will have an editor-in-chief; all daily newspapers are issued once a day, not once every two days.

A **sector** refers to a collection of industries. For example, the media sector is a collection of newspaper, magazine, television, and radio industries and so on. As shown in Chapter 4, "Economies," there is no universal standard for what the media sector is constituted of. In this book, industry and sector are used interchangeably, even though nation-states and international organizations have very strict definitions of what industries and sectors mean. We choose not to adhere to such a strict definition, because digital technologies have blurred the boundaries between traditional industries and sectors.

The media sector is even more complicated when we look beyond a national boundary. The biggest media organizations are **transnational corporations**: they operate in more than one country, one sector, one industry, and one market. Although it is possible to slice and dice the business activities of a transnational corporation and classify them into sectors, industries, and markets, such classification is not always meaningful to understand the media economy. The value of combined industries in one corporation is precisely the **synergy** that it produces: the value of media goods is greater when different units in a corporation work together.

Most of the media goods produced worldwide come from business organizations whose main goal is to make a profit. These organizations are called commercial media. Do business organizations in the media industry operate like those in other industries? Media economists would argue that they operate in the same way. Political economists and production studies scholars would argue that they do not. The disagreement is rooted in whether media goods are **public goods** or **private goods**. In contrast to **private goods** that are produced to satisfy individuals' wants and needs, public goods are produced for the greater societal good. Some other public goods are infrastructure, education, and healthcare. Public goods are necessary for a healthy and sustainable society. If infrastructure, education, and healthcare are all private goods, those who are willing to pay more will get better services. One consequence of seeing public goods as private goods is that the society as a whole will be worse off. A society will be weakened if most of its population is uneducated, sick, and has limited access to infrastructure such as road and transportation. For the same reason, some argue that media products should be seen as public goods, because socially meaningful media products will benefit the society as a whole. The question of whether media goods should be seen as private or public goods will be discussed in Chapter 7, "Civil Societies."

Keywords in Critical Political Economy

Capitalism, Class, and Social Relations

In this section, we will identify keywords and concepts in a critical political economy of communication. People who take this approach do not believe that any political economic system is natural and eternal. Yet, politicians and the media often suggest that **capitalism** is the best and the most natural political economic system in the contemporary world. As a result, social beings living in a capitalist society have accepted a specific way of allocating resources; they rarely ask if this way is the fairest and the most just. Critical political economists thus want to point out the **unnaturalness** of the system by showing the assumed logic of capitalism. They also want to provide alternative schemes of resource allocation to achieve a fairer, more just, and more equitable society.

Most citizens in today's world live in a capitalistic society. The few exceptions may be found in North Korea, Cuba, and a few small-scale tribal and indigenous societies. If we look back to societies in the 17th century, we will find most citizens lived in different kinds of society: agrarian, feudal, slave. Even in the 1960s, communism was a dominant political economic system in parts of Asia, Russia, and Eastern Europe. The unnaturalness of capitalism can be revealed if we contrast it with other systems.

Capitalism has a few distinctive characteristics. The first one is **property rights**: who has the rights to own what. Under capitalism, economic resources are owned by private individuals and institutions (such as production plants, service companies, transportation companies). The owners invest resources into the production of goods and services in order to make a profit. The profit will be partially pocketed by the owners and partially reinvested in the production process. Goods and services are priced based on the supply and demand of the market (see keyword "supply and demand" under media economics). Property rights have not always been seen as a private right. An agrarian society views property as communal—no one single individual owns land and raw resources. A communist society views property as "people-owned" (even though the state regulates the ownership), and the state decides what to produce and how resources will be allocated.

Another characteristic of capitalism is **class**. Political economists follow a Marxist understanding of class by seeing it as a **social relation**. Social relations are made to appear to be natural in a capitalist society. The unequal social relation between owners and workers keeps on reproducing, resulting in the rich getting richer and the poor getting poorer. Slave society is an example that shows how another political economic system creates a specific social relation. Because slaves are private properties of owners, they do not earn a wage. Children of slaves are also seen as the private properties of the owners; therefore, they can be sold to other owners. Slaves are only given basic necessities to renew their labor power in order to produce more goods, hence profits, for the owners.

Labor, Value, and Commodity

A labor market has to exist for workers to sell their labor power (Stilwell, 2002). **Objectified labor**—the third characteristic of capitalism—is as unnatural as capitalism and class are. In precapitalist societies, some humans owned their labor: they decided when to work, where to work, and how much they worked. For example, hunters and gatherers probably did not work from nine to five in order to sustain themselves and their families. This is not to say that their lives were easier and less structured than contemporary lives are, but they made their own decisions of how to deploy their labor. The same could be said of an agrarian society in which farmers work on their own land. Their work is determined by seasons and weather rather than by profits.

Capitalism, however, has changed how labor was conceived, because capitalists who owned the means of production could purchase **labor power** from workers. When land became private property and when machines sped up the production of goods, farmers and artisans found themselves becoming workers in a labor market. Karl Marx analyzed labor as **wage labor**. Workers sell their labor for wages, which they receive from capitalists. Capitalists have to standardize the quantity and quality of labor, because not all kinds of labor are the same. Labor of the sick and the elderly is not valued as highly as that of healthy, strong adults. In this case, only **productive labor** produced by fit and sound adults is valued in the market, because it produces surplus value.

51

Related to the concept of objectified labor is that of **exchange value**. Marx differentiated use value from exchange value. **Use value** is subjective; it is attributed by the users. For example, a mobile phone of an outdated model may not be worth much, but it has enormous use value to the users, especially if the phone has a lot of useful data on it or sentimental value. On the other hand, exchange value is objective; its value is determined by the market. Recalling the theory of supply and demand, the price of a good can be seen as the exchange value of the good. In a capitalist society, exchange value is privileged over use value. As a result, the market is flooded with products that may have low use value but high exchange value. An example is diamonds. Except for some industrial use, diamonds are stones with little use value. However, they command a high exchange value because they symbolize love, commitment, wealth, and so on.

Not only do workers produce **commodities** (defined as goods that have exchange value in the market), but their labor is also a form of commodity. Labor as a commodity has an objective exchange value that is determined by market supply and demand. If the market has an oversupply of workers, the exchange value of labor will be driven down. In contrast, labor shortage will drive up wages. Once workers sell their labor as a commodity, their labor power is said to be **alienated** from them; they no longer own their time or power. Marx called this a process of **exploitation**, because capitalists are only interested in buying productive labor in order to make a profit. The profit made by capitalists are not reinvested in the workers, but in more profit.

Students may find the Marxist theory of class, value, and labor irrelevant to their lives, because we tend to define workers as those who are less educated. We may think that bus drivers and cleaners are workers, but that media workers are not. Therefore, some theorists coin different terms to describe media workers. Hesmondhalgh (2013) uses the concept **cultural labor** to refer to workers in industries that "deal primarily with the industrial production and circulation of texts" (p. 16). As such, **cultural work** is the "work of symbol creators" (pp. 17, 20). In Chapter 9, "Labor," we will introduce concepts coined to characterize labor in the media, such as **free labor** and **affective labor**.

Ownership and Control

When Marx wrote about capitalism, the owners of the means of production were individuals. Nowadays, the scale of firms owned by individuals can hardly be compared to that owned by shareholders. In Chapter 4, "Economies," we will differentiate **private companies** from **public companies**. Since the 1980s, the scale of corporations is so immense that they exercise significant power on governments. Political economists are interested in examining how they exercise power through **ownership** and **control**. We will explain both terms at length in Chapter 4, but as a preview, ownership refers to who *owns* the media and who *profits* from them; control is about who *makes decisions* about the media.

A question that political economists ask about **ownership** is how much market share a corporation owns in a single market. Generally speaking, there are four types of market: **monopoly** (one firm in the entire market); **oligopoly** (a few firms in the entire market); **perfect competition** (many firms in the entire market); and **monopolistic competition** (many firms in the entire market, each firm sells a different product). Among the four types, economists generally agree that monopoly is the most harmful to consumers, whereas perfect competition is the most beneficial. Political economists, however, do not entirely agree with this assumption. Perfect monopoly (as in the past case of many telecommunications companies) is seen to be harmful to the market because it stifles competition. However, monopolies that are properly regulated by the state can benefit the public, because they are the most efficient in allocating resources. For example, there is usually only one railway company in one city, because it is not cost effective to have two sets of railroads leading to the same destinations. In most countries, the railway companies are state monopolies.

Among the four types of market, stable oligopolies are believed to benefit media firms the most, because newcomers find it hard to enter. As a result, existing firms can continue making the most profits. A lot of media markets are oligopolies: broadcasting, film production, motion picture theaters, book publishing, and recorded music (McCheseny, 1999a). Political economists, however, point out that the media markets are not really oligopolies but monopolistic competition (Graham, 2006). In other words, media corporations offer similar but not identical goods. For example, Disney and NBCUniversal have amusement parks, but Time Warner does not. Instead, Time Warner licenses characters to Universal theme parks. The amusement parks of Disney and NBCUniversal are also different: while Disney targets families, NBCUniversal targets teenagers and young adults.

These corporations are not competing with each other on price, but on product differentiation.

Media economists also examine the nature of a market, but their motives are different from political economists. While media economists want to describe and analyze a market so that they can propose ways to make it the most efficient, political economists want to understand the nature of a market so as to critique **a concentration of power**. They pay particular attention to the strategies that corporations use to consolidate power, such as mergers and acquisitions (that one company buys another company; or two companies merge) and global expansion (that one company sets up branches overseas). Not all mergers and acquisitions consolidate power. For example, Myspace, which was acquired by News Corporation in 2005, did not add to the profit margins or enhance the parent company's brand image (Silkos, 2005; Jin, 2013; see also Chapter 6, "Technologies," which has more examples on "de-convergence"). Mergers and acquisitions have made Silicon Valley a powerful global player: not only are a number of hi-tech companies located there, but there are also many "start-up" firms waiting to be absorbed by the few giants. Mergers and acquisitions are used to eliminate competition, resulting in an unfair and unjust market that poorly allocates resources (McCheseny, 1999a).

What are some consequences of a concentration of power in the media? There are a few implications. First, there is a debate of whether the most wealthy and powerful people—through owning the media—are able to impose their values on audiences. The impact may not be as direct as owners' viewpoints being imposed on the audiences; the impact may be more indirect because owners' influence is exerted through cultural production and distribution (Hesmondhalgh, 2014). For example, media corporations tend to steer clear of certain topics because they are assumed to have little market interest.

The second implication of a concentrated market is that it hurts democracy. Because democracy is about a marketplace of diverse viewpoints, a concentrated media will diminish the range of viewpoints. A narrow range of viewpoints is particularly detrimental to journalism, because the press is believed to play a watchdog function of the state. If journalists are indirectly asked to provide news of a narrow range of viewpoints, they will do a disservice to society.

The third implication is that the few firms in a market will do **price-fixing**, because the lack of competition among companies in a market will reduce the desire to use a low price to attract consumers (Downing, 2011). An often-cited case study is the breakup of AT&T. After the monopoly was broken up, consumers could choose their services from many telephone companies. As a result, companies competed for customers by offering low-cost service. However, the reconsolidation of telecommunications corporations reduced the number of providers. Consumers usually can only choose between a handful of providers who offer a very similar price. Once again, they do not compete based on price but on brand differentiation.

Market

Market is a keyword used in all three approaches. It can be defined as institutions or organizations that make economic decisions, where particular goods or services are bought and sold at prices negotiated between buyers and sellers. Political economists such as Meehan and Torre (2011) believe that this conventional definition has a few false assumptions. First, the market is assumed to be an actual and singular place where people go to sell or buy goods and services; second, the sellers and buyers are assumed to have only one motive; and third, the transaction is assumed to involve only one commodity. This highly abstract definition of a market assumes the **autonomy** of all market participants: that they enter the market voluntarily and with a clear purpose. The abstraction of market is supposed to be free and competitive; thus it guarantees economic growth and political stability for all nations in the global economy (Meehan & Torre, 2011). We will cover in Chapter 4, "Economies," that an abstraction of the market is false because of a number of reasons. For example, different kinds of markets coexist: some are legal, some are illegal; some involve face-to-face interaction, some virtual; some are more free with no state intervention, some are less free with red tape. We will talk about different types of economies in Chapter 4.

Regulation

Political economists do not shy away from discussing the role of the state in resource allocation, because government policies are related to property rights, markets, and class relationships by regulating the operation of markets for labor, capital, land, and commodities (Stilwell, 2002). **Regulation** refers to laws and policies that stipulate what is allowed and disallowed in a society. Regulation works at different levels: from town/city, state/province, national, and regional to international. Regulation is related to control: how a society organizes itself, manages its affairs, and adapts (or fails to adapt) to the inevitable changes that all societies face (Mosco, 2009). In this vein, control is a political process, because the government shapes social relations within a community and a nation.

We mention the concept of **public goods** earlier. Public goods do not just exist; they exist because of regulations. A public good is "an item for which one person's use of or benefit from the product does not affect its use by or benefit to another person" (Baker, 2002, p. 8). In the same vein, some argue that media—in particular journalism—should be supported by the government. Regulations that are useful to generate media as public goods include direct funding to media organizations, scholarships for journalism students and professionals, and tax cuts for firms that produce goods.

Keywords in Production Studies

Production studies is a relatively new field in media studies; therefore, it may be less familiar to media scholars and students. Production studies scholars are interested in "how media producers make culture, and, in the process, make themselves into particular kinds of workers in modern, mediated societies" (Mayer, Banks, & Caldwell, 2009, p. 2). Based on this definition, we introduce two keywords—"media work" and "authorship/creativity"—in this section.

Media Work

Media production scholars analyze **work**. Media economists and critical political economists tend to reduce work to labor, but work is more complicated than just labor. Hesmondhalgh (2014) pointed out that the working lives of media workers are neglected by most media scholars. Prospective workers seek jobs in the media and cultural sectors not only because they want to exchange their labor for wages, but also because they enjoy the content as audience members. Media products are readily available in different venues; they are a visible way for the workers to show others what they have done. In addition, media work is usually seen as creative work that can be found in global cities. The aura surrounding media work is not accidental, because it is carefully planned by the industries and the states. Hesmondhalgh (2014) pointed out that **cultural labor** (or creative labor) has become "a special case of some emergent features of contemporary capitalism, and so has a neighboring set of labor practices, in new media" (p. 15). In other words, media work is necessary because it is seen as a new kind of labor that generates profit for capitalism. Unlike industrial labor that is slowly dwindling in industrial societies, there is a presumed demand for and supply of creative labor.

According to Deuze (2007), cultural labor has four elements: (1) the organizations that hire cultural labor are a combination of public service and companies; (2) the organizations that deal with the industrial and creative production and circulation of culture; (3) the production of spoken and written words, audio, still or moving images; and (4) the production of platforms for the production and exchange of content. The four elements are integrated in media work, thus making it hard to assess what it really is. Suffice it to say, anyone dealing with the production and circulation of content, connectivity, creativity, and commerce can be counted as cultural workers.

Media work is highly dependent on technologies. For example, computer engineers can write "bots" for sports and business reporting. Readers are not able to differentiate stories written by humans from those written by algorithm. In another example, consumers have become "prosumers" and "playbor." (We will explain these terms in greater detail in Chapter 9, "Labor.") We produce content by consuming social media and technologies. Therefore, media work needs to be understood in the process of adaptation to technological development (Deuze, Elefants, & Steward, 2010).

Authorship/Creativity

Unlike other manufacturing industries, such as automobile and chemical, the media industries make cultural products that are aesthetic, symbolic, and expressive. This means that the products are embedded with the signature of the creators. The concept of **authorship**—the emphasis on individual creators—thus highlights the relationship between the products and the originators. Authorship implies that **creativity** is incremental: that artists innovate a small step at a time; at each time, they modify conventions and challenge boundaries (Hesmondhalgh, 2014). In other words, "the new idea, process or product that is created must be original and be judged to be so in at least one social setting" (McIntyre, 2012, p. 41). Something is deemed creative if the creators can develop something original, of high quality, and appropriate to the task at hand (Redvall, 2016). Any study of creativity in the media focuses on three major interests: the creative person, the creative process, and the created object (McIntyre, 2012). Creativity is not only required for the arts, but also for scientific findings, digital inventions, and sustainable new social programs (Sternberg & Lubrat, 1999). The Apple ad campaign "Think Different" illustrates the concept of creativity well. Famous figures such as John Lennon, Albert Einstein, and Martin Luther King Jr. show the audience who did things differently so that the entire humankind could benefit. Many may also add Apple founder Steve Jobs to the list of highly creative people.

Authorship implies the creators often work alone and in isolation. According to Hesmondhalgh (2014), there is a great emphasis on the achievements of great individuals (as reflected in the list of people in the Think Different campaign). We discussed in Chapter 2 that the majority of books published on the business of media are about individuals rather than teams. Media products, however, are almost always done in teams; this is especially the case when they are produced in a conglomerate. Newspapers and films, in particular, need hundreds, if not thousands, of people on a single project. This raises the question of who does what to "create" a product and what it means when one says "a film, TV program or album is '*by*' someone" (Hesmondhalgh, 2014, p. 149; emphasis added). Some try to weigh in on the question by using the concept "**utterance**": whoever intentionally "utters" any action to express an idea is the author. Sellors (2007) thinks utterance is a useful concept, because it implies an **agency** and an action. Thus, analyzing a textual utterance relies on identifying what constitutes an utterance.

The concept of utterance may be less salient with work that emphasizes commercial success. Names such as movie stars are attached to blockbusters. In such a case, the authorship of the media text is not highlighted in marketing and publicity, even though the stars may not have as much creative control over the work as the director (Hesmondhalgh, 2014). This calls into question the ongoing conflicts between media work as creative and it being constrained by market. Therefore, media researchers need to take into account that media workers are both creators of meaningful work and servants to capitalism (Whitney & Ettema, 2003, cited in Mayer, Banks, & Caldwell, 2009). At the same time, media corporations need to balance their respect for producers' creativity and the company's economic sustainability.

Conclusion

The three approaches discussed here—media economics, critical political economy, and production studies—hold different positions on how the business of media can be studied. Two reasons to explain the differences are ontological standpoints and the central object of studies. As shown in Table 3.1, the three approaches have differing views of whether the reality of "economy" and "market" exists: media economists do not question their existence; political economists question them as results of historical outcomes; and production studies scholars believe they are intersubjective constructs. The central objects of study are also different: media economists study the economies and markets; critical political economists study capitalism and social relations; and production studies scholars study media work and workers' identity. Despite the differences, we believe that prospective media practitioners can better position themselves in the job market if they are able to examine the business of media from the three approaches. Asking more than one set of questions allows future media workers to be critical thinkers, which in turn enables them to become change agents in transforming the media industry.

Critical political economy and production studies both emphasize the transformative power of change agents. Political economists illustrate change by adopting a historical approach to show the continuous unfolding of events in real historical time. They emphasize a dynamic approach to analyzing the world around us, illuminating the forces that provoke and steer the processes of change (Stilwell, 2002). Therefore, the end goal of a critical political economic critique is to promote social justice and democracy in the media and the broader society. Production studies also believes in workers being change agents. Change occurs when they are able to articulate their lifeworlds through languages. The industry may appear like a fixed structure, but participants' activities constitute this structure.

In the following six chapters, we will examine the six lenses (economies, politics, technologies, civil societies, cultures, and labor) from which we can examine the business of media. In each of the chapters, we will describe how the three approaches view the lens. Then we will draw on some of the keywords and concepts we introduce in this chapter to explain the lens.

References

Albarran, A. (2002). *Media economics: Understanding markets, industries and concepts*. Malden, MA: Wiley.

Bank, M., Corner, B., & Mayer, V. (2016). *Production studies sequel: Cultural studies of global media industries*. London: Routledge.

Baker, E. (2002). *Media, markets, and democracy*. Cambridge: Cambridge University Press.

Caldwell, J. (2008). *Production culture: Industrial reflexivity and critical practice in film and television*. Durham, NC: Duke University Press.

Cunningham, S., Flew, T., & Swift, A. (2015). *Media economics*. London: Palgrave Macmillan.

Davies, M. (2006). Production studies. *Critical Studies in Television: The International Journal of Television Studies, 1*(1), 21–30.

Deuze, M. (2007). *Media work*. Cambridge, UK: Polity.

Deuze, M., Elefante, P., & Steward, B. (2010). Media work and the recession. *Popular Communication, 8*(3), 226–231.

Downing, J. (2011). Media ownership, concentration, and control: The evolution of debate. In J. Wasko, G. Murdock, & H. Sousa (Eds.), *The handbook of political economy of communication* (pp. 140–168). Malden, MA: Wiley-Blackwell.

Doyle, G. (2002). *Media ownership: The economics and politics of convergence and concentration in the UK and European media*. London: Sage.

Garnham, N. (2000). *Emancipation, the media, and modernity*. Oxford: Oxford University Press.

Graham, P. (2006). Issues in political economy. In A. Albarran, S. Chan-Olmsted, & M. Wirth (Eds.), *Handbook of media management and economics* (pp. 493–521). London: Lawrence Erlbaum.

Golding, P., & Murdock, G. (2005). Culture, communications and political economy. In J. Curran & M. Gurevitch (Eds.), *Mass Media and Society* (4th ed., pp. 60–83). London: Arnold.

Hesmondhalgh, D. (2013). *The cultural industries* (3rd ed.). London: Sage.

Hesmondhalgh, D. (2014). Media industry studies, media production studies. In J. Curran (Ed.), *Media and society* (5th ed., pp. 145–163). London: Bloomsbury.

Jin, D. Y. (2013). *De-convergence of global media industries*. London: Sage.

Keane, M., & Sanson, K. (2016). *Precarious creativity: Global media, local labor*. Berkeley, CA: University of California Press.

Low, L. (2000). *Economics of information technology and the media*. Singapore: Singapore University Press.

Mayer, V. (2016). The places where audience studies and production studies meet. *Television and New Media*, 1–13. Retrieved from http://journals.sagepub.com/doi/abs/10.1177/1527476416652482

Mayer, V., Banks, M. J., & Caldwell, J. T. (2009). Introduction: Production studies: Roots and routes. In V. Mayer, M. J. Banks, & T. J. Caldwell (Eds.), *Production studies: Cultural studies in media industries* (pp. 1–13). London: Routledge.

McChesney, R. (1999a). *Rich media, poor democracy: Communication politics in dubious times*. New York: The New Press.

McChesney, R. (1999b). The political economy of communication and the future of the field. *Media, Culture & Society*, 22(1), 109–116.

McIntyre, P. (2012). *Creativity and cultural production: Issues for media practice*. London: Palgrave Macmillan.

Meehan, E., & Torre, P. (2011). Markets in theory and markets in television. In J. Wasko, G. Murdock, & H. Sousa (Eds.), *The handbook of political economy of communication* (pp. 62–82). Malden, MA: Wiley-Blackwell.

Mosco, V. (2009). *The political economy of communication* (2nd ed.). London: Sage.

Owers, J., Carveth, R., & Alexander, A. (2004). An introduction to media economics theory and practice. In A. Alexander, J. Owers, R. A. Carveth, C. A. Hollifield, A. N. Greco (Eds.), *Media economics: Theory and Practice* (3rd ed., pp. 3–48). Mahwah, NJ: Lawrence Erlbaum.

Pindyck, R., & Rubinfeld, D. (1998). *Microeconomics*. Upper Saddle River, NJ: Prentice-Hall.

Redvall, E. (2016). Craft, creativity, collaboration, and connections: Educating talent for Danish television drama series. In M. Banks, B. Corner, & V. Mayer (Eds.), *Production studies sequel: Cultural studies of global media industries* (pp. 75–88). London: Routledge.

Samuelson, Paul A. (1976). *Economics* (10th ed.). New York: McGraw-Hill.

Sellors, P. (2007). Collective authorship in film. *The Journal of Aesthetics and Art Criticism*, 65(3), 263–271.

Silkos, R. (2005, July 18). News Corp. to acquire owner of MySpace.com. *New York Times*. Retrieved from www.nytimes.com/2005/07/18/business/news-corp-to-acquire-owner-of-myspacecom.html?_r=0

Sternberg, R. J., & Lubart, T. I. (1999). The concept of creativity: Prospects and paradigms. In R. J. Sternberg (Ed.), *Handbook of creativity* (pp. 3–31). Cambridge, UK: Cambridge University Press.

Stilwell, F. (2002). *Political economy: The contest of economic ideas* (3rd ed.). Oxford: Oxford University Press.

Thussu, D. (2006). *International communication: Continuity and change*. London: Bloomsbury.

Wasko, J., Murdock, G., & Sousa, H. (Eds.). (2011). *The handbook of political economy of communication*. Malden, MA: Wiley-Blackwell.

Whitney, C., & Ettema, J. S. (2003). Media production: Individuals, organizations, institutions. In A. Valdivia (Ed.), *A companion to media studies* (pp. 157–187). Oxford: Blackwell.

Winseck, D., & Jin, D. Y. (Eds.). (2011). *The political economies of media: The transformation of the global media industries*. London: Bloomsbury.

Economies

At the end of the chapter, students will be able to:

- explain why an economy is both an objective reality and a subjective perspective, both a state and a process, and both macro and micro concepts;
- suggest how the three approaches (media economics, political economy of communication, and production studies) conceptualize an economy;
- state five reasons why an economy is difficult to measure. Give an example to illustrate each of them;
- state the different types of international, regional, national, and business organizations that measure media economies. Suggest why they collect and analyze economic data;
- explain what an informal economy is. Give examples of what kinds of media activities belong to the informal economy;
- explain the different business models by applying the concepts of ownership and control.

If there is no [live] show, then all those people who want to hear the musical will be sad. If all those people are sad, they might not go to work tomorrow. If they don't go to work tomorrow, the economy will collapse. And if the economy collapses, the country will be doomed.

(*Sesame Street* special episode "Elmopalooza,"
aired on ABC on February 20, 1998)

The television show *Sesame Street* not only teaches children about the alphabet and numbers, but it also teaches them how an entertainment show is related to the national economy. In a special *Sesame Street* episode "Elmopalooza," host Jon Stewart was locked inside a dressing room. A worrying monster explained to others that if the live show is canceled, then no one will go to work and the nation will be doomed. The worrying monster may entertain the young viewers by talking about the economy in a comical way, but his concerns may not be entirely lost on the adult viewers who regularly hear about how the economy affects our daily lives, the nation, and the world.

We frequently hear the word "economy" in television news and daily life conversations. For example, the news media tell us that developed countries such as North America, Europe, and Japan have been experiencing slow economic growth in the past few decades. Worse still, from the 1990s to the 2010s, Latin American countries had experienced a recession resulting in slow income growth (Weisbrot, 2011). On the contrary, the Chinese economy had enjoyed double-digit growth during the same time period. In daily life conversations, we hear a bad economy would lead to a tough job market while a good economy would lead to more consumer spending, home sales, and job gains. Both news reports and daily life conversations tell us that there is only one single *economy*, and *that* economy can be measured, compared, and predicted. Moreover, we are told that *the* economy affects our lives in multiple ways, in our ability to find a job, afford a house, and buy things. If there is only *one* economy, then why do we use the plural form "economies" for the chapter title?

How Is the Concept "the Economy" Different From "Economies"?

The term "economies" is preferred to "economy," because the plural form implies there are many coexisting and concurrent economies. Economies are fluid, because the technical definition and public perception of an economy changes. We prefer to see the economy not as a single entity or "thing," but as a *fluid concept* that encompasses *both an objective "reality" and a subjective perception, both a state and a process, both a macro and a micro concept.*

How is an economy objective and subjective at the same time? An objective economy can be measured and quantified. Some objective measurements are the gross domestic product (GDP) and the consumer confidence index. Regardless of our socioeconomic status, the GDP and the consumer confidence index stay the same. Yet each of us has a subjective perception of an economy. For example, stock market performance directly affects stockowners' net worth, but it may not directly impact that of a low-income person. But stock market performance may indirectly affect a low-income worker's ease in finding work, because the affluent population may reduce spending on household services that employ low-income workers. In another example, when the news announces a high consumer confidence index, shoppers may loosen up their purse strings more because they feel everyone is spending more in a good economy.

How is an economy *a state* and *a process* at the same time? Economists characterize economies in different time periods as different states. For example, the US suffered from an economic collapse in the 1930s after the stock market crash. The European economy was damaged after WWII and had to go through a recovery period in the late 1940s. The Japanese economy went through a "bubble" in the late 1980s. Argentina has been suffering from high inflation since 1991. Even a layperson could associate these economic states with specific hardships in daily life. For example, jobs were hard to find during the Great Depression in the US; food rationing was implemented in Europe after WWII; the housing price was high during a bubble economy; and people could not afford daily necessities during an inflation. However, an economy is also a process, because plenty of economic activities are taking place even during a recession, only they slow down. As long as people are working for money and buying daily necessities, economic processes take place. We can say that an economy is in process as long as human beings engage in economic activities.

An economy is studied at both the *micro* and *macro* levels. Students are usually introduced to economics by taking either microeconomics or macroeconomics classes: the former deals with economic behaviors of individuals and firms; the latter deals with national economies such as inflation, growth, and unemployment. Even to someone who has never heard of microeconomics and macroeconomics, we are constantly making economic decisions in daily situations, some of which are affected by national economies. For example, we know a set meal in a restaurant costs less than à la carte dishes do because it takes less labor to make a large quantity of the same kind of food. We also know that the price of a meal depends on a number of factors: labor cost, rent, and overhead. Some of our micro-level daily decisions are impacted by macro-level governmental policies. For example, the government may decide workers' minimum wage or food subsidies.

Bearing in mind that "economies" is a more useful concept than "the economy," we ask four key questions in this chapter:

- How is an economy being talked about in the news media and daily lives? The economy is regularly mentioned in the news, but laypersons may think the concept is too complicated for noneconomists to understand. As a result, the media economy is seen as something that needs years of schooling to understand.
- Which international, regional, and local organizations collect data about media economies? Why do organizations collect these data and for what purpose? Despite the plentiful data, we argue that it is hard to estimate the size of the *entire* global media economy, because different organizations use different categories to classify data.
- What are some economic activities that are not measured in the formal economy? What is an informal economy in relation to the media? Is it possible to estimate the size of the informal economy? What are some economic activities that contribute to an informal media economy?
- How are economic models related to business models? Certain business models may be favored in certain economic models, but by no means does an economic model limit the variety of business models.

How the Three Approaches Conceptualize the Economy

Among the three approaches introduced in this book, the media economic approach and the political economic approach are the most explicit at describing and explaining media economies, while the production studies approach is the least explicit at describing it.

Media Economics

The media economic approach sees the economy as an object of study. Media economists are primarily interested in understanding media markets and how they operate in an economy. Albarran (2002) states that the media are economic institutions whose chief purpose is to produce and distribute media contents to consumers. Based on this, "media economics is the study of how media industries use scarce resources to produce content that is distributed among customers in a society to satisfy various wants and needs" (p. 5). Media economists tend to focus on microeconomic issues, such as firm behaviors (for instance, why Amazon.com began as an online book retailer but became a distributor of films, television shows, and music), characteristics of specific markets (for instance, why the market for printed news is shrinking), and consumers' preferences and activities (for example, what kinds of audience tend to watch prerecorded shows).

In a sense, media economists do not see the media industry as different from other industries (such as the food and beverage industry or the hospitality industry), because like any other industry, firms allocate limited resources to satisfy consumers' needs and wants. In another sense, media economists are aware that the media market is different from other markets. For example, Napoli (2009) calls the media market a dual goods market: while producers deliver contents to the consumers, they also deliver consumers to the advertisers. The media market is a dual goods one because advertisers partially pay for the goods that media consumers buy. For example, the price of a subscribed magazine is lower than the cost to produce one copy of the magazine. The subscription price is kept artificially low so that consumers will continue subscribing to them and magazines can deliver a readership to advertisers. Free magazines rely solely on advertising money. In return, they are distributed in affluent areas for consumers who have disposable income. Media economists are also aware that media goods are different from other goods, because customers' taste plays a more important role than prices in the media market. For example, iTunes charges the same price for every song, because a song that has a lower price tag will not make it more popular. In contrast, customers' taste may play a lesser role in the food and beverage market. While customers may prefer a certain brand, they may prefer a product that has a lower price tag.

A Political Economy of Communication

The critical school of political economy of communication also sees the economy as an object of study, but political economists do not see economies as a separate entity from politics and cultures, because they are interested in understanding *who* have the power to distribute and control resources and *how* they exercise the power. They do not see the economy as an autonomous entity that is devoid of human intervention and power struggle. Returning to the example of iTunes, political economists would argue that the reason why iTunes is the dominant online music retailer is not necessarily that it is the best in the market, but that Apple Computer has the money and power to negotiate with record labels and artists. Also unlike media economists, political economists do not believe an understanding of the economy can be reduced to mathematical calculation. However, like media economists, political economists also want to understand an economy by examining market structures, firm behaviors, competition, and consumer behaviors.

Production Studies

In contrast to the two approaches of media economics and a political economy of communication, the production studies approach is the least explicit at analyzing the economy. It does not mean that they ignore the economic factor of media production, but they see the economy as a condition under which media practitioners negotiate their sense of identity and agency in the industry. In a post-Fordist economy and a neoliberal capitalist society (see Chapter 2, "The History of the Study of the Business of Media" for definitions), media workers are asked to see themselves as empowered individuals and active economic beings. In a neoliberal capitalist society, media workers are asked not to see themselves as passive workers, like waged labor in a fast food restaurant. Instead, media workers are asked to exercise their own sense of agency, which would aid them in figuring out their economic worth and plotting their career move. This economic self is both subjective and objective. On the one hand, media workers reckon that they are willing to take financial risks because they love what they do. On the other hand, they are asked to be business savvy and learn how much they can charge for their work in the market. From this approach, an economy cannot be reduced to concepts such as market

Table 4.1 *How the three approaches conceptualize an economy*

	Media Economics	Political Economy of Communication	Production Studies
Object of study	The economy at a microeconomic level	The economy at a macroeconomic level	The economy as a condition under which workers' identity is negotiated
Primary interests	Media markets; How the markets operate in an economy	Power to control and distribute resources	Identity and agency in a neoliberal capitalist society

structure and competition, but also how participants negotiate their identities, roles, and functions in a media economy.

Advanced media technology and flexible labor seem to have disrupted the market and economies. For example, search engine companies such as Google and Baidu are said to have changed how advertising models work. Mass advertisements are said to be less effective than targeted advertising. However, which *economy* do these companies disrupt? Because there are different concurrent economies, it is hard to argue the existence of these companies have changed all the economies in the same way.

What Is an Economy?

After reviewing how the three approaches—media economics, a political economy of communication, and production studies—study an economy, we look at what an economy is. As previously mentioned, economies are both a state and a process, objective and subjective, and macro and micro concepts. However, when an economy is mentioned in the news, it is predominately described as an objective "thing" at a macro level.

The word "economy" is frequently mentioned in the news media and daily life conversations. Despite the frequent mentions of the word and the perception that the economy impacts our personal and work lives, a layperson often feels an economy is too complicated to understand. In addition, the word "economy" is ambiguous because its meanings are context-driven. In this section, we look at how the word is used in different contexts and why the word is ambiguous.

A search for the word "economy" on Google News in any day would yield an inexhaustible number of articles. When we drafted this chapter, the two most popular pieces were "Will the US economy slip into recession in 2016?" from *CBS MoneyWatch* (Sherter, 2015) and "China's Economy: Seven Predictions for 2016" from the *Los Angeles Times* (Yang & Li, 2015). In the first article, the US economy is said to be influenced by a number of factors: unemployment rate, consumer confidence, interest rate, economic growth, market demand from overseas buyers, corporate profits, Americans' optimism, job creation, GDP, and household debt. The second article, "China's Economy: Seven Predictions for 2016," explicates the tie between the US and Chinese economies. The US economy is said to depend on the Chinese one because of tourism, real estate sales, Chinese investment, and US farm exports. The Chinese economy is said to be weakened as a result of slower growth rate, lower currency value, and less money spent on gambling. Both articles share a few themes about *the* national economy: present and past data can be used to predict future economic performance; the Chinese economy affects the American one more than vice versa; and the economy can be explained with a plethora of factors: labor supply, market demand, foreign investment, and so on. However, it is unclear if all factors influence the economy in a similar way to a similar degree. It is also unclear which factors are the causes or effects. Because an economy appears to be a "thing" that moves on its own and cannot be controlled, it is no surprise that a layperson feels the economy is too complicated to understand! To a layperson, the economy appears to be a result of too many factors, and each factor is already a complicated concept on its own.

However, some populations may not learn about the economy from news but from daily lives. There are many online resources, books, and television shows about wise spending. Some common advice is to have a budget and stick to it; shop alone and do it quickly; use coupons and compare prices. The same tips are presented in various ways for different audiences. Laypersons may have an easier time understanding what an economy means by reflecting on their own spending habits. After all, even young children may know if they choose one thing, they cannot choose another. While news reports tend to see the economy as an uncontrollable "thing" that cannot be readily understood, articles about wise spending paint the economy as a personal plan. In news articles, an economy is an objective state that occurs at a macro level. In articles about wise spending, an economy is a subjective process at the micro level. Neither concept of the economy is wrong, because the economy is always both a *state* and a *process*, *objective* and *subjective*, *macro* and *micro*.

Throughout this chapter, we apply a political economic assumption that economies are not a separate entity from politics and cultures. The above three examples show precisely why they do not belong to three separate spheres. For example, why do economists and business analysts in the United States pay so much attention to the performance of the Chinese economy? In the 1940s–1960s, it was a struggle to find a headline about the Chinese economy in mainstream news. The development of the Chinese economy is a result of the open-door policy implemented by Chinese leader Deng Xiaoping in the 1970s, which led to the reintegration of the Chinese economy with the developed economies. The prominence of the Chinese economy was a political decision made some decades ago that resulted in Americans' business interest in the Chinese economy since the 1980s. China had an economy from the 1940s to the 1960s, but it did not impact the US economy. In the example of wise spending tips, individuals are asked to see themselves as informed consumers who must make wise choices among the many options in the retail industry. This consumer culture is fostered in an affluent society where consumption is seen as a pastime and a leisure activity. In a society that focuses on production— which is what most societies were prior to WWII—most consumed because they had to sustain life, not because they saw it as a leisurely activity.

Why Is an Economy Difficult to Measure?

Laypersons may find economies to be a complicated matter, but they would have faith that an economy can be measured and predicted by economists. We question this faith by suggesting that the media economy cannot be accurately measured because of five reasons. First, as we see in Chapter 1, "Introduction and Overview," media corporations have expanded the boundary of the media industry. Traditionally, media refers to mass communication such as print (newspapers, magazines), broadcast (television, radio), film, and music. Nowadays, media conglomerates have business interests in "mass" media, social media, telecommunications, and information technologies. For example, the British news agency Reuters was acquired by the Canadian information firm Thomson in 2008, and the joint company was renamed as Thomson Reuters. Not only does the new conglomerate produce news, but it also produces information for professionals in the financial, education, medical, and legal sectors. Likewise, Walt Disney Company produces mass media products as well as goods in the arts, entertainment, and recreation sectors. Disney musicals, ice-skating shows, theme parks, and packaged tours are not media products, but goods in the live entertainment, recreation, and tourism sectors. However, the value of one arm of the company will increase the value of others. For example, when Disney has a hit movie like *Frozen*, its entertainment unit will benefit because it can create a Disney musical of the same title. In contrast, a company like General Electric may not enjoy the same benefits. While the consumers see General Electric as an electrical appliance company, this association may not increase the value of its former media branch: the television and film company NBC Universal.

The second reason why the media economy is difficult to measure is that privately owned companies do not disclose their revenues to the public. As discussed in Chapter 3, "Theories and Approaches to Study the Business of Media," there are two kinds of companies: public and private. While public companies are required by some countries to publish their financial information for investors, private companies are not required to disclose this information. As a result, the revenue of privately held companies may only be estimated from available figures, such as the number of employees and market shares. This estimation is further complicated by the fact that some privately held companies own diverse businesses. For example, Chinachem Group in Hong Kong began as a chemical company but evolved into a major real estate developer, investment company, hotel chain, and theatrical chain. But Chinachem Group does not invest in any other kinds of media business other than movie theaters. Therefore, it is hard to estimate how much of its revenue and profits come from the movie business. In Latin America, TelMex and América Móvil are two privately held telecommunications companies partially owned by one of the wealthiest persons in the world, Carlos Slim of Mexico.

The third reason why the media economy is difficult to measure is that a lot of nonmedia businesses produce media content for promotion, customer relations, and internal use. Some of the content is produced in-house rather than contracted out to a third party, such as an advertising and marketing firm. In-house production of nonmedia firms is not counted in the media economy. In addition, the popularity of the social media platform also complicates the measurement of a media economy, because an amateur could launch a social media campaign. Many small businesses do not pay outsiders to design an advertisement; instead, they rely on tech-savvy young employees to launch a social media campaign.

The above three reasons explain why a media economy is difficult to estimate in a *formal* economy. The fourth reason why a media economy is difficult to measure is that there are media activities in the *informal* economy. In the formal economy, economic activities are reported, measured, and counted towards the national economy. In this economy, media businesses report their profits and losses; employees report their income; and the government taxes media businesses' profits and individuals' income. In contrast, economic activities in the informal economy are not reported, measured, or counted towards the national economy. Some of the informal economic activities are legal; some of them are not. An example of a legal economic activity is street musicians getting tips for their performance and selling self-produced CDs. Although street musicians are supposed to report their income to the state, there is no record of their income, as they do not work for a company.

The fourth reason to explain why an economy is difficult to measure is that the informal economy is sometimes constituted of illegal activities. Some examples are illegally duplicated media such as software and DVDs; stolen cell phones and computers resold in local and international black markets; and the production and distribution of particular types of pornographic materials. It is extremely difficult to estimate the size of the informal economy, because cash transactions are difficult to track. Participants have to be secretive when producing, distributing, and consuming illegal content and technologies, so they tend to avoid paying with credit cards. Cash is a preferred form of payment because the authorities cannot trace who the traders are. In other situations, some governments are aware of the black market and illegal activities but tend to ignore the consequences, because those illegal activities greatly benefit the economy. For example, smuggling is pervasive in Paraguay because there is virtually no industry regulation; bankers, politicians, and soccer club barons who are involved in illegal economic activities make hefty campaign contributions to keep their businesses afloat (Guevara, 2014).

The fifth reason why an economy is difficult to measure is that there are ambiguous cases, in which some economic activities belong to the formal economy and some do not. Digital currency, such as bitcoin, also complicates the distinction between formal and informal economies. Bitcoin is not a currency recognized by any government. It is not issued by a central bank and the supply of bitcoin is not regulated. It is a digital currency that can be used at online merchants that recognize it. In a sense, bitcoin is like in-game currency: video game players can earn virtual money as long as other players recognize it. Because bitcoin is not regulated or overseen by a central bank of a government, it could be used as a currency for illegal transactions, such as drug trade.

The above five reasons explain why a media economy is difficult to measure. However, what if some economies cannot be measured at all? For example, a worker's emotional investment in a job. To give an example, although the compensation of famous movie stars and directors are high and the salary of production assistants is low, the personal investment of a production assistant may be as great as that of a movie star. Can and should this kind of subjective investment be measured? We cannot say that the personal investment of a movie star is significantly greater than that of a production assistant just because the movie star has a much higher compensation. A movie star may spend extensive time researching into a character in order to feel emotionally connected to the role. Similarly, a production assistant may spend extensive time researching into the skills required for the job in order to feel emotionally connected. If we expand an understanding of an economy to include everything that involves an investment of emotions and feelings, then we realize there are multiple, concurrent economies that take place in both public and private lives.

How to Measure Media Economies and Why It Should Concern Prospective Media Practitioners

Media industries in the digital age include more than mass media industries (such as broadcast, print, film, and music); they also include computing, telecommunications, and hi-tech industries. To estimate the size of the media industries, different international, regional, and national bodies measure media economies for different purposes. Governments and business consulting firms collect industry data to inform government officials, business executives, and investors for decision-making purposes. These bodies make decisions such as which media sector should be developed, what kinds of media goods should be exported, and how much money should be invested in the industries. These industry data might appear to be irrelevant to aspiring media practitioners, because the data appear to reflect the economy on a very grand scale. However, these data are relevant to the job prospects of media workers, because statistical figures could influence how states and businesses invest in the sectors. In the following, we examine five types of bodies that collect and publish data of media industries.

International Bodies

International bodies are not always international, because not all countries are member states. However, they aim to gather data of all regions. We review two international bodies here: the International Telecommunications Union (ITU) and the World Trade Organization (WTO).

The International Telecommunications Union (ITU)

Established in 1865, the ITU is a United Nations agency that addresses issues concerning information and communication technologies. It does not have an authority over national governments regarding telecommunications development, but it makes recommendations about international telecommunications standardization and regulation. It collects data that indicate the state of telecommunications development, such as penetration rates of telecommunications technologies in both the developing and developed worlds.

To the ITU, access to and ownership of telecommunications technologies are key indicators of how economically developed a region is. The ITU tends to see the developed world as a model for the developing world to emulate. For example, ITU data show that the developing world is quickly "catching up" with the developed one in terms of mobile phone subscriptions. In 2005, there were 82 subscriptions per 100 inhabitants in the developed world, but only 23 subscriptions in the developing world. A decade later in 2015, the figures jumped to 121 in the developed world and 92 in the developing world (ITU, n/a).

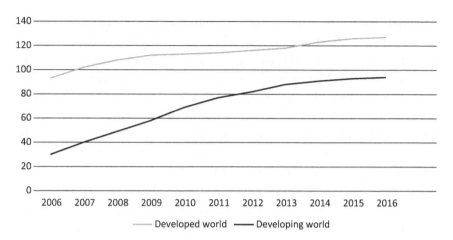

Figure 4.1 *Mobile phone subscriptions (per 100 inhabitants)*
Source: ITU

The narrowing gap of mobile telephony subscription rate between the developed and developing worlds may inform governments and businesses that it is better to invest in mobile telephony than in fixed telephony in the developing world because of the rapid growth.

The World Trade Organization (WTO)

Established in 1995, the WTO regulates international trade between countries, such as how much goods a country can export to other countries. In relation to media economies, the WTO gathers data on the import and export of office and telecom, and telecommunications equipment (WTO, n/a).

Table 4.2 *Import and export of office and telecom, telecommunications equipment (2014)*

Office and telecom equipment		Telecommunications equipment	
Top five exporters	Top five importers	Top five exporters	Top five importers
China	The EU	China	The US
The European Union (EU)	China	The EU	France
Hong Kong	The US	Hong Kong	India
The US	Hong Kong	The US	Canada
Singapore	Germany	The Netherlands	Russia

Source: WTO

Governments and businesses rely on these data to decide in which sector to invest and what competitive advantages they have internationally. For example, African and Latin American countries exported an insignificant amount of telecommunications equipment when compared to major Asian exporters. African and Latin American states may not want to invest in manufacturing telecommunications equipment, because they do not have an advantage when compared to Asian countries. On the other hand, they may find themselves more competitive in exporting raw materials to manufacture telecommunications equipment, such as zinc exported from Peru, China, and Australia to make circuit boards for telecommunications equipment.

Regional Organizations

Regional organizations also collect data on media economies. A well-known regional organization that collects such data is the European Union (EU). The EU is a regulatory body of the politics and economies of 28 member states. In terms of media-related data, the EU collects data on the number of people employed in the cultural sector. The EU has a broad definition of cultural workers; it ranges from people who work in the manufacturing, wholesaling, and retailing of printed and recorded media; to service providers in motion pictures and video activities, radio and television, arts facilities, news agencies, libraries, and museums; to—quite bizarrely—workers who repair motor vehicles and motorcycles. Like the ITU, the EU also tracks Europeans' access of online information technologies by collecting data such as subscriptions of mobile phone and broadband services, levels of computer and Internet skills, and participation in e-commerce, such as online shopping.

In addition to political economic bodies like the EU, regional organizations also include trade blocs whose primary interest is to facilitate trades between countries in the region. Trade blocs usually do not explicitly touch upon political issues unless those issues deal with the economy. For example, the US, Canada, and Mexico signed the North American Free Trade Agreement (NAFTA), which eliminated export restrictions in the three countries. Since the signing of the agreement, the US has increased its exports of computer and electronic products to the two trade partners (Office of the United States Trade Representative, n/a). Another regional trade bloc is the Association of Southeast Asian Nations (ASEAN). This organization tracks the imports and exports of media commodities such as printed books, newspapers, manuscripts, and typescripts in the region; imports and exports of telecommunications, computer, and information services; and personal, cultural, and recreational services (ASEAN, n/a). (See also Chapter 5, "Politics," on the nature of regional bodies.)

National Organizations

In addition to international and regional organizations, some countries also track economies of media industries, particularly if the countries have national policies to develop media industries for the purposes of exporting goods or seeking foreign investment. For example, the Australian government has led a strong push to develop the creative industry sector, which includes publishing, performing arts, visual arts, screen production, screen services, facilities (such as location filming and post-production), and music. The Department of Communications and Arts in Australia is in charge of administering programs to develop the creative industries. Some measures are funding innovation start-ups, giving tax credits to companies that engage in research and development (R&D), investing in broadband infrastructure, and investing in educating students at all levels (Department of Communications and the Arts, 2011). (In Chapter 5, see the case study of the Korean Wave and Cool Japan.)

Trade Organizations, Trade Unions, and State-Affiliated Commissions

Trade organizations, trade unions, and state-affiliated or state-sponsored commissions also collect data about media economies. Each of them represents the interests of a specific group: trade groups represent business interests; trade unions represent workers' interests; and state-affiliated or state-sponsored commissions assist businesses and workers with finding work in a specific region. All of these bodies focus on a niche area such as film, television, publishing, or music.

We use filmmaking as an example to illustrate the different roles played by trade organizations, unions, and state-affiliated commissions. Because of the long history of filmmaking in Hollywood and the economic power of the US film industry, US film workers and companies are highly organized and well represented by unions and trade associations. For example, the Motion Picture Association of America (MPAA) established in 1922 represents the interests of six major Hollywood studios. To the general public, MPAA may be better known as the organizer of the annual Academy Awards or the body to enforce film ratings. MPAA is less known to the public as a lobbyist on behalf of the studios. For example, it lobbies the US government to give tax breaks to film studios by showing the significance of the film economy to the country. It also lobbies the government to enforce tougher measures to prosecute offenders of DVD dubbing, because piracy is said to hurt the profits of film studios. MPAA is not only a lobbyist, but it is also a regulator of media economies. By enforcing the movie ratings system, it prohibits some audience segments from viewing films with indecent content. The ratings system may in name protect "family values," but it also determines what kinds of films should be made and distributed by major studios. Major studios would steer away from producing materials that are deemed unsuitable for young audience members, because those films will have a hard time finding a distributor.

The second type of organization is trade unions, which represent workers' interests. They collect data to show how much workers contribute to the local and national economies. A common concern among Hollywood workers and unions today is the outsourcing of production and post-production jobs from California to other states and countries. (See Chapter 9, "Labor," on what unions do.) Labor unions point out that outsourcing jobs would weaken a state's economy, because workers have less to spend and small companies are not making money.

The third type of organization is state-affiliated or state-sponsored commissions that assist businesses and workers in lobbying the state to invest in media industries and to lure investors to the region. They also collect data to show the economic significance of an industry. Many US states have set up offices to attract Hollywood producers to take their production outside Southern California. For example, the Massachusetts Film Office assists out-of-state producers in taking their production to this East Coast state. It provides databases of film professionals, locations, and previous work produced in the state. It keeps track of how much investment out-of-state producers bring to the state, how many people are employed, and how much money is retained in the state.

Trade associations, trade unions, and state-affiliated or state-sponsored commissions all collect economic data to lobby the government to provide a favorite condition. Each of them represents a different segment of the industries—large studios, smaller firms, and workers. As suggested, the US film industry is exceptionally organized; not all countries and industries have such well-organized forces. A country with a small film industry (such as Singapore) may not have well-organized trade associations. Emerging industries, such as video game design or apps design, may also be less organized: it is hard to know how many people are employed and how investment in the industry would make a national economy competitive in a global stage. However, the industries of video game and apps have a lot of room to grow in a digital age. In contrast, the studio-dominated film industry in the US may have reached a saturation point. Hence, it can be expected that in the near future, more data will be collected about the economic significance of emerging media industries, such as video games and apps.

Financial Services and Business Consulting Firms

Last but not least, financial services and business consulting firms collect economic data about media industries. Unlike those collected by international, regional, and national organizations, these data are not publicly available and are expensive to acquire. These data are marketed to investors and businesses that make decisions on investment. For example, Mergent is a financial service company that offers subscriptions of industry analysis. It provides analysis reports of the media, telecommunications, IT, and technology industries in four regions: North America, Latin America, Europe, and Asia Pacific. Their business analysis reports not only provide statistics of the industries, such as the revenue of major companies, but they also offer analysis of the region's broader social, economic, and political environment, industry profiles, and market trends and outlook.

Size of the Global Media Economies

After learning the range of organizations that provide data on media economies, readers may want to know the size of media economies: how many people are employed worldwide; what the sales figures of media products are; what the revenues of all media companies are. The answer is "no one knows"; it is not possible to know the size of global media economies. There are a few reasons to explain why this is the case: first, different organizations define the industries differently:

some see media workers as service workers in entertainment, tourism, and hospitality; some see media workers—along with opera singers and ballet dancers—as cultural performers. Some organizations, such as ITU, only look at access to information technology and mobile telephony, not ownership of television and radio sets. In addition, data about emerging media industries, such as video gaming and mobile phone apps design, are not widely collected. Second, some highly organized industries provide a plethora of information of export figures and employment figures, others much less so. Third, international organizations rely on self-reporting data from member states. Not all countries collect data of the media industry. The data collected by international organization and business firms are not really that international. For example, Mergent only collects data of the media and telecommunications sectors from five countries (Australia, China, Japan, South Korea, and Taiwan) and one city-state (Hong Kong) in the Asia Pacific region. The data do not cover Southeast and South Asia. Interestingly, it ignores India, even though it has the world's largest middle class and Bollywood produces more films annually than Hollywood does.

Readers may ask why the economic data matter to aspiring media workers, especially if they do not plan to work overseas. We argue that they matter to future media workers, because these data inform governments, investors, and businesses on which media industries will be globally competitive and what kinds of workers are needed to compete internationally. As previously shown, the Australian government promotes to media producers abroad that the country has the capacity to do post-production work. Video editors in the US, the UK, and Canada may compete with their Australian counterparts for work. The competition will be keen, because English is the primary language in all these countries. In addition to labor supply, exchange rate also affects the labor market. When the US dollar is strong, producers are likely to take American jobs overseas. A media student in the US may not spend too much time thinking of the media industry in Australia or the strength of the US dollar, but he/she may find some jobs are outsourced abroad. In another case, business analysis reports influence investment decisions from international firms. Because a financial service firm such as Mergent excludes a large number of Asia-Pacific countries, a media student in Singapore who is as talented and ambitious as a student in Hong Kong may not find the same opportunities in the media industry. What are measured or not have direct impact on media students around the world.

"Nonformal" Media Economies

We review above how different international, regional, and national organizations, state-affiliated commissions, and business consulting firms estimate the size of global media economies. We have suggested a number of reasons why the size of media economies is hard to estimate. This section focuses on another reason why it is impossible to estimate the size of media economies: many economic activities that produce and distribute media content are not reported to the states. Hence, these activities are not counted towards the formal economy. We call these "nonformal" media economic activities. They include the production of media for nonmedia companies; illegally dubbed media for sales in a black market; user-generated content; and open source software and common licensed media content.

As mentioned in Chapter 2, "The History of the Study of the Business of Media," an economic activity is any kind of production, distribution, and consumption that produces a value in a market. Any economic activity requires time and labor investment. While the definition of economic activity may appear to be straightforward, many examples illustrate that it is not as clear-cut as it may sound. For example, if bakery workers are asked to post images of the baked goods in their leisure time, is it a form of economic activity? If an intern in a media organization is neither paid nor has any job responsibility, is it a form of economic activity? If a father uploads his baby girl's photos on social media daily, is it a form of economic activity? According to the definition, they are all economic activities even though the media producers are not paid. They are economic activities because they have the potential to create value in a market, and these activities are done at the expense of someone's time and labor. For example, a bakery worker may not be paid to provide media content for the employer, but the images may attract more customers to patronize the business. An unpaid intern may not have any job responsibility, but he/she pays an opportunity cost: she could have spent the time and labor on a paying job. The father who produces social media content for private consumption on his own leisure time may not receive monetary compensation for the pictures, but his posts generate data for social media companies. Therefore, the father's uncompensated time and labor still produce a value in a market, albeit in an indirect way: the value is created when the marketers buy aggregated data from social media companies. (See Chapter 9, "Labor," on the concept of "free labor".)

The above three examples show economic activities that take place outside the media sector where producers are not paid for producing media content. Yet their activities are economic because they produce potential value in a market. In Chapter 7, "Civil Societies," and Chapter 9, "Labor," we explore in detail some of the following activities:

- "Nonmedia" market economy is contributed by workers who produce media content for nonmedia firms. Many small businesses do not have an in-house advertising/marketing unit, and they do not hire an outside firm to produce content on social media. Employees—usually young and tech-savvy ones—may assume the responsibility of producing content. Although workers are compensated for their work, the production of media content is not specified in the job description.
- "Nonmarket" media economy: the production, distribution, and consumption of media content by amateurs in their leisure time. While some amateurs hope to break into the professions by demonstrating their talents on social media, the majority create content for their own personal use. However, "nonmarket" media activities can be transformed into activities in a formal economy because of how social media companies distribute content. In a pre-digital age, amateurs used to produce content with analog technology, such as a manual camera or a camcorder. Sharing analog content was difficult, costly, and time consuming. Analog content could not be easily distributed by amateurs or media companies. Advanced technology allows amateurs to distribute content more easily, and it allows companies to monetize content not produced for the market. We will explore more of this issue in Chapter 9, "Labor."
- "Gift" economy: content produced to be shared at no cost for users. The content is shared in the commons as public goods. Some examples are online sharing of open source software and licensing content with nonexclusive terms. In the case of open source software, the code is collaboratively written by professionals and enthusiasts. Software could have had a market value if the collaborators had chosen to sell the code in a market. Similarly, a

photographer who licenses her picture under a Creative Common license could have sold the exclusive rights of the photos to a private entity, such as a news agency. These economic activities are said to contribute to a "gift" economy, because the content producers share their skills and products as a gift to others; in return, they do not expect any monetary compensation. We will examine the gift economy in the section about alternative media and platforms in Chapter 7, "Civil Societies."

The Informal Economy

In the previous section, we listed three cases of activities that are not counted towards a media economy even though those activities are related to the media. In this section, we focus on activities in the *informal* media economy; these activities are also not counted towards the formal economy because they are not reported to the state. One example is extracting scratch metals from "recycled" hardware dumped in developing countries (Maxwell & Miller, 2012). Another example is street musicians performing for tips. They are supposed to report the tips as income to the state, but they seldom do.

Some informal media activities are legal; others are illegal. While everyday consumers may knowingly break the law, such as by photocopying a copyrighted book, the state targets organized illegal activities, such as organized pirating of software, films, and television shows and sales of stolen electronic hardware, such as mobile phones and computers in a local or international black market. Illegal activities are carefully kept out of state surveillance. For example, human trafficking from Latin American countries to the United States and Canada is a good, yet unfortunate, example of an informal economy. Many of the victims come to North America with a legal work or visitor visa, but they stay after the visas expire (Woolhouse, 2014). More so than activities in the formal media economy, the value of informal media activities is even harder to estimate, because cash is the preferred form of money transactions.

Examples of Informed Media Activities

Pirating copyrighted software, films, and television shows is a criminal activity. International organizations, such as the WTO and the WIPO (World Intellectual Property Organization), and trade associations, such as MPAA and the Recording Association of America (RAA), are some bodies that collect data about illegally dubbed media. According to the lobbyist Software Alliance, nearly half of installed PC software was unlicensed. In 2013, the value of illegally dubbed software was $62.7 billion. Individuals can be prosecuted for dubbing copyrighted materials, but organized criminals are the major targets of the state.

Illegally dubbed copies may be sold within the country of origin, but many are sold abroad for a number of reasons. First, illegal copies are much cheaper than legal copies. To some populations, illegal copies of software are the only affordable kinds. Most of the unlicensed software is installed in computers in emerging countries. International textbook publishers have different prices for the same textbook: students in developing countries would pay less for the same content. However, it is illegal for anyone to buy the cheaper version in one market and sell it in another. Nonetheless, it is possible to buy the cheaper version of the textbooks online from an international marketplace, such as Amazon.com. Second, some countries such as China have a film quota that restricts the number of foreign films imported into the country. The local Chinese audience may have to turn to illegal copies to enjoy films that are not distributed in the country. The MPAA, on behalf of studios, has been lobbying the US government to pressure the Chinese government to increase the limit of the film quota. Third, some media products are released on different schedules. For example, *Game of Thrones* is the most illegally downloaded television show in history. Fans in the UK and Australia were eager to watch the show that was broadcast later in their countries, so they had to turn to peer-to-peer file sharing sites to satisfy instant gratification. Fourth, immigrants may buy or download illegal copies of movies from their home countries, because distributors tend not to buy rights to distribute films and television shows that have a limited audience. Last, illegal copies of films and TV shows are also circulated in countries where certain materials are banned. For example, copies of South Korean dramas are leaked across the border to North Korea (Kim, 2013). South Korean dramas are not broadcast in its northern counterpart, because they are criticized for promoting materialism and decadence.

The second kind of illegal media economic activity is the sale of stolen electronic goods, such as mobile phones and laptop computers. It has been established that 40% of robberies in major US cities are thefts of mobile phones. In 2014, 1.6 million cell phones were stolen in the

US (Smith, 2013). According to a 2014 *Huffington Post* report, Bogotá, Colombia, is a destination and entrepôt of stolen cell phones: "the traffickers take stolen phones from the United States to an electronics market at a shopping center in downtown Bogotá, where the devices are refurbished and then smuggled across borders" (Smith, 2014, para. 11). The smugglers find ways to disguise the stolen cell phones and transport them by air, sea, or ground. Older models of stolen mobile phones and laptop computers may also be shipped overseas, because new models are too expensive for some populations.

Online auction sites, such as eBay, and community marketplaces, such as craigslist, are also places for traders to sell stolen goods. Sometimes the unsuspicious buyers are not aware that the goods are stolen until the phones fail to connect to the network. The boundary between legal and illegal economies is not clear. Illegal media products can contribute to the formal economy because the sellers report the sales of illegal products. For example, many counterfeit CDs are sold on Amazon.com, which cannot tell the difference between authentic and counterfeit goods (Karp, 2016).

The third kind of illegal media economic activity is more unfortunate; it involves the production, distribution, and consumption of child pornography. The online trade of child pornography in the US alone was established to be $20 billion in 2006. The disturbing news is that 139 countries don't have laws to prosecute the circulation of child pornography (Bialik, 2006). Given that many countries do not outlaw child pornography and do not collect data about the trade, the economy of child pornography is probably much higher than $20 billion.

Business Models and Economic Models

We have argued that the concept "economies" is more useful than "economy" because an economy is both objective and subjective, both a state and a process, and both a macro and micro concept. We have further looked at why the size of media economies is difficult to estimate. In this section, we look at the relation between business models and economic models.

An economic model suggests how resources should be allocated to satisfy needs and wants. At a macro level, a state decides on an economic model and designs appropriate policies to implement resource allocation. Some states emphasize an equitable distribution of wealth by heavily taxing those who earn the most (as in the case of Scandinavian countries); others emphasize a free market by offering a low tax rate for businesses (such as Hong Kong and Singapore). At a micro level, a business firm also follows an economic model to allocate resources. In addition, a business organization also has a business model that describes what a company aims to achieve and how the goal can be achieved. The business model can include a customer base, strategies, and processes. The economic goal is not the only goal of a business organization; it also has social, cultural, and political goals.

There is an assumption that the media sector is necessarily a business in a free market economy and a democracy. This is not strictly the case. Here we describe business models based on ownership and control. As we recall in Chapter 3, "Theories and Approaches to Study the Business of Media," ownership refers to *who* owns the media, *who* invests in the organizations, and *who* profits from the ownership. Owners can be shareholders, wealthy individuals, business entities, the public, or the state. Control refers to *who* makes the major decisions of the business. The owners, managers, workers, or board of directors could control the business. The ones in control may not run the business on a daily basis, but they might make major decisions, such as acquisitions and layoffs. For a large organization, the power of control rests on an executive team that may consist of the chief executive officer (CEO), the president, the chief operating officer (COO), the chief financial officer (CFO), the chief technology officer (CTO), and various vice presidents. Smaller organizations may be controlled by the president and various managers. Table 4.3 summarizes four types of model in terms of ownership and control.

Table 4.3 *Ownership and control of four business models*

	Ownership	Control
Corporation	Shareholders	Managers overseen by a board of directors
Privately held	Individuals and/or private companies	Owners and/or managers
Publicly owned	The public	Managers overseen by a board of directors
State-owned	The state	Managers/officers appointed by the state

The first type of business model is the corporation. According to Forbes (Le, 2015), some of the world's largest media and telecommunications corporations are: ComcastUniversal (US), Disney (US), 20th Century Fox (US), Time Warner (US), Time Warner Cable (US), WPP (UK), Columbia Broadcasting System (US), Viacom (US), and Sky Broadcasting (UK). Corporations consist of public companies whose shares are traded in the financial market. Wealthy individuals and investment bankers who have good connections with the founders may be able to acquire a fair amount of the stock. An average person does not have the financial means or the influence to acquire such stocks. A corporation is owned by shareholders, such as wealthy individuals—who may be the executives or the founders—and business entities that are not directly involved in the media (such as investment banks and insurance companies). A corporation is controlled by an executive team that is composed of the CEO and other chief officers. A corporation is overseen by a board of directors that is charged to safeguard shareholders' interests and ensure that executives make sound decisions. The board members are leaders from business, government, academia, and the community. Their professions are related to the business of the corporation. For example, the board of directors of Google consists of angel investors of start-up companies, executives of other hi-tech firms, and university presidents.

The second type of business model is the privately held company. The number of privately held media companies is dwindling, because small businesses have been driven out of competition by large corporations or have been acquired by them. For example, the print newspaper business has experienced a rapid change in its business model because of decreasing readership. News Corporation of the US has acquired many small, privately held newspapers in the UK and Australia. Its acquisition of *Wall Street Journal*—a privately held company of financial publications—was the latest triumph of the company. However, there are still huge privately held companies owned by wealthy individuals or angel investors. For example, Bloomberg L.P., a financial services, media, and technology company, is a privately held company owned by the billionaire Michael Bloomberg. Facebook was a privately held company with a sizable revenue before it became a public company in 2012. Angel investors had put money in Facebook hoping to make money once it became a public company. Angel investors are either individuals or corporations who invest in start-ups.

They make money when the invested companies become public or are acquired by a large corporation (such as YouTube acquired by Google, Instagram acquired by Facebook). Huge, privately held media corporations can also be found in the Middle East, Latin America, and Asia. For example, Al Jazeera Media Network is a huge family-owned media company based in Qatar. China's Dalian Wanda Group started as a real estate company but has moved quickly into the businesses of film distribution and movie theaters. Recently, this Chinese company has acquired the AMC Theaters chain.

The third type of business model is publicly owned media funded by taxpayers' money, hence owned by the public. The most notable example is the British Broadcasting Corporation (BBC) founded in 1922. It had been funded by license fees paid by television and radio audiences. (See Chapter 7, "Civil Societies," on public media.) Similar to the control of a corporation, the executive board oversees the direction of the BBC. Some board members are the directors of different divisions, such as radio and television. In recent years, the call for privatization has forced BBC to create profit-making entities, such as BBC Worldwide, that licenses shows outside the UK. Nordic countries (Sweden, Finland, Denmark, Norway, and Iceland) also have a long tradition of public media. Public media can be used to reinforce a sense of national identity, particularly in the Scandinavian case due to robust public support and a small population.

The fourth type of business model is state-owned media. What worries critics the most is not who owns the media but who *controls* media content. If the state exercises control over the content and oversees daily operations, then dissidents' voices would be silenced. Worse, critics may be prosecuted, jailed, or "disappeared." China, North Korea, and Iran are some commonly cited countries where the states own and control media, but this business model is also commonly found in Latin America (Cuba), Africa (Libya), the Middle East (Syria), and Asia (Burma). Not all media industries are owned by the state. In some countries, such as China, the state is more interested in owning media that produce news content, such as broadcast media and newspapers. It is less interested in the "entertainment" media (magazines, music, and films), even though it sanctions entertainment content. It has the least interest in telecommunications and Internet companies. Therefore, non-Chinese businesses are allowed to own telecommunications and technology companies (such as Microsoft and Yahoo), but not content-based media companies. Nevertheless, the state has required websites and web portals to censor opposing voices and to attend workshops on "correct" political content.

We need to emphasize that media corporations exist in Western, capitalist societies as well as non-Western, noncapitalist societies. The difference is a matter of degree. Likewise, state-owned and state-controlled media exist in both types of societies. To give an example, Chinese Internet companies such as the search engine Baidu and the web portal Alibaba are huge media corporations. US-based Yahoo owned shares of Alibaba whose business performance is better than Yahoo's. In Italy, former Prime Minister Silvio Berlusconi owned Mediaset, which often acted as the mouthpiece of his political party and thus helped him accrue political and economic power (Sanderson, 2017).

Case Study: Google vs. Bloomberg

Let's look at what we have learned in this chapter before we conclude it with a case study: we have looked at why the concept "economies" is more encompassing than "economy"; how different media organizations measure a formal media economy; what informal media economies are; and the four different models of business models. In the final section, we present a step-by-step approach to compare the economies of two information companies: a public company, Alphabet—the parent company of Google—and a private company, Bloomberg. This case study shows how to locate economic data of both types of companies. Students can conduct their own analysis by substituting other media companies located in the United States or abroad.

Step 1: Public or Private

The first step is to identify whether a company is public or private. As stated earlier, shares of a public company are traded on a stock exchange, whereas those of a private company are not traded. Go to the website of the company and look for a page called "investor relations." Public companies have this page, which provides financial information for investors. A private company may have an "About us" page but no "investor relations" page. Another way to identify a public company is to look up the stock symbol online. For example, Alphabet, the parent company of Google, has the symbol GOOG. Most online pages also list where the stock is traded (such as NASDAQ, NYSE

[New York Stock Exchange], or LSE [London Stock Exchange]). In contrast, Bloomberg L.P. is a privately held company, so it does not have a stock symbol.

Step 2: Financial Information

The second step is to locate financial information from websites and databases. It is easy to find out financial information of public companies, because they are required to disclose the information to investors in some countries. The financial information is independently audited and certified to be as accurate and truthful as possible. Public companies usually have a copy of the annual report online for viewing (called 10K filing in the US); a hard copy may also be requested and sent to a mailing address. Public companies also provide quarterly financial reports, but they are not needed for our purpose.

Unlike public companies, private companies are not required to disclose financial information, so the data are less readily available. However, there are other ways to locate the information. For example, the Bloomberg website has a "history and facts" section on which it states the number of subscribers, overseas offices, and employees. These numbers may not tell us about the revenue and profit/loss of the company, but they give an idea of the size of the company. Business databases such as Mergent and Standard and Poor's may have information about Bloomberg, such as sales figures. This kind of database requires a subscription but may be available at a university or public library. Financial newspapers such as *The Wall Street Journal* (US, Europe, Far East, international editions) and the *Financial Times* (UK, international) have searchable databases of large companies. A reliable source that should not be overlooked is nonfiction books on the company history and the founder's biographies.

Step 3: Ownership and Control

What should you look for after collecting data about the companies? There will be an overwhelming amount of information, and some may sound foreign to you. Here we show how to use the data to illustrate two concepts (ownership and control) that we learned in this chapter and two others (market and competition) that we have already come across in Chapter 3, "Theories and Approaches to Study the Business of Media."

Ownership refers to who owns the company. The owners could be wealthy individuals or business entities (such as investment banks and insurance companies). Alphabet is a public company, so the major stockowners are listed on reliable sources such as Nasdaq.com. As of February 2017, the top five institutional owners of Alphabet are all investment banks based in the US (Vanguard, Fidelity, State Street, T. Rowe Price, and Blackrock), and the top three individual owners are the two founders Sergey Brin and Lawrence Page, and former president Eric Schmidt. The owners of a private company are more difficult to identify. Because Michael Bloomberg is a public figure—owing to his wealth and political life—it is easy to find out that he is the major owner of Bloomberg L.P. However, it is not easy to find out who the co-owners are.

Control of a company means who has the power to make major decisions concerning the company direction. For public companies, the owners do not necessarily control decision-making in the company; this is particularly the case when the major stockholders are institutional shareholders. For a public corporation, the executive board and the board of directors assume the control of the company. The names of executives and the board of directors are listed under "Directors, Executive Officers and Corporate Governance" in the annual report. To fully understand how the board of directors shapes the direction of the corporation, we have to find out the official titles of the directors and on what other companies' boards they also sit. For a prominent company like Alphabet, the directors include presidents of elite higher education institutions, owners and executives of large corporations, and angel investors. In contrast, the board of directors of private companies is hard to identify. Bloomberg lists the board of directors as both "insiders" (executives of the Bloomberg) and "outsiders" (owners of other companies).

In Chapter 3, we have come across the concepts of market and competition. Originally, market refers to a physical place where sellers and buyers trade. Now market can be viewed as constituted by sellers of similar products. Competition is the rivalry between different sellers in a market. A big corporation like Alphabet (which owns Google) or Bloomberg may have its business in more than one market. Their competitiveness is not the same in different markets. Generally speaking, a new business has the least market advantage when the market has the least competition and is the most concentrated. In other words, a business can hardly compete when only a few companies share the market.

Table 4.4 *Competitiveness of markets that Google is in*

Two markets that Google is in	search engines	advertising
Type of market	oligopoly	perfect competition
Is the market competitive?	No	Yes
Is the market concentrated?	Yes	No

Google's annual report states that it is in the markets of search engines and information services; e-commerce websites; social networks; and advertising. Some of the markets are more competitive than others are. For example, the search engine market is an oligopoly: only a few companies are in the search engine market. The market is thus not too competitive and very concentrated. In comparison, the advertising market is more competitive, because many agencies can place advertisements on behalf of clients. It is a competitive market because it has many sellers.

After learning whether a market is competitive or not, we can then estimate the competitiveness of a company. One way to measure whether it is competitive or not is its market shares. Market share is defined as the portion of the market that a company owns. The more market shares one company has, the more competitive it is, which is unrelated to the type of the market. In a highly concentrated market such as a search engine market, the biggest companies can equally share it so that no one dominates others. In a competitive company with many sellers, one company can stand out because its sales are overwhelming. For example, there are many booksellers in the market, but few will be as competitive as Amazon.com and national chains. These big companies are very competitive, while independent bookshops are not competitive at all. For one thing, Amazon.com can give deep discounts of certain books so that its competitors will lose out. If small booksellers follow suit, they may not make money at all; if they don't, the business will be lost to Amazon.com.

How competitive is Google in the search engine market? According to Netmarketshare.com, there are seven major search engine companies in the world. We can conclude that it is an oligopoly market, because a few markets own the majority of the market (see Chapter 3). As of February 2017, Google has about 80% of the market share. The next three have only single digit shares: Microsoft's Bing, Baidu, and Yahoo. Because Google dominates the search engine market, it can be said to be very competitive. It can set advertising prices and make changes to the interface without worrying too much about losing market shares. On the other hand, its competitors have to closely watch Google's moves so as not to lose market shares. However, not all Google products are competitive. Google once owned a social networking site called Orkut. It was not a major player in the social networking market. It was only competitive in Brazil and India. However, a decade after its launch in 2004, Google killed the project. The social networking example of Google shows that even if one product of a company is very competitive in a market, other products may not be. Therefore, it is essential to find out in which markets a company is competing and to analyze the market shares the company has in every market.

Conclusion

We introduced the first lens, "economies," in this chapter. We prefer to see an economy in its plural form because an economy is both objective and subjective, both a state and a process, and both a macro and micro concept. Then we stated how people following each of the three approaches understand an economy: those taking the media economic and political economic approaches tend to see an economy as an objective state, while those taking the production studies approach tend to see it as a subjective, micro-level process. Because an economy is not a monolithic concept, therefore, any measurement of an economy is partial. We have suggested why an economy is difficult to measure; a digital era complicates the measurement because the circulation of money can take place outside the state surveillance, as shown in the examples of the information economy. Despite the difficulties in measuring the economy, international, regional, and state agencies collect data about media economies. Data about economies can be used for planning and lobbying purposes. We last show how an information economy can be analyzed by applying the concepts of ownership and control, market shares, and competitiveness of two information companies.

References

Albarran, A. B. (2002). *Media economics: Understanding markets, industries, and concepts* (2nd ed.). Ames, Iowa: Iowa State Press.

Association of Southeast Asian Nations. (n/a). *ASEAN Stats*. Retrieved from www.asean.org/resource/statistics/asean-statistics/

Bialik, C. (2006, April 18). Measuring the child-porn trade. *Wall Street Journal*. Retrieved from www.wsj.com/articles/SB114485422875624000

Department of Communications and the Arts. (2011, August). *Creative industries: A strategy for the 21st century Australia*. Retrieved from http://arts.gov.au/sites/default/files/creative-industries/sdip/strategic-digital-industry-plan.pdf

Gomis, B., & Botero, N. C. (2016, February 5). Sneaking a smoke: Paraguay's tobacco business fuels Latin America's black market. *Foreign Affairs*. Retrieved from www.foreignaffairs.com/articles/paraguay/2016-02-05/sneaking-smoke

Guevara, M. W. (2014). Smuggling made easy: Landlocked Paraguay emerges as a top producer of contraband tobacco. *The Center for Public Integrity*. Retrieved from www.publicintegrity.org/2009/06/29/6343/smuggling-made-easy

ITU. *Statistics*. Retrieved from www.itu.int/en/ITU-D/Statistics/Pages/stat/default.aspx

Karp, H. (2016, October 13). Fake CDs hit online sales. *Wall Street Journal*, p. B3.

Kim, S-Y. (2013). For the eyes of North Koreans? Politics of money and class in *Boys Over Flowers*. In Y. Kim (Ed.), *The Korean Wave: Korean media go global* (pp. 93–105). Abingdon, Oxon: Routledge.

Le, V. (2015, May 22). The world's largest media companies of 2015. *Forbes*. Retrieved from www.forbes.com/sites/vannale/2015/05/22/the-worlds-largest-media-companies-of-2015/#6843780d2b64

Maxwell, R., & Miller, T. (2012). *Greening the media*. New York: Oxford University Press.

Napoli, P. M. (2009). Media economics and the study of media industries. In J. Holt & A. Perren (Eds.), *Media industries: History, theory, and methods* (pp. 161–170). New York: Blackwell.

Office of the United States Trade Representative. (n/a). *North American Free Trade Agreement (NAFTA)*. Retrieved from https://ustr.gov/trade-agreements/free-trade-agreements/north-american-free-trade-agreement-nafta

Sanderson, R. (2017, January 4). Berlusconi study sheds light on politics and profits. *Financial Times*. Retrieved from www.ft.com/content/eb86eb6c-d284-11e6-9341-7393bb2e1b51

Sherter, A. (2015, December 23). Will the US economy slip into recession in 2016? *CBS Money Watch*. Retrieved from www.cbsnews.com/news/will-the-u-s-economy-slip-into-recession-in-2016/

Smith, G. (2013, July 22). Inside the massive global black market for smartphones. *HuffPost Tech*. Retrieved from www.huffingtonpost.com/2013/07/13/smartphone-black-market_n_3510341.html

Smith, G. (2014, December 10). How stolen smartphones end up in the hands of Colombian cartels. *The Huffington Post*. Retrieved from www.huffingtonpost.com/2013/12/10/stolen-smartphones_n_4384211.html

Weisbrot, M. (2011, May 18). Latin America's growth picks up after decades of failure. *Foreign Policy Digest*. Retrieved from http://cepr.net/publications/op-eds-columns/latin-americas-growth-picks-up-after-decades-of-failure

Woolhouse, M. (2014, October 21). Most victims of human trafficking enter the US legally, study says. *Boston Globe*. Retrieved from www.bostonglobe.com/business/2014/10/20/most-victims-human-trafficking-enter-legally-study-says/Ix9eMinYLLzN0FBDj4QCSO/story.html

WTO. *Trade and tariff data*. Retrieved from www.wto.org/english/res_e/statis_e/statis_e.htm

Yang, Y., and Li, A. (2015, December 23). China's economy: Seven predictions for 2016. *Los Angeles Times*. Retrieved from www.latimes.com/business/la-fi-china-economy-201620151210-story.html

Politics 5

At the end of the chapter, students will be able to:

- define "nation," "state," and "nation-state";
- suggest whether the power of a nation-state is weakened as a result of globalization;
- suggest how the three approaches (media economics, political economy of communication, and production studies) conceptualize politics;
- name the main political bodies that govern and regulate the media economy at the national, regional, and international levels;
- suggest how policies have brought along a multi-platform era;
- suggest how corporations influence digital media policies;
- discuss how the Japanese and South Korean governments developed media politics.

Infinite is a South Korean boy band formed in 2010. As one of the most popular idol groups, Infinite has become the poster child for K-pop to the global audience. They have done two global tours; the more recent one kicked off in January 2016 in Vancouver (Canada), followed by Los Angeles (US), Mexico City (Mexico), Santiago (Chile), New York

(US), and concluded in Hong Kong. Infinite's world tour was a huge success, as many K-pop fans around the globe gathered in local cities to see some of South Korea's most famous pop stars. Infinite joined the league of many K-pop idol groups in the global touring business: stars such as Girls' Generation, Kara, and TVXQ have performed in many regions, including North America and Western Europe.

Since the late 2000s, K-pop has become a global sensation. Korean pop musicians have gained popularity in the global cultural markets. The most visible case was Psy's single "Gangnam Style" that enjoyed remarkable success in the global music market in 2012. Even to a non-Korean-speaking audience, the occasional English words such as "sexy ladies" reflect the global nature of the Korean Wave. The music video for "Gangnam Style," which mixes humor with glamor, has more than two billion views on YouTube and was the most watched video at one point. However, the global success of K-pop was a relatively new phenomenon; it was not something seen before 2010. Aside from K-pop, the Korean Wave also includes television dramas, films, and digital games. The wave symbolizes both the rapid growth of Korean local cultural industries and exports of cultural products to the global markets.

Several dimensions could explain the emergence of Korean cultural industries in the global market; one major dimension is the state. It has been a major player in orchestrating the commercial success of the Korean Wave by making cultural industries a centerpiece of its policy in the midst of neoliberal reform (see Chapter 2 for the definition of neoliberalism). In the 1980s, long after the Korean War (1950–1953), Korea was still a relatively underdeveloped country. Korean cultural industries were not very exceptional by global standards in terms of both quality and quantity. Furthermore, as is the case in many other developing countries, the Korean cultural industries also were not active in global market development. However, this is no longer the case in the early 21st century. The cultural sector has become a significant segment of the Korean economy, and the number of cultural industry corporations and employees and the amount of revenue have grown dramatically (Jin, 2011a; 2011b).

Undoubtedly, the commercial production and consumption sides of the Korean Wave have played significant roles for its emergence, but the government's favorable cultural policies have supported the growth of K-pop in a big way. For example, in 2013, in order to boost the music industry, the Korean government decided to construct a mega K-pop studio that accommodates an audience size of 15,000 (Ministry of Culture, Sports and Tourism, 2014a). The government also increased its budget for cultural industries from 16.8 million Korean won in 1998 (US$10,000) to 305.7 million Korean won (US$270,000) in 2014 (Ministry of Culture, Sports and Tourism, 2014b).

The Korean government has taken a developmental state perspective in creating the Korean Wave in the midst of neoliberal globalization. Contrary to a belief that small governments would give way to the market in order to facilitate a fast-growing economy, the South Korean state plays an active role in developing its popular music industry. Interestingly, Korea is not the only case where the state has a strong push for its cultural industries. Many countries—including Canada, France, China, Japan, and Taiwan—have also advanced their cultural industries and cultural sovereignty. For example, the Chinese government attaches great importance to the development of the cultural industries (Yantao, 2016), while the Japanese government commissions a "Cool Japan" project to make Japanese cultural industries and popular culture more competitive on the global stage.

Given the paramount role that the state may play in developing media industries, we ask in this chapter:

- What are some political bodies that are in charge of media and cultural sectors at the national, regional, and international levels? Why would governments want to be involved in the business of media?
- What political bodies are involved in bringing media convergence? Why did they do that?
- What are the roles of corporations in relation to the states in bringing political changes? Why would business be involved in politics?

Politics is defined as activities of governing. For example, debating the pros and cons of a proposal in the city hall is an activity of governance. Policies are the outcome of the debate; they stipulate the courses of action that a political party will carry out. Bearing in mind the definitions and the above three questions, we ask, what are the relations between politics and the business of media? To some, a digital era means the state should have less control of media industries, because digital technology allows for cheaper content production, hence the industry does not have to rely on state subsidy. While this may be true, a digital era has not changed the macro relation between politics and the economy of media. Therefore, we believe the different relations between politics and the economy are not a dichotomy, but rather fall on a spectrum. On one end there is the free market and minimum state intervention approach to media industries, such as the case in the United States. On the other end, there is a state-controlled and state-owned approach to media in countries such as North Korea and Cuba, where journalists could be harassed, intimidated, and detained by the state (Freedom House, 2015). In the middle, there is a strong sense of civil and public media in Europe (see Chapter 7, "Civil Societies") and a state-initiated media market in East Asia.

Definitions of Nation, State, and Nation-State

The notion of nation-state is one of the most significant and controversial topics in the study of globalization (see Chapter 2 to see what globalization is), therefore it is critical to understand the concepts "nation," "state," and "nation-state" and to differentiate the concept of "nation-state" from that of "country," particularly in tandem with media and cultural sectors.

The term "nation-state" is the convergence of two different concepts: "nation" and "state." The term nation is "derived from the Latin [word] *natio*, meaning a social grouping based on real or fancied community of birth or race. In later usage, the term was expanded to include such other variables as territory, culture, language, and history" (Rejai & Enloe, 1969, p. 141). Based on that, we may define a nation as "a relatively large group of people who feel that they belong together by virtue of sharing one or more such traits as common language, religion or race, common history or tradition, common set of customs, and common destiny" (ibid.). As we will explore in Chapter 8, culture has especially been significant in the notion of nation-state, and it is easy to see why many governments have continued to develop their own cultural sectors to reinforce a sense of national identity.

State refers to something else; it is about "an independent and autonomous political structure over a specific territory, with a comprehensive legal system and a sufficient concentration of power to maintain law and order" (Rejai & Enloe, 1969, p. 143). In other words, "state" is primarily a political-legal concept, whereas "nation" is primarily psycho-cultural. The former is about how a group of people should be governed; the latter is about who should belong to the group.

Although nation and state coexist most times, they may also exist independently of one another: a nation may exist without a state, and a state may exist without a nation. For example, many premodern kingdoms may be considered nations because local landlords and warlords could set their own laws, but there were no national laws to govern a group of people who shared the same cultural roots. At present, there are also states without nations, for example, Hong Kong and Macau are city-states, not nation-states, because both are administrative regions of the People's Republic of China (PRC). These two city-states do not share the same administrative, executive, and judiciary structures as the PRC. However, the majority of the populations in both city-states are Chinese, thus they share many cultural traditions and rituals with the mainland Chinese populations. Depending on whom is asked, Taiwan can be a nation-state to the Taiwanese government, but a state to the People's Republic of China. There are also some territories that are neither a nation nor a state, such as Puerto Rico, British Virgin Islands, and Gaza Strip. The term "country" can be used interchangeably with "state," but not with "nation-state." However, since government represents the nation-state, "government" and "nation-state" are seen as identical. In this book, we use "country," "government," and "nation-state" without distinguishing them unless we use the terms in a very specific way.

After exploring the concepts "nation" and "state," we look at the concept "nation-state." UNESCO defines this concept as "one where the great majority are conscious of a common identity and share the same culture" (Yuval-Davis, 1997, cited in UNESCO, 2016). Further, Kazancigil and Dogan (1986) pointed out "the nation-state is an area where the cultural boundaries match up with the political boundaries. The ideal of nation-state is that the state incorporates people of a single ethnic stock and cultural traditions" (p. 188). Because of global migration in the 20th century, few nation-states actually fulfill the above definition. Japan—with its strict immigration policy and emphasis on cultural purity—is one of the few nation-states where most populations share the same cultural and ethnic roots. The Nordic country Iceland may also pride itself on most of the population sharing the same cultural heritage and indeed bloodlines. However, ethnic groups coexist in immigrant countries such as the US, Canada, Australia, and Brazil. These countries have many cultural traditions within the political boundary. At the same time, immigrant countries also induce a sense of cultural togetherness for all populations, such as teaching school students the official language and national history.

Is Nation-State Still a Relevant Concept?

In the 20th century, several globalists (Ohmae, 1995; Giddens, 1999) argued that nation-states have lost their own authority in national affairs, including the realms of media and culture. During the height of globalization theory in the mid-1990s, these scholars claimed that the role of the nation-state would need to change primarily as a result of borderless economic integration. For example, the establishment of the European Union in 1993 brought along the eurozone. Sharing a currency reduces member states' ability to control their monetary policies. In a similar way, the FTAA (Free Trade Area of the Americas) was proposed in 1994 at the First Summit of the Americas in Miami. This agreement asked member states to reach a consensus on trade liberalization, market access, economic integration, and intellectual property rights in the two Americas. This proposal was never approved, though; instead, the US and six other countries signed the Central American Dominican Republic Free Trade Agreement (CAFTA-DR) in August 2004. This agreement has since increased the total trade of goods by 71% (Amadeo, 2016).

Economic globalization often goes hand in hand with neoliberalism (see Chapter 2). Many countries in both Western and non-Western regions have initiated new policy measures to guarantee the private sector with maximum profits. These measures have privatized many key public sectors, such as social welfare, education, and public broadcasting and telecommunications. As a result, many states reduced their subsidy to social welfare and education by making the public pay more for them. Also, broadcasting and telecommunications are no longer seen as a free or low-cost service for the public (see Chapter 7, "Civil Societies") but as a commodity that consumers need to pay for.

Economic globalization and neoliberalization negatively impact less-advanced economies. International organizations such as the International Monetary Fund (IMF) could intervene with the governance of indebted nations by restructuring their public sectors. Economic restructuring has affected many South American and African countries, because the states were stripped of power from governing their own finance. Thus, Denning (2004, cited in Van Elteren, 2011) argued that neoliberalization has undermined the legitimacy of national authorities, especially in the aspect of economic self-governance. In other words, international organizations such as IMF seem to have "joined the chorus of hyperglobalist thinkers of globalization, who contend that transnational capitalism, international governance, and hybrid global culture have effectively put a halt to the modern nation-state" (Van Elteren, 2011, p. 152).

In the realm of culture, several theoreticians (Morley & Robins, 1995; Sinclair, 2007) believe that the nation-state has seemingly lost its power in regulating the national economy and culture. This is particularly true in the media and telecommunications sectors, because transnational corporations could have overwhelming power over nation-states. Media corporations from a few Western countries (mainly the US) have become major forces in the realm of global cultural and information flows. For example, Disney negotiated long and hard with city governments to build Disneyland theme parks. Very often, Disney reaps most of the profits while investing little in the parks. East Asian corporations such as Samsung, Sony, and Nintendo also dominate the consumer electronic markets in the region and beyond. Beginning in the early 1980s, the US government, alongside several transnational media corporations, forced many other governments to undertake neoliberal reforms, including relaxing the imports of cultural goods, thus intensifying the dominance of Western cultural influence. The nation-states may also lose some control of their national economies with Internet commerce. Online consumers can access the so-called global marketplace to acquire goods that are unavailable in their home countries.

As will be discussed more in the next section, international treaty liberates the cultural industries of other countries. Some treaties that concern the flows of media and cultural goods are the North American Free Trade Agreement, the General Agreement on Tariffs and Trade (GATT), the World Trade Organization, and recently the Free Trade Agreement (FTA) (Wasko, 2003; Jin, 2011a). While the major goal of the FTAs is fair competition in global trade, it also stipulates that national governments adopt open and transparent rule-making procedures as well as nondiscriminatory laws and regulations in several areas, including the elimination of content quotas in the cultural sector (Office of the US Trade Representative, 2009). Because the US government could pressure other nations of less economic power in the negotiation of the FTAs (Jin, 2011a), nation-states in several regions—in particular, South America—have had no choice but to liberalize their cultural markets to the global society in the name of progress in domestic markets. (See Chapter 4 on how NAFTA has facilitated imports and exports of cultural goods between Canada, the US, and Mexico.)

However, not all countries submit to US-led trade liberalization. Several countries (such as Canada and France) have continued to resist forced neoliberal reform in the realms of media and telecommunications with protective policies, such as restrictions of media imports. However, many less developed economies, including Mexico, Brazil, South Korea, and China, have adopted US-led neoliberal globalization. Nevertheless, this does not mean that neoliberalism is a uniform or monolithic project, because it takes different shapes in different contexts and works in highly uneven and unpredictable ways. For example, the Canadian government developed cultural policies to create a strong national culture through state intervention, which resulted in domestic cultural industries being protected from direct market competition. However, the Canadian cultural policies are nonetheless neoliberally oriented, because the state wants its cultural sector to be as competitive as the one in the United States (Milz, 2007). As Weiss (1997) pointed out, globalists have overstated and overgeneralized the degree of state powerlessness; they ignore the significance of state politics even in the age of neoliberal globalization.

Non-Western countries (such as Chile, Mexico, Brazil, Korea, and China) that have adopted neoliberal policies also simultaneously developed cultural policies to support their cultural industries. Consequently, the global cultural market has been a battleground among nation-states, mainly between the US and local governments in many parts of the world. In addition, there is also regional competition in the media and cultural sectors, such as the competition between Japanese and South Korean governments in the East Asian market. Therefore, it is not always the case that neoliberalism has completely eroded nation-states' role in developing cultural industries, because some nation-states have continued to initiate and support their own cultural industries.

How the Three Approaches Conceptualize Politics

Among the three approaches introduced in this book, the media economic approach has the least concern for the role that politics plays in the business of media. The political economic approach—as reflected in the name—has much to say about how macro-level political power influences the regulation and structure of the industries. In contrast, the production studies approach mainly concerns micro-level political power, such as how media workers experience a neoliberal and globalized workplace.

Media Economics

Media economists believe politics plays a minimal role in the economy. Because media economics refers to "the business and financial activities of firms operating in the various media industries" (Owers, Carveth, & Alexander, 1993, p. 3), economists taking this approach believe that the nation-state should only be involved when there is a market failure. Some state-employed strategies include protective measures and media funding (see Chapter 7, "Civil Societies"). Winseck (2011) has clearly pointed out that the liberal wing of the neo-classical school is:

> more open to the idea that markets sometimes fail and that governments will occasionally need to step in to set things right. However, . . . state intervention should be minimized to providing meritorious public goods, bringing a small number of essential services to areas not served by private business, and striking a balance between the public good qualities of information versus protecting its status as valuable property.
>
> (p. 16)

The media economic approach assumes the market autonomously allocates resources by responding to consumers' demands (Mosco, 2009). As such, perfect competition—defined as a market in which many suppliers offer homogeneous products to buyers, and both sellers and buyers have perfect knowledge of all available substitutes—is believed to be the most efficient in resource allocation. Therefore, media economists only ask that the government work as the market regulator and that it be given minimal power to interfere with market behaviors (Doyle, 2002).

A Political Economy of Communication

In contrast to the media economic approach, the political economic approach focuses on the relations between politics and the economy at the macro level. This approach offers a lot about international and national politics in both capitalist and socialist states. It responds to the rise of corporate power by examining the relationship between media/communication systems and the broader social structure of society, such as *who* makes the decisions to allocate resources (Schiller, 1999). It also emphasizes "how ownership, support mechanisms such as advertising, and government policies influence media behavior and content" (McChesney, 2000, p. 110). In addition, it sheds light on the structures and processes of communication that are deeply embedded within the wider structures and processes of a given social formation: "who can say what, in what form, to whom, for what purposes, and with what effect" (Garnham, 2000, p. 4) and simultaneously determines and is determined by the structure of economic, political, and cultural power in a society. Unlike the media economic approach that emphasizes a free market ideology, the political economic approach focuses on diversity and democracy in tandem with media and telecommunications, and therefore, it follows that the government has a critical role to play in intervening and supporting the media and cultural industries.

Production Studies

Unlike how political economists conceptualize politics at a macro level, production studies scholars tend to look at politics at a micro level, such as how a neoliberal state affects work conditions of media workers. Because production studies scholars look at workers who make audiovisual products and their work culture, they pay attention to issues such as how media producers make culture and how they morph themselves into particular kinds of workers in a mediated society. For example, production studies scholars John Caldwell and colleagues offer a nuanced and richly textured approach to study media workers' lived experience by "explor[ing] both the stylistic implications of screen media labor routines and the ways workers understand, represent, and theorize their labor" (Caldwell, 2008, cited in Keane and Sanson, 2016, p. 9).

In view of the Marxist tenor of some political economic thought, production studies scholars are critiqued as saying relatively little about the contributions of labor as determinants of cultural meanings and value (Davies, 2006). In production studies analysis, politics is understood to be situational more than structural. For example, production studies scholars may see gender playing a role in shaping aspiring workers into professionals, but gender is seen as a lived experience more than a political structure. Furthermore, production studies scholarship is critiqued as stopping short of linking their analysis to a global political economy by offering specific claims about the internal dynamics of media industries and workplaces. They also tend to be suspicious of totalizing frameworks, preferring to see power as heterogeneous and capillary rather than centrally anchored by the logic of capital (Keane & Sanson, 2016).

As reflected in the above, the three approaches show some significant differences in understanding the relation between politics and the business of media. Depending on the question at hand, sometimes we cannot rely on one single approach to conduct a satisfactory analysis;

Table 5.1 *How the three approaches conceptualize politics*

	Media Economics	Political Economy of Communication	Production Studies
Role played by politics in an economy	Minimal role in an economy.	Inseparable from an economy.	At a micro level in daily life situations.
Primary political entities	Nation-state.	Governments at the levels of international, regional, national, provincial/state, city/town; for-profit and nonprofit organizations are considered political as well.	Social beings and groups; also consider governments at the levels of international, regional, national, provincial/state, city/town; for-profit and nonprofit organizations are considered political as well.

therefore using two or three approaches may provide better solutions to analyze the rapidly changing media environments.

Who Are the Main Political Bodies That Govern and Regulate the Media Economy?

There are three kinds of governing and regulating bodies: national, regional, and international. Governing refers to how a political body conducts its affairs. Regulating refers to how this political body uses laws, policies, and guidelines to achieve governance. A state can govern without relying on regulations. For example, it can govern by randomly punishing or rewarding people without explicitly stating how the population should be governed. However, most democratic, modern nation-states have laws and policies to stipulate what kinds of actions would be punished or rewarded.

In this and the next sections, we conceptualize the nation-state and international political organizations as modern governing bodies. International political organizations are "younger" policy-making bodies than nation-states are; they only gained prominence after WWII. The UN, probably the most well-known international organization, was established with the goal of facilitating mediation among nations before conflicts arose.

Media regulations fall into three broad categories: content regulations, ownership regulations, and trade regulations. Content regulations concern what can be shown to whom through which media under what kinds of circumstances. Ownership regulations concern who can own what kinds of media and technology under what kinds of circumstances. Trade regulations concern who can import or export what kinds of media, cultural, and technological goods under what kinds of circumstances. National regulators are usually concerned with all three categories, while regional and international regulators tend to be more concerned with ownership and trade, and less with content.

A national regulator in the United States is the Federal Communications Commission (FCC). The FCC was founded to regulate radio frequency in the country. Similar agencies in the UK are the Independent Television Commission and the Radio Authority. Some examples of regional governing and regulating bodies are NAFTA (North American Free Trade Agreement) and the European Union. Some examples of international bodies are the WTO (World Trade Organization) and the Group of Eight (intergovernmental organizations where leaders of developed economies summit). In the following, we suggest how media regulations at all three levels have implications on the business of media.

National Regulators

Because of the histories of media technologies, we may find different governmental agencies being responsible for different media policies. Traditionally, broadcast media are the most regulated because signal transmissions rely on limited radio frequencies. The airwaves are seen as a kind of natural resource, just like water and natural scenery. If radio frequencies are not regulated, then there may be unfair allocation of this natural resource. As the often-told story about *Titanic* goes, the disaster happened because wealthy passengers monopolized the telegraph system for their private purposes, such as checking stock prices. The accident might have been prevented if there had been a designated radio frequency for safety communication. In contrast to broadcast media, print media is historically less regulated, because there can be as many publication titles as possible. Publishers usually self-regulate to make sure the contents are not offensive. There are also no consistent policies on Internet regulation at the global level. Internet regulations, like all kinds of communication means, can be broken down to content, ownership, and trade regulations. Countries that respect the freedom of the press usually control less of the information accessed on the Internet, whereas countries that restrict freedom tend to control more. The following shows how countries differ in broadcast and Internet regulations: the case in the US shows broadcast regulations are separated from those of Internet; the case in South Korea shows they are integrated.

The US Federal Communications Commission is one of the most discussed regulators in the media economy. The FCC is the United States' primary authority for communications laws, regulation, and technological innovation. It regulates radio, television, wire, satellite, and cable, but it does not regulate the print media, the Internet, video games, and films. Regulating broadcast media is more than determining what can be shown on air or not; it also determines *who* has the rights to own *what*. For example, most of the broadcast media in the

US are owned by commercial interests, but this does not have to be the case. If the FCC had ruled that at least half of broadcasting licenses be granted to nonprofit entities, the entire US media industry would have been very different. In the FCC's own words, the Commission takes advantage of economic opportunities in global communications. It capitalizes on its competencies in a few areas, such as promoting competition, innovation, and investment in broadband services and facilities, supporting the nation's economy by ensuring an appropriate competitive framework for the unfolding of the communications revolution (Federal Communications Commission, 2016).

Likewise, governments in other Western countries and non-Western countries have agencies similar to the FCC that deal with domestic telecommunications industries, though they may take a different stance in tackling the global media economy than the FCC does. For example, the Canadian Radio-television and Telecommunications Commission (CRTC) (2016) emphasizes public interest and citizenry more than does the FCC. The CRTC strives to ensure Canadians have access to a world-class communication system and to provide tools for citizens to make informed decisions in the marketplace. It supervises and regulates over 2,000 broadcasters, including TV services, AM and FM radio stations, and the companies that bring telecommunications services to consumers.

In Asia, South Korea probably has the most comprehensive response to the convergence of digital technology in the broadcasting and telecommunications sectors. Unlike the FCC in the US, the Korea Communications Commission (KCC) also deals with Internet regulation and broadcast contents. Therefore, the KCC uses a more integrated approach to media and telecommunications regulations than the FCC does. The president launched the Korea Communications Commission (Korea Communications Commission, 2016) as a ministerial-level central administrative organization to harness technological convergence; to ensure the freedom, public nature, and interest of broadcasting; and to achieve balanced growth of broadcasting and telecommunications so as to enhance national competitiveness. KCC is also responsible for policy-making for a general programming channel and an all-news channel; formulating and implementing policies to protect users and their privacy; preventing circulation of illegal and harmful information on the Internet; policies for broadcast advertising; and programming evaluation, media diversity, inter-Korean exchanges, and international cooperation in communications (KCC, 2016). KCC then has a more comprehensive regulating framework than has both the FCC and the CRTC.

National regulators can also constrain the freedom of the media. For example, the Social Responsibility in Television and Radio Law in Venezuela forbade contents that incite hatred, intolerance, and racism (Doleac, 2015). Chinese media regulators ban offensive content, including "wronged spirits and violent ghosts, monsters, demons, and other inhuman portrayals, strange and supernatural storytelling for the sole purpose of seeking terror and horror" (Beijing Newsroom, 2008). In Iran, the press cannot express opinions that insult the fundamental principles of Islam, even though the press is said to enjoy freedom of expression. The press cannot propagate "luxury and extravagance" (Bruno, 2009); violators may face jail time, fines, and even lashings.

Regional Regulators

Regional regulators make policies within a region. Some examples of regional regulators are the Association of Southeast Asian Nations and the European Union. Regional regulators tend not to stipulate what kinds of media content can be regulated in its member states. For example, Germany has outlawed any circulation of Nazi symbolism, so it is impossible to buy Nazi-related memorabilia in the country. However, other EU member states do not outlaw the circulation of Nazi symbolism. Instead, regional regulators tend to control the imports and exports of media and cultural goods in the region (see also Chapter 4, "Economies").

As introduced in Chapter 4, the North American Free Trade Agreement signed between Canada, the US, and Mexico in 1994 has facilitated media flows between the three countries. The agreement was believed to create the largest free trade region in the world, generate economic growth, and raise the living standard of the populations in the region. Indeed, NAFTA has prodded Canada to strengthen the rules and procedures governing trade and investment and thus has proved to be a solid foundation for building Canada's prosperity and set a valuable example of the benefits of trade liberalization for the rest of the world (Global Affairs Canada, 2016).

Although NAFTA is primarily seen as an economic agreement, the imbalanced power between the three countries and the overwhelming power of US media corporations have detrimental effects on the imports and exports of media goods between the three member countries. Unlike other goods, such as raw resources and manufactured goods, cultural and media products bear symbolic values; thus, an imbalanced media flow may mean a foreign country's culture could erase the local one (Lozano, 2008). NAFTA has been critiqued to have inadequately addressed how local cultures might be affected because of the flow of cultural goods. This is especially the case when the three countries have different attitudes towards their cultural industries. Implied in NAFTA is that cultural goods should be like other commodities, such as agricultural goods; it gives no specific attention to how cultural products may have political impact (Lozano, 2008).

International Regulators

Finally, international bodies may touch upon media regulations. Organizations such as the WTO and Groups of Eight/Fifteen tend to focus on the economic aspect of media industries, but the unbalanced power relations between countries have implications on global media and cultural industries. For example, Groups of Eight/Fifteen are "elitist" semi-formal organizations made up of leaders from the most economically developed countries. The summit leaves out the majority of nation-states in making decisions that may have global implications. Moreover, WTO membership is not automatic; nation-states have to apply to become a member. In order to be considered an eligible member, nation-states have to agree to a list of international trade standards, such as strengthening intellectual property laws. WTO and Groups of Eight/Fifteen do not explicitly deal with international digital communication, which is the domain of International Telecommunication Union (see Chapter 4, "Economies"). But international economic policies have implications on international digital communication.

The 1997 WTO Telecommunications Agreement culminated in a drive for liberalization. Consequently, these regional and international organizations presumably replace the role of the nation-state (Milz, 2007). The 1997 WTO agreement exemplified a sweeping liberalization of the global telecommunications sector. Signed by 69 countries, the Agreement on Basic Telecommunications Services requires member states to open their domestic markets to foreign competition and to allow foreign companies to buy stakes in domestic operations (Jonquireres, 1997). The WTO agreement on basic services attracted

Table 5.2 *Top five spenders in six sectors from the communications/electronics industry in political lobbying in the US (2016)*

Electronics manufacturing and equipment
1. Microsoft
2. Oracle
3. Entertainment Software Association *
4. Qualcomm
5. Hewlett Packard

Telecommunication services
1. Comcast
2. NCTA - The Internet and Television Association *
3. Cellular Telecommunication and Internet Association *
4. Deutsche Telekom
5. Charter Communications

TV/movies/music
1. National Association of Broadcasters *
2. National Amusements
3. 21st Century Fox
4. Recording Industry Association of America *
5. iHeartMedia Inc.

Internet
1. Alphabet
2. Amazon
3. Facebook
4. Yahoo
5. eBay

Telephone utilities
1. AT&T
2. Verizon
3. US Telecommunication Association *
4. CenturyLink
5. National Telecommunication Cooperative Association *

Printing and publishing
1. RELX Group
2. News Media Alliance *
3. Magazine Publishers of America *
4. News Corporation
5. Association of American Publishers *

* Trade groups that represent companies in the sector/industry.

Source: OpenSecrets.org

widespread attention because it succeeded—on a global scale—in establishing the free trade principle in basic telephony service—an area previously closed to foreign intervention. This agreement brought along a wave of merging and acquisition as a result of giant global telecommunication firms moving aggressively into deregulated domestic markets around the world and transnational corporations forming joint ventures with each other and with local investors (Jin, 2005).

However, some nation-states doubt if the globalization trend in the 1990s has done their countries well; therefore, there is a deglobalization trend as well. For example, the UK decided the country should leave the European Union in June 2016 (Rosenfeld & Kemp, 2016). A major implication will be the degree of control that the nation-state has over its own political, economic, and cultural destiny. While some have pointed out the economic loss that the UK would face after leaving the EU, the nation-state can resume a pivotal role in the national economy and culture. The 2016 US election also showed there is a rise of anti-globalization nationalism. The call for limiting free trade and immigration shows a protectionist stance against global markets. Manufacturing laborers who lost jobs are especially vocal in protesting job exports.

What Are Some Major Political Decisions That Brought Along a Multi-Platform Era?

The previous section covered national, regional, and international political bodies that regulate media content, ownership, and trade. In this section, we focus on political bodies that actively develop a specific area of the media and cultural industries to strengthen their national economy and to facilitate exports. These agencies may not be regulators who make laws and policies; they may be commissions and task forces that recommend that governments, businesses, and regulators take certain actions. Because some countries—most notably the US—believe that certain industries should perform the best when they are the least regulated, they ensure a free market for these industries. Similarly, some countries actively persuade international organizations to adopt standards and procedures to promote a free global flow of media and cultural products.

National Agencies

As covered in Chapter 4, "Economics," film policies are usually made at the state level. Nation-states have a lot of catching up to do regarding comprehensively supporting digital media industries, such as video games, apps, and social media. States tend to use a combination of strategies to develop new industries: channeling money into higher education; giving tax breaks and small loans; developing innovation centers and industrial parks. However, the film industry seems to hold a special status in national media development, probably due to its glamorous aura, potentially high export value, and enhancements to a country's "soft power" (see Chapter 8, "Cultures").

Western and non-Western states sometimes provide financial support to the domestic film sector by providing seed grants for filmmakers to produce their work. Some countries, such as Australia and South Korea, categorize film policies as part of the cultural policies, whereas others, such as the US and Hong Kong, view them separately from other creative industries. In some countries—most notably the US—competition for investment even occurs at the state level. The US government's support for its film industry is unique; it has devoted "massive resources to generate and sustain 'private-sector' film in the interests of ideology and money, and the industry has responded in commercial and ideological kind" (Miller & Maxwell, 2016, p. 41). As suggested in Wasko (2003) and Miller & Maxwell (2016), the government supports the film industry in different ways, such as by offering tax-credit schemes, representing the industry in the global markets, offering loans and support to the independents, and providing police services to block city streets for film sets. The Brazilian state also highlighted film industry as an industry of growth. Unlike the US, though, this South American film industry is characterized by small production companies.

In Canada, both the federal and provincial governments offer a diverse range of financial supports for eligible film and television productions that take place in the country (McMillan, 2011). The Canadian experience is particularly telling of how the state could actively develop an industry from infancy to a more mature stage. In the 1980s and 1990s, government policy had succeeded in creating audiovisual production clusters in three major cities: Toronto, Vancouver, and Montréal. Prior to 1984, independent film production did not exist, and state-owned corporations dominated the very limited amount of production. A brief foray into tax-incentive financing for feature films had ended disastrously in the late 1970s (Grant & Wood, 2004). However, the Canadian government has switched its emphasis from tax incentives to direct investment and support for international co-production since the late 1980s. With this combination, an industry gradually came into being (Grant & Wood, 2004).

In Canada, film policy is seen as part of wider cultural policies. The Cultural Industries Sectoral Advisory Group (1999) said, "As a nation, Canada has developed a vibrant cultural sector, with numerous cultural institutions, a diverse publishing industry, a talented music industry, a dynamic cultural new media industry and critically acclaimed film and television industries" (para. 1). They may have responded to an increased level of economic integration by strengthening domestic cultural industries and cultural expression to maintain the country's sovereignty and the citizens' sense of identity. The advisory group explained that the government uses a combination of financial incentives, Canadian content requirements, tax measures, rules on foreign investments, and intellectual property tools to promote Canadian culture. The dual end goals are to take advantage of global goods and to preserve Canadian culture.

In addition to cultural policies, the Canadian government is also aware that digitization and convergence of the broadcasting, cable, satellite, and telecommunications sectors could undermine the state's authority to ensure that Canadians have access to domestic cultural products. Thus, national policies need to adapt by attracting multinational corporations and by vertically integrating the production and distribution sectors. Canada is not alone in this respect; nations in Latin America (Chile and Mexico) and the Asia Pacific region (New Zealand, Australia, South Korea, and China) keep their small domestic film production industries alive with government supports through tactics such as financial subsidies and legal means.

Some Asian governments have recently taken the initiative to advance their own cultural industries with export capacities. For example, the Japanese government has started to highlight cultural industries since the 1990s. In July 2011, it established the Creative Industries Division within the Japanese Ministry of Economy, Trade and Industry (METI). The Division is to supervise Japan's promotion of "cool" products abroad and assist domestic small and midsize culture-related firms to pursue a global strategy. The state focuses on providing the infrastructure needed for the development of the cultural industries (such as building an industrial park for a specific type of industry), supporting the technology needed for delivering and consuming cultural content (such as providing infrastructure for the Internet, cable television, or satellite broadcasts), and ensuring the availability of venture capital for producing movies, television programs, animation, and computer games (Jin & Otmazgin, 2014, p. 48).

Likewise, the Korean government has also taken a deep interest in developing the cultural industries. It has been strongly supporting the development of the "creative contents industries" and promoting Korean popular culture as an export industry. In 1998, former president Kim Dae Jung announced that the promotion of cultural industries was strategic for Korea's future (Jin & Otmazgin, 2014). As a result, since the early 1990s, the Korean government has been supporting the audiovisual sector, which became a springboard for the Korean Wave. While there are several elements in the formation and development of the Korean Wave, it can be argued that the state support of the cultural industries was the most important driver for the growth of the Korean cultural industries, both domestic and for export. To illustrate the immense support from the state, the Korean broadcasting industry has continuously increased its exports of television programs (such as dramas and reality competition shows) from only US$18.9 million in 2001 to US$340 million in 2014 (Korea Creative Content Agency, 2015).

Another way to promote domestic production is to restrict the imports of foreign media, as indicated by screen quota systems in Canada, France, Korea, China, and Mexico. Screen quota means only a limited number of foreign films can be shown in theaters. In Europe, France has the strictest screen quota system, limiting the imports of Hollywood movies; the government also actively encourages other European production companies to work with French ones. Not only does the French government limit the imports of US films, but it also restricts the inflow of US television programs. The French government aims to protect a European identity in the media sector by protecting the French film industry. In Latin America, Mexico had a 50% "screen quota" before the signing of NAFTA. The signing of the treaty destroyed the local film industry, because Hollywood films have since dominated local screens (Paxman, 2009).

Regional Agencies

Unlike Mexico, NAFTA did not affect the film industry in Canada as much, largely because the local film industry had been very marginalized. Canada has continued to restrict the influx of American popular culture to the country. Because of the overwhelming power of Hollywood in the global film market, the market share for domestic films in Canada has not been strong. In the late 1980s, Hollywood dominance in the Canadian film market was the strongest. When NAFTA came into effect in the early 1990s, Canada could not find any momentum to revive its film industry in terms of market share as well as production (Telefilm Canada, 2005).

However, with the passing of the Canada-United States Free Trade Agreement (CUSFTA) in 1987, Canada succeeded in excluding cultural industries from being free trade goods. In the FTA era, the Canadian government has initiated and continued its support of the Canadian film industry by, for instance, providing Canadian producers a refundable tax credit of about US$60 million a year. Despite these proactive cultural policies, local productions have only a small share in most Canadian film and television markets. American cultural products—including films, television programs, and magazines—flow rather well to the northern border, because Canada's protection measures for the cultural industry are not effective (Jin, 2011a).

International Agencies

In this section, we look at the Internet Corporation for Assigned Names and Numbers (ICANN) and the World Summit on Information Society (WSIS). The former is a nongovernmental, nonprofit organization based in the US governing IP addresses; the latter is a UN initiative to bring equitable information development to the developing world. Both ICANN and WSIS deal with Internet governance, such as institutional and policy problems related to the global coordination of Internet domain names and addresses. It is generally recognized that Internet regulation is difficult, if possible at all. By nature, the Internet is global, and any national attempts to regulate it will be fruitless (Andrews, 1999, cited in Klein, 2002). Therefore, global collaboration is needed for Internet governance.

The United Nations first organized the World Summit on Information Society in 2003, where states, businesses, and civil societies met to discuss how the digital gap can be narrowed between developed and developing countries and how developing countries can harness the potential of the Internet for international development. In addition, the UN has created the Internet Governance Forum (IGF) for states to talk about public policy relating to the Internet.

ICANN is a nonprofit entity based in the US. Internet governance is tricky, because the Internet began as a military project and continued as an academic project. At the very beginning, a college professor coordinated all the Internet Protocol Identifiers as a hobby. As the number of websites exploded, it was impossible for an individual to keep track of all IP Identifiers. Because the earliest Internet architects were suspicious of state and business involvement in the digital space, the US government recommended that a nonprofit organization be formed for this purpose. The Internet Corporation for Assigned Names and Numbers was thus created in 1998. It is a new type of international, nongovernmental model; it is a US-constructed unilateral global regime (Van Eeten & Mueller, 2013), yet the government has no involvement in its running.

ICANN aims to ensure that the Internet is secure, stable, and interoperable. At the same time, it fosters competition and helps develop protocol for the Internet's unique identifiers. It makes policies for global protocol parameters, Internet number resources, and domain names. However, the expansion and evolution of the Internet are not the responsibility of ICANN. It is more like a coordinator among website addresses rather than an Internet architect. By putting in place all the mechanisms needed for the creation, promulgation, and enforcement of regulations, ICANN makes effective Internet governance possible for the first time (Klein, 2002). Thus, ICANN has the potential to radically change the nature of the Internet. However, countries such as China and Russia complained that ICANN controls domain names. China wanted domestic users to register domain names through government-licensed providers. This process does not guarantee anonymity and the government would know who disseminated the content. To Western democratic countries, this type of Internet governance counters the ideal of the Internet being open and unconstrained by national boundaries.

What Kinds of Roles Do Business Organizations Play in Political Decisions?

In Chapter 2, we discussed that in an age of trade liberalization and deregulation, the state minimizes its role in many aspects of social life, whereas the private sector takes over some aspects. Therefore, the business sector influences a lot of political decisions in the cultural sector. Many governments—be they in the developed or developing world— have no choice but to accommodate media and telecommunications corporations in decision-making. One such tactic is through lobbying. We discuss in this section how lobbying is commonly used among platform companies to push for policies.

The development and expansion of US digital platforms throughout the world is partially a result of direct government intervention and support from the State Department (Jin, 2016). However, hi-tech firms in the platform business have been vehemently involved in political decisions through several mechanisms, including hiring lobbyists to persuade lawmakers to take the companies' positions into consideration. For example, Google spent about US$6 million lobbying 13 government agencies in the single year 2009. An issue that Google lobbies for is the freedom of speech on the Internet, probably because of the search engine's highly publicized battles with the Chinese government in 2010. The Chinese government asked Google to censor searches of politically "sensitive" topics such as "human rights" and "Taiwan independence." Google decided to move its operation from mainland China to Hong Kong instead of complying with the Chinese government. Afterward, Google urged the US Congress to adopt policies that assure a neutral and open Internet at home and put pressure on foreign governments that censor the Web (Goldman, 2010). Other issues that Google lobbied for range from patent reform, cloud computing, and driverless cars to renewable energy. From 2007 to 2010, Google increased its lobbying expenditure spending by more than $1 million each year. In 2013, the company spent a record $14.06 million on lobbying (Chiu, 2011; Consumer Watchdog, 2014).

Even though Google maintains a youthful company image, its expenditure on lobbying far exceeds some well-established industries, such as automobile and energy: "The rise of Google as a top-tier Washington player fully captures the arc of change in the influence business. Google has soared to near the top of the city's lobbying ranks" (Hamburger & Gold, 2014, para. 10). Other platform corporations are also lavish spenders on lobbying. According to Consumer Watchdog (2016), Facebook lobbied for issues concerning government surveillance, Internet advertising, child online protection, and immigration reform; Apple lobbied for issues concerning corporate tax reform, energy efficiency, mobile payments, safe driving, and patents. Microsoft, Twitter, and Uber are other hi-tech firms that have increased their spending on lobbying lawmakers. Hi-tech companies not only lobby for issues that are closely related to their businesses, but they also lobby for issues that the founders and executives care about. See Table 5.2 on p. 113 for the top spenders in the communications/electronics industry in political lobbying.

Case Study: State Strategies of "Japanese Cool" and the "Korean Wave"

In this last section, we show how two cultural phenomena, "Japanese Cool" and "Korean Wave," were actually results of state-private sector collaboration. We list the state agencies that are responsible for promoting the two creative industries by discussing the ways in which the business community works with state policies.

Step 1: Japanese Cool

The Japanese government used to pursue a minimal state intervention policy within the realm of the cultural sector. It had no direct ties to the cultural sector in terms of developing and promoting cultural programs (Jin, 2011b). The public broadcasting system NHK has the primary responsibility for providing Japanese programming abroad (Broadcast Law Article 2). One of the missions of the Broadcast Law and NHK's charter is to furnish programming to Japanese living abroad, as well as to foreigners. The Japanese government used to intrude little in the television content industry, partly because Japan did not want to appear to violate Broadcast Law (Article 1) that prohibits an infringement on the freedom of the press and expression (Jin, 2003). The state's minimal intervention has changed in the 21st century. The Japanese government realized the increasing importance of cultural products for the national economy; therefore, the state shifted its broadcasting policies and developed new policy measures to promote the broadcasting industry and television programs exports. The state grew to be aware that cultural exports could be economically profitable and could boost Japan's image overseas, so the government became more supportive of promoting cultural exports (Otmazgin, 2003; Ministry of Economy, Trade and Industry of Japan, 2012).

At the same time, the Japanese government began to pay attention to the film industry by acknowledging the importance of film as a cultural commodity in the Japanese economy. In 2001, the Japanese government created the Fundamental Law for the Promotion of Culture and Arts, which authorized financial support for producing and exhibiting theatrical films (Ministry of Education, Culture, Sports, Science and Technology, 2009). In accordance with this law, in 2002 the Japanese government formulated the Basic Policy for the Promotion of Culture and the Arts. The Basic Policy intends to enhance Japanese cultural power and to disseminate and promote Japanese culture and international cultural exchanges (Article 1). The government has highlighted media and cultural goods, such as animation, manga, and films, as exports (Agency for Cultural Affairs, 2008). The Japanese Ministry of Economy, Trade and Industry (METI, 2016) has also helped with exporting culture by promoting overseas an internationally appreciated "Cool Japan" brand, cultivating creative industries and promoting these industries in Japan and abroad.

Step 2: The Korean Wave

Unlike the Japanese government, the Korean government has been deeply involved in the development of the Korean cultural industries. It was involved in the production and promotion of the Korean Wave since the early stage. Since the early 1990s, it has liberalized and deregulated the cultural market in response to strong requests by the US government. However, unlike neoliberal globalists' expectations, the Korean government has maintained and continued its influence as a regulator of the cultural sector. For example, it financially supported the broadcasting industry between 2002 and 2016. During this period, the government made a "broadcasting-visual content production supporting system" and financially supported a total of 277 programs. Among them, documentaries were the largest category (151 programs), followed by dramas (39) and educational programs (35). The government also supported finished programs in order to sell them in the global markets (Ministry of Culture, Sports and Tourism of Korea, 2013).

Meanwhile, since the mid-1990s, the Korean government has initiated the resuscitation of the film industries while applying the logic of globalization to the cultural industries. In the early 1990s, Korean cinema experienced the worst recession of its domestic film market share in the midst of neoliberal reform. The market share of domestic films was only 15.9% in 1993, so the government had to develop high-level policy changes to revive Korean cinema. In

December 2006, the Ministry of Culture and Tourism (2006) established the "Film Development Fund" to promote the export of domestic films and support small producers. The Korean government's favorable cultural policy, including financial subsidies, clearly gave preference to domestic companies (including large conglomerates) in an effort to integrate them into the domestic film industries. Likewise, the Korean government has developed several supporting mechanisms for the music and digital games industries. Admittedly, the Korean Wave also depends on other dimensions, but it is undeniable that the Korean government has become a primary driver of the Korean Wave, which promotes the emergence of local popular culture in the global markets.

Interestingly, the Korean government pursued both hands-on and hands-off policies at different times, depending on which political party was in power. The state followed a hands-off policy during the liberal administration between 1998 and 2008. The government employed indirect measures to promote domestic cultural products. The state preferred an indirect measure, because it tried to avoid appearing to instigate Korea's cultural invasion into other countries. The state was afraid that state involvement in the cultural sector would harm the Wave's popularity in Asia (Jin, 2016). However, during the conservative administration between 2008 and 2017, the government changed gears and developed a hands-on policy by using direct measures to promote Korean Wave as part of their foreign policy that emphasizes soft power (Nye & Kim, 2013). By developing favorable cultural policies, it has played a major role by not only developing the cultural industry, but also promoting the export of Korean pop culture (Jin, 2016).

In sum, nation-states still play a significant role in the formation of cultural policy and the promotion of cultural products. Neoliberal globalization challenges the ability of nation-states to protect their national culture; however, the two most capitalist regimes in East Asia have employed robust cultural policies to protect their cultural products and national cultures (Jin, 2011b). In the age of neoliberal globalization, many national governments continue to function as key players in the realm of culture. Therefore, it is critical to understand the changing role of the nation-state under neoliberal globalization in order to address politics in tandem with the cultural industries.

Conclusion

We asked in this chapter whether neoliberal globalization has influenced how a political entity makes decisions relating to the media and hi-tech industries. In other words, do nation-states still have the same degree of autonomy when the revenue size of the largest corporations are larger than the national economies of some nation-states? We have not found conclusive evidence to show that this is the case. A comparison between national policies of countries that invent and export media and cultural products show the state is involved in different ways to different degrees. On the other hand, corporations are not without their influence; lobbying is a commonly used strategy to influence politicians to make policies that favor corporations.

References

Agency for Cultural Affairs. Government of Japan. (2008). *Promotion of international cultural exchange*. Retrieved from http:// www.bunka.go.jp/ english/index.htm

Amadeo, K. (2016). FTAA: Agreement, members, pros and cons. *The Balance*. Retrieved from www.thebalance.com/ftaa-agreement-member-countries-pros-and-cons-3305577

Andrews, E. (1999, November 18). German court overturns pornography ruling against Compuserve. *New York Times*.

Beijing Newsroom. (2008, February 14). Regulators now spooked by ghost stories. *Reuters*. Retrieved from www.reuters.com/article/us-ghosts-idUS N1442888920080214?feedType=RSS&feedName=oddlyEnoughNews

Bruno, G. (2009, July 22). The media landscape in Iran. *Council on Foreign Relations*. Retrieved from www.cfr.org/iran/media-landscape-iran/p19889

Caldwell, J. (2008). *Production culture: Industrial reflexivity and critical practice in film and television*. Durham, NC: Duke University Press.

Canadian Radio-Television and Telecommunications Commission. (2016). *About us*. Retrieved from www.crtc.gc.ca/eng/acrtc/acrtc.htm

Chiu, E. (2011, February 17). Google, Facebook lead new generation of technology companies pressing government for favorable treatment. *OpenSecrets.org*. Retrieved from www.opensecrets.org/news/2011/02/goo gle-facebook-lead-new-generation.html

Consumer Watchdog. (2014, January 22). *Google leads pack as 10 tech firms pump $61.15 million into 2013 lobbying efforts*. Retrieved from www.con sumerwatchdog.org/newsrelease/google-leads-pack-10-tech-firms-pump-6115-million-2013-lobbying-efforts

Consumer Watchdog. (2016, April 21). *Uber, Twitter are spending big on political lobbying*. Retrieved from www.consumerwatchdog.org/story/uber-twitter-are-spending-big-political-lobbying

Cultural Industries Sectoral Advisory Group on International Trade. Government of Canada. (1999, February). *New strategies for culture and trade Canadian culture in a global world*. Retrieved from www.international. gc.ca/trade-agreements-accords-commerciaux/topics-domaines/ip-pi/ canculture.aspx?lang=en&_ga=2.235831617.190048148.1493907139-1729186741.1493907139

Davies, M. (2006). Production studies: Critical studies in television. *The International Journal of Television Studies, 1*(1), 21–30.

Doleac, C. (2015). Insufficient media reforms in Latin America: Urgency to go further. *Council on Hemispheric Affairs*. Retrieved from www.coha.org/ insufficient-media-reforms-in-latin-america-urgency-to-go-further/

Doyle, G. (2002). *Media ownership: The economics and politics of convergence and concentration in the UK and European media*. London: Sage.

Duran, R. (2013, September 23). Film industry in Brazil. *Brazil Business*. Retrieved from http://thebrazilbusiness.com/article/film-industry-in-brazil

Federal Communications Commission. (2016). *The FCC's mission*. Retrieved from www.fcc.gov/about/overview

Freedom House. (2015). *Freedom of the press: Cuba*. Retrieved from https://freedomhouse.org/report/freedom-press/freedom-press-2015#. WQs9ANxZqUk

Garnham, N. (2000). *Emancipation, the media, and modernity*. Oxford: Oxford University Press.

Giddens, A. (1999, April 11). Comment: The 1999 Reith lecture: New world without end. *Observer*.

Global Affairs Canada. (2016). *North American Free Trade Agreement (NAFTA)*. Retrieved from www.international.gc.ca/trade-agreements-ac cords-commerciaux/agr-acc/nafta-alena/index.aspx?lang=eng

Goldman, D. (2010). How Google plays the angles in Washington. *CNN Money*. Retrieved from http://money.cnn.com/2010/03/30/technology/ google_washington/#

Grant, P., & Wood. C. (2004). *Blockbusters and trade wars: Popular culture in a globalized world*. Vancouver, Canada: Douglas & McIntyre.

Hamburger, T., & Gold, M. (2014, April 12). Google, once disdainful of lobbying, now a master of Washington influence. *The Washington Post*. Retrieved from www.washingtonpost.com/politics/how-google-is-transforming-power-and-politicsgoogle-once-disdainful-of-lobbying-now-a-master-of-washing toninfluence/2014/04/12/51648b92-b4d3-11e3-8cb6-284052554d74_ story.html

Jin, D. Y. (2003). Globalization of Japanese culture: Economic power vs. cultural power, 1989–2002. *Prometheus, 21*(3), 335–345.

Jin, D. Y. (2005). The telecom crisis and beyond: Restructuring of the global telecommunications system. *International Communication Gazette, 67*(3), 289–304.

Jin, D. Y. (2011a). A critical analysis of US cultural policy in the global film market: Nation-states and FTAs. *International Communication Gazette, 73*(8), 651–669.

Jin, D. Y. (2011b). Cultural politics in Japanization and the Korean Wave: The changing role of nation-states in the midst of cultural globalization. In D. K. Kim & M. S. Kim (Eds.), *Hallyu: Influence of Korean popular culture in Asia and beyond* (pp. 91–129). Seoul: Seoul National University.

Jin, D. Y. (2016). *New Korean Wave: Transnational cultural power in the age of social media.* Urbana, IL: University of Illinois Press.

Jin, D. Y., & Otmazgin, N. (2014). Introduction: East Asian cultural industries: Policies, strategies, and trajectories. *Pacific Affairs, 87*(1), 43–51.

Jonquireres, G. (1997, February 18). Template for trade tariffs. *Financial Times*, p. 6.

Keane, M., & and Sanson, K. (2016). *Precarious creativity: Global media, local labor.* Berkeley, CA: University of California Berkeley Press.

Kazancigil, A., & Dogan, M. (1986). *The state in global perspective: Comparing nations: Concepts, strategies, substance.* Paris: Gower/UNESCO.

Klein, H. (2002). ICANN and Internet governance: Leveraging technical coordination to realize global public policy. *The Information Society, 18*, 193–207.

Korea Communications Commission. (2016). *About KCC.* Retrieved from http://eng.kcc.go.kr/user.do?page=E01010100&dc=E01010100

Korea Creative Content Agency. (2015). *2015 Content industries production.* Naju: KOCCA.

Lozano, J-C. (2008). NAFTA and international communication. *Blackwell Reference Online.* Retrieved from www.blackwellreference.com/public/tocnode? id=g9781405131995_chunk_g978140513199519_ss1–1

McChesney, R. (2000). The political economy of communication and the future of the field. *Media, Culture & Society, 22*(1), 109–116.

McMillan. (2011). *We've got you covered in Canada.* Retrieved from www.mcmillan.ca/files/Overview_film_television_production_in_Canada_s3.pdf

Miller, T., & Maxwell, R. (2016). Film and globalization. In O. Boyd-Barrett (Ed.), *Communication, media, globalization and empire* (pp. 33–52). Bloomington, IN: Indiana University Press.

Ministry of Culture and Tourism of Korea. (2006, December 22). *Establishment of Film Development Fund.* Seoul: MCT.

Ministry of Culture, Sports and Tourism of Korea. (2013). *2012 Contents industry white paper.* Seoul: MCST.

Ministry of Culture, Sports and Tourism of Korea. (2014a). *2013 Music industry white paper.* Seoul: MCST.

Ministry of Culture, Sports and Tourism of Korea. (2014b). *2014 Budget: Fund summary.* Seoul: MCST.

Ministry of Education, Culture, Sports, Science and Technology of Japan. (2009). *Promotion of culture and arts and international cultural exchange.* Retrieved from www.next.go.jp/english/org/struct/038.htm

Ministry of Economy, Trade and Industry of Japan. (2012, January). *Cool Japan strategy.* Tokyo: METI.

Ministry of Economy, Trade and Industry of Japan. (2016). *Cool Japan/Creative industries policy*. Retrieved from www.meti.go.jp/english/policy/mono_info_service/creative_industries/creative_industries.html

Milz, S. (2007). Canadian cultural policy-making at a time of neoliberal globalization. *ESC, 33*(1/2), 85–107.

Morley, D., & Robins, K. (1995). *Spaces of identity: Global media, electronic landscapes and cultural boundaries*. London: Routledge.

Mosco, V. (2009). *The political economy of communication* (2nd ed.). London: Sage.

Nye, J., & Kim, Y. (2013). Soft power and the Korean Wave. In Y. Kim (Ed.), *The Korean Wave: Korean media go global* (pp. 31–42). London: Routledge.

Ohmae, K. (1995). The end of the nation state. In F. J. Lechner & J. Boli (Eds.), *The globalization reader* (3rd ed., pp. 223–227). Malden, MA: Blackwell.

Office of the US Trade Representative. (2009). *Summary of the US-Korea FTA*. Washington, DC: USTR.

Otmazgin, N. (2003). Japanese government support for cultural exports. *Kyoto Review of Southeast Asia*. Retrieved from http://kyotoreview.org/issue-4/japanese-government-support-for-cultural-exports/

Owers, J., Carveth, R., & Alexander, A. (1993). An introduction to media economic theory and practice. In A. Alexander, J. Owers, & R. Carveth (Eds.), *Media economics: Theory and practice* (pp. 3–46). Hillsdale, NJ: Lawrence Erlbaum.

Paxman, A. (2009). *Who killed the Mexican film industry? The decline of the Golden Age, 1949–1960*. Rio de Janeiro, Brazil: Latin American Studies Assn. conference. Retrieved from www.academia.edu/189946/Who_Killed_the_Mexican_Film_Industry_The_Decline_of_the_Golden_Age_1949-1960

Rejai, M., & Enloe, C. H. (1969). Nation-states and state-nations. *International Studies Quarterly, 13*(2), 140–158.

Rosenfeld, E., & Kemp, T. (2016, June 25). Welcome to the world after Brexit: Here's what happens next. *CNBC*. Retrieved from www.cnbc.com/2016/06/23/welcome-to-the-worldafter-brexit-heres-what-happens-next.html

Schiller, D. (1999). *Digital capitalism*. Cambridge, MA: MIT Press.

Sinclair, J. (2007). Cultural globalization and American Empire. In G. Murdock & J. Wasko (Eds.), *Media in the age of marketization* (pp. 131–150). Cresskill, NJ: Hampton Press.

Telefilm Canada. (2005). *The role of federal government support the development of the Canadian feature film industry*. Retrieved from www.telefilm.gc.ca/document/en/01/17/StandingCommitteeCanadianHeritage.pdf

UNESCO. (2016). *Nation-state*. Retrieved from www.unesco.org/new/en/social-and humansciences/themes/international-migration/glossary/nation-state/

Van Elteren, M. (2011). Cultural globalization and transnational flows of things American. In P. Pachura (Ed.), *The systemic dimension of globalization* (pp. 149–172). Rijeka, Croatia: InTech.

Van Eeten, M., & Mueller, M. (2013). Where is the governance in Internet governance. *New Media & Society, 15*(5), 720–736.

Wasko, J. (2003). *How Hollywood works*. London: Sage.

Weiss, L. (1997). Globalization and the myth of the powerless state. *New Left Review, 225,* 3–22.

Winseck, D. (2011). The political economies of media and the transformation of global media industries. In D. Winseck & D. Y. Jin (Eds.), *The political economies of media: The transformation of the global media industries* (pp. 3–48). London: Bloomsbury.

Yantao, B. (2016, April 5). When will Chinese TV dramas play their part? *China Daily.* Retrieved from www.chinadaily.com.cn/culture/2016-04/05/con tent_24291279_2.htm

Yuval-Davis, N. (1997). *Gender and nation*. London: Sage.

Technologies

At the end of the chapter, students will be able to:

- explain why technology alone does not change the business of media;
- explain why information and communication technologies were seen as a stimulus of the economy;
- define media and technological convergence;
- suggest how the three approaches (media economics, political economy of communication, and production studies) conceptualize technologies;
- explain how technologies could be a disruptive force in the media business landscape;
- give an example to show how a new media company (e.g. Amazon.com, Apple, Netflix) has disrupted the old business model;
- suggest if media companies and technology companies tend to work with or compete against each other;
- suggest how information can be commodified;
- suggest how free labor is created in a digital economy;
- suggest how technology can be a change agent, power consolidator, or a curse. Give one example in each of the cases;

- give one example to show how cell phones are used in Africa and suggest if the cell phone is used for the same function as in the developed world.

The smartphone may appear to have changed everything: from people's daily lives to media corporations' business strategies. When Apple introduced the first iPhone in 2007, it changed the meaning and function of a mobile phone: users could listen to music through earplugs as well as watch television dramas and films on the small touch screen. The smartphone has also changed how young people communicate. They quickly cut the cord to the landline telephone, using the mobile phone as their sole telephone. Gradually, they do not even use the smartphone to make calls, but instead communicate through instant mobile messengers, such as WhatsApp, WeChat, Line, and Kakao. The use of the smartphone has prodded both traditional media and telecommunications corporations to shift their business models, because the mobile phone takes advantage of media and technological convergence. To respond to the rapid changes in media consumption habits, newspaper companies set up mobile news teams to develop multi-platform journalism, and film festivals create film awards to commend indie films shot on a smartphone.

The recent smartphone growth in many countries has dramatically changed digital culture and economy. Young people tend to be heavy smartphone users: they use applications to play games, communicate with friends and relatives, watch new movies, and check their daily schedules. Business owners also rely on the smartphone to do things that used to require multiple machines (such as desktop computer, calculator, and telephone). The pervasive use of the smartphone drives the advancement of the digital economy as well. The popularity of the smartphone and apps prompt many industries to become smartphone-centric. For example, smartphone pioneer Apple now relies less on the sales of computers, software, and music and more on the sales of iPhone to drive company performance. Another global mobile phone company, Samsung, previously focused on semi-conductors and television monitors, but now it relies on the sales of smartphones to produce impressive annual revenue. Social media companies have changed their business model as well. Facebook had to develop smartphone-based functions to attract mobile advertising revenue, which accounted for approximately 84% of all advertising revenue in the fourth quarter of 2016 (Facebook, 2017).

The importance of the smartphone in digital culture and economy demands an examination of the mobile technology surge from several different perspectives: media economics, political economy, and production studies. Economists would see the smartphone as a cutting-edge technology to garner profits from production and consumption activities. However, from a political economic perspective, a smartphone economy shows that the expansion of contemporary digital capitalism heavily relies on users' online activities; platforms such as Facebook, Google, and YouTube make profits by monetizing users' energy and time. Meanwhile, we also need to understand the smartphone from a production studies perspective by looking into those who make cultural products and how they work with technologies.

Since users play a key role in developing audiovisual content by uploading texts, pictures, and videos, it is critical to consider that users constitute a free labor force. As Terranova (2004) aptly argues, free labor can be interpreted as unpaid labor: it is voluntarily given and unwaged, enjoyed and exploited at the same time. Although gamers find excitement, satisfaction, and pleasure during gameplay, their time and energy contribute to the profits of smartphone companies. Free labor is closely tied to a commodification process, in which media and information technology corporations and advertising agencies systematically exploit users (Jin, 2015a). Mason (2015) suggested that information technology "has reduced the need for work, blurred the edges between work and free time and loosened the relationship between work and wages" (para. 2).

Based on the above, we discuss in this chapter how digital technology can be analyzed from the three perspectives, in particular media economics and a political economy of communication. However, it needs to be emphasized that technology is in the background of all the lenses: economies, politics, civil societies, cultures, and labor. Many have suggested that technologies have transformed the media business, but technologies alone would not change the entire business landscape. Therefore, we insist that all the lenses are interdependent. For example, the case of the smartphone shows that the global economy is related to digital technology, because the latter is seen as a driving force of the former. However, we also critically analyze the influences of digital technologies on modern capitalism in conjunction with digital platforms. For example, how technologies transform digital distribution and promotion in the media industry and how online retailers (such as Amazon and Netflix) gradually become content producers.

A few questions addressed in this chapter are:

- Are technologies a disruptive force in the media landscape? A brief review of the history of technologies in the media shows that new technology can aid small media companies to become major players. The case of Netflix shows that not only did the company make DVD rental shops obsolete, it also branched out to become a media producer and distributor.
- Is technology a change agent, a power consolidator, or a curse to companies? Evidence shows that technology can make or break a company. Hi-tech companies such as Google, Facebook, and Amazon experienced exponential growth due to media convergence. However, some media companies need to "de-converge" themselves, because their acquisitions of tech companies have not produced the synergistic effect as they hoped. To some former hi-tech pioneers, they could lose their competitive edge if they could not accept new innovation.
- How can information and labor be commodified? Search engine giant Google always brands itself as a company that provides services akin to public goods. Yet, political economists think Google underwent a process of commodification that make something publicly available into something proprietary.
- We last look at mobile phone use and the telecommunications market in Africa as a case study. Although the continent is assumed to be a laggard in technology, mobile phone use has become prevalent in Africa. However, the telecommunications industry has also been quickly privatized and liberalized, which could have a stifling effect on technological adoption in Africa.

Platform Technologies in the Business of Media

Information and communication technologies (ICTs) contribute to a networked society: from the earliest World Wide Web to social media and digital platforms, new ICTs have greatly influenced the daily lives of most of the world's populations. The recent growth of the smartphone has shown that mobile technologies and applications (hereafter apps) are woven into people's daily activities and routines, such as gamers playing mobile games on their cell phones while commuting on public transit. Therefore, it is critical to understand the roles of ICTs in tandem with the global economy, because ICTs are one driving force for the growth of digital capitalism.

Since the mid-1990s, ICTs have played a key role in the economy; technologies were seen as a stimulus to a sluggish economy. In the 1970s, the US experienced "stagflation": prices went up but wages remained the same. The economy failed to grow as dramatically as the post–WWII period, when the automobile industry had transformed the economy of the country. With the introduction of the commercial Internet in the mid-1990s, some economists believed that new ICTs were the answer for lifting the economy up (McChesney, Wood, & Foster, 1998). Alan Greenspan, the chairman of the US Federal Reserve at that time, believed that ICTs would bring unprecedented and continuous growth to the economy. As a result, the global economy has rapidly embraced the Internet and other new media technologies, such as broadband cable, mobile technologies, and digital games. To governments and corporations around the world, ICTs have been seen as an important infrastructure for economic development, not only because of the size of the industries, but also because of their indispensable role in communication and information dissemination. All major industries rely on ICTs to some extent, whether they are agriculture, manufacturing, or service.

ICTs have transformed the telecommunications sector: the infrastructural growth has expedited that of the Internet and broadband services. The large-scale and sustained growth of the fixed telephone network was fundamental in providing an infrastructure to support the explosion of Internet service. From 1994 to 2002, there had been a 17.5-fold growth in global Internet users: from 38 million users to over 665 million (Computer Industry Almanac, 2002). The growth continued; by the end of June 2016 the number of Internet subscribers worldwide reached over 3,611 million (International Telecommunication Union, 2000; Internet World Stats, 2016).

Digital technology made possible the convergence of voice, data, and video; the transmission of digital data is much faster than analog signals and is thus quickly expandable (Jin, 2013). Together with a plethora of other types of user equipment, such as video game consoles, ICTs are shifting how information is transmitted, received, and managed in the networks (Frieden, 2001).

But the explosion in digital technology cannot be explained by technology alone. In the context of deregulation in both developed and developing countries (see Chapter 2, "The History of the Study of the Business of Media"), private companies were allowed to enter into state-owned industries in order to compete and expand into Internet service businesses. In the late 1990s, no company—in particular, no telecommunications company—could afford to neglect the Internet either as a tool to expand its business or as a business itself (ITU, 2000). One result was large-scale mergers and acquisitions: media and telecommunications corporations bought up each other in order to invest in the international ICT market (Jin, 2013).

Later came new forms of digital technologies, including social media and platform technologies. On the one hand, social media, such as social network sites (hereafter SNSs) and user-generated content sites (such as YouTube), have quickly gained popularity due to their functionality and playfulness. SNSs are deeply embedded in the everyday lives of young people; SNSs such as Facebook and Twitter have hundreds of thousands of young users spending immense time and energy to update their personal profiles with a blog-type interface in which their latest postings or photos appear on top of the SNS (Jin, 2015b). Social media sites allow users to present themselves, articulate their social networks, and establish or maintain connections with others (Boyd, 2007; Ellison, Steinfield, & Lampe, 2007; Hargittai, 2007). SNS users participate in creating their own content and expressing themselves because SNSs provide a new time-space for self-expression, connectivity, and self-creation among young people (Livingstone, 2008).

On the other hand, the economy of digital platforms has rapidly grown since the 2010s. Platform technologies, such as social network sites, search engines (e.g., Google), smartphones (e.g., iPhone) and operating systems (e.g., Android), have swiftly become some of the most significant digital technologies and cultures throughout the world. These digital platforms have substantially shifted and influenced people's daily lives, because platform technologies have enabled a fundamental shift from the mass-mediated public sphere to platform-driven public sphere (Benkler, 2006). Therefore, platforms provide opportunities for people to mobilize themselves effectively for social change (Jin, 2015b). To van Dijck and Poell (2013), a platform is a "mediator" because it shapes the performance of social acts. They emphasize that a platform is not simply a delivery system but plays a major role in developing content, as many users upload their texts and videos on SNSs.

How the Three Approaches Conceptualize Technologies

Media economists tend to see technology as an extraneous factor to nontechnology firms; that is, technology may stimulate production but is not integrated into the entire chain of production, distribution, and consumption. Political economists have written extensively about the hi-tech industries; in particular, how digital technology has facilitated media convergence. Production studies scholars recognize that digital media blurs the boundary between producers and consumers.

Media Economics

The media economic approach tends to see industries as separate entities, such as media, telecommunications, and technology. As such, media economics does not capture the fluidity and the interplay between the interrelated industries. Media economists are mainly interested in how ICTs assist with the growth of different markets, and how this growth contributes to the national and global economies. This approach tries to understand the business practices, operations, and content of the media industry in tandem with technology, with an emphasis on the digitization of media platforms. As Albarran (2002) points out, media institutions are economic institutions, therefore their main goal is to produce and distribute media content to consumers in order to make profits. In other words, "media economics is the study of how media industries use scarce resources to produce content that is distributed among customers in a society to satisfy various wants and needs" (Albarran, 2002, p. 5). As addressed in Chapter 4, media economists tend to focus on microeconomic issues such as firm behaviors, characteristics of specific markets, and consumers' preferences and activities. In a sense, media economists do not see media technology as different from other resources, such as energy and food, because the industry allocates limited resources to produce goods to satisfy consumers' demands.

A Political Economy of Communication

In contrast to media economics, a political economy of new media technology focuses on the power relationship between several major players: the government, corporations, software/app developers, and consumers. In other words, a political economy of new media technology should seek to understand the way in which power is structured and differentiated, where it comes from, and how it is renewed (Garnham, 2000, cited in Mansell, 2004). Political economists study new media technology to show how global networks are structured, how digital information flows, and how a consumption of ICTs is informed by predominant principles, values, and power relations of a specific political economic system. A political economy of new media technology insists on examining the circumstances that give rise to any existing power distribution and consequences for consumers (Mansell, 2004; Mansell, Samarajiva, & Mahan, 2002). As Mansell (2004) pointed out,

> Distinctions between the older and newer media relate to how and why scarcity conditions emerge and the extent to which they contribute to the reproduction of unequal social conditions. Without research that gives a central place to power as a "headline" issue in new media studies, we can only speculate how inequality may be reproduced and then seen as the "natural" outcome of innovations in new media technologies.
>
> (p. 98)

Since a political economy of communication emphasizes the close relationship between politics, economy, and cultures, its primary interests are to identify the major owners of power and the ways in which their power executes.

Production Studies

Meanwhile, production studies looks at technology as a condition of possibilities of media production. As discussed previously, production studies researches into the people who make audiovisual products and how these people work (Davies, 2006). Since media producers form communities of shared practices, languages, and cultural understanding of the world (Mayer, Banks, & Caldwell, 2009, p. 2), the rise of new media has changed the identity of workers in fields from journalism to the creative industry (Ross, 2010). In particular, it is crucial to understand the role that digital media plays in media production—whether

Table 6.1 *How the three approaches conceptualize technologies*

	Media Economics	Political Economy of Communication	Production Studies
How technologies are related to an economy	As an extraneous factor that could simulate an economy.	Technology corporations are integral to an economy.	Not directly related but as a condition of possibilities of media production.
How the approach sees digital technology	Not too different from analog technology.	As a catalyst to converge media industries and corporations.	As knowledge that empowers/ disempowers media production.

it is old media (such as newspapers and television broadcasting) or new media (such as the Internet and mobile telecommunications). In this regard, production studies scholars believe that the use of new media technology benefits media corporations; for example, the use of computer graphics in media production, in particular big-budget Hollywood films (Johnson & Lamb, 1990). New media has also blurred the line between consumers and producers. SNSs and user-generated content platforms allow consumers to create their own content and to upload it; thus the consumers can brand themselves as producers. As Ross (2010) pointed out, "experience and knowledge of the audience are central to production" in the early 21st century, and new media technologies enable consumers "to mediate ideas to a third party" through digital platforms and "to bring people to the next idea" (p. 922).

How Do Technology Companies Collaborate and Compete With Media Companies?

Traditionally, technology companies collaborated with media companies because media products are after all technological products. For example, Kodak had a long-standing relationship with Hollywood studios. Sometimes the early adoption of new technologies allows smaller media companies to compete with their more established competitors. For example, the use of Technicolor by Disney made it a household name in color films; the use of sound made Warner Bros. a major player in the film industry.

Digital technology, however, brought technology companies into direct competition with media companies. A few cases prove that technology innovation in both hardware and software has expanded the market of technology companies and helped them gain a competitive edge in the global media industries. We review the cases of Apple, Amazon.com, and Google in the following.

Apple's iTunes has changed how music is distributed and consumed. Apple released iPod, a portable music player that needs to be synced up with a computer. Previous portable music players, such as the Sony Walkman and Discman, separated the software and hardware. Apple integrated the software and hardware: to upload music files on the hardware, users have to organize their music through iTunes either by copying files from a CD to the computer or purchasing music from Apple directly. Apple's iPod became obsolete when iPhone could also play music. However, the file managing system iTunes stays on. This case illustrates how Apple has tied together hardware, software, and media. Although users can purchase music on iTunes and play it on non-Apple software, it requires extra work and computer literacy from users.

Amazon.com began as an online book retailer and took businesses away from brick-and-mortar bookstores. Not only did many small, independent bookstores go out of business because of the convenience provided by Amazon.com, but the big US bookstore chain Borders also went out of business, even though it did enter the online book-selling market later. Meanwhile, Amazon.com expanded itself into a general online retail store that sells everything from clothing and dog food to books. It also expanded into the music, television, and film online retail markets. Users can rent or buy digital copies of music products, but it requires them to download a piece of Amazon software. Because of the domination of Apple in online music retailing and Netflix in online streaming and DVD rental, Amazon is not a leader in the online media market. It has tried to attract users to download software by partnering with big names, such as Lady Gaga, in music to sell eagerly anticipated albums at an extremely low cost (one-tenth of the original price). Amazon also produces its own shows, hoping its exclusive offering would attract users to download the software.

Google also expanded into the media industry by tapping on its domination in the search engine business. Strictly speaking, Google does not produce or distribute media goods, because its role may appear to be merely letting users search for what already exists on the Internet. However, the existence of Google as a search engine has facilitated media production and distribution in a new way. Some Google users do not merely receive media content but also actively produce content to be uploaded on YouTube. Google rewards online media celebrities who have a sizable following by giving them the name "YouTuber." Google also fosters a culture in which one's online presence and reputation can be measured by how many "views" one has on YouTube. Similarly, many bloggers measure their online presence by the position of links to their sites. Because users rarely scroll beyond the first page of search results, landing on the first page has become a valuable prize to bloggers. In addition to amateur producers who upload their own content, other users also upload copyrighted materials on YouTube. Although major media companies have asked Google to prohibit the distribution of copyrighted materials, Google prefers to remove copyrighted materials only if someone flags them. At the same time, Google Books is a massive operation that relies on both copyrighted and non-copyrighted books. During the scanning of library books, Google knowingly scanned copyrighted materials and uploaded them online. Instead of asking permission from copyright holders, it chose to go to court to settle with publishers and other copyright holders.

Netflix: From Retailer to Producer and Distributor

Netflix is another technology company that has drastically changed the media industry. Netflix is the dominant company in the on-demand media industry. According to the popular investment site Investopedia (2015): "by providing on-demand content, creating compelling original shows, using user data to better serve customers and letting customers consume content in the way that they prefer, Netflix is forcing cable companies to change the way they do business" (para. 2). Netflix began as a DVD mailing rental company. Later, it set up its own production company, Red Envelope, which distributes its own media goods. Although Netflix may appear to rely on media companies to supply content, its role is more complicated than that. For one thing, the company is highly valued by investors not only because of its almost monopoly status on DVD rental and online streaming, but also because of its aggregated data on consumers' tastes: what users watch, when they watch, and how long they watch.

Netflix's humble beginning as a mailing DVD rental company had formidable competitors in the market. Its competitors were brick-and-mortar retailers, such as the chain Blockbuster, and small, independent shops. Blockbuster once dominated the retail market with thousands of locations, millions of customers, massive marketing budgets, and efficient operations. In the 2000s, Netflix asked Blockbuster to buy the company for US$50 million, but the offer was declined. Netflix has quickly proven that there was a need for convenience: consumers could receive their DVDs through the mail instead of visiting a video store. Consequently, Blockbuster went bankrupt in 2010, even though it had tried to enter the online DVD rental market, while Netflix became a $28 billion dollar company in 2014 (Greg, 2014).

Mail-in DVDs, however, could not satisfy instant gratification and spontaneity, so an online streaming subscription service became the answer (O'Neil, 2011). Netflix had wanted to split into two companies: one in online DVD rental, the other in online streaming. Poor response from customers made it halt the plan. However, Netflix has been gradually and quietly reducing the options of their DVD plan; it is possible that online streaming will become the only service provided by Netflix.

Netflix is not the only online streaming company. Amazon Prime and Hulu Plus (a consortium of 21st Century Fox, Walt Disney, and NBCUniversal) are also in the same business. By the end of 2014, over 40% of all US households with a TV and/or broadband Internet subscribed to a video on-demand service (Nielsen, 2015). However, Netflix is believed to have the most extensive library, because it partners with both major and minor media companies, unlike Hulu Plus that limits itself to the libraries of a few companies only. Netflix is also the most international on-demand service. International audiences can watch television shows originally aired in other countries, thus bypassing the local television stations.

Netflix expanded into the content market and competed with television for original content. Its production arm, Red Envelope Productions, made documentaries about the media industry, and those productions are available on Netflix only. It has also become a distributor of television shows. Working with established television companies, such as Lionsgate, it distributes an award-winning show titled *Orange Is the New Black*. By being a producer and distributor of media content, Netflix has challenged television consumption in two ways: first, the audience needs to subscribe to the service to watch the shows. A few cable channels, such as HBO and AMC, have also been actively producing big budget television shows so that audiences would subscribe to their online streaming service *just* to watch one or two shows. Second, Netflix does not release a new episode once a week like traditional television. It releases the entire season so that viewers can "binge watch" the entire season in one setting.

Technology Companies as a Disruptive Force?

Is technology a disruption to the media industry? On the surface, technology companies such as Apple, Amazon.com, Google, and Netflix seem to have brought a disruption because they are more proactive in thinking of the relation between hardware, software, and content. Rather than first producing the content then thinking about outlets like traditional media content providers do, technology companies expanded the ways in which media products can be consumed: on a television set, a computer, a handheld device, or a game console. Very often media companies reacted to newcomers by finding legal loopholes in how they operate. For example, when Sony first released its VCR, media companies were busy suing Sony for copyright violations. They were not interested in exploring how the VCR could help with their businesses. Seeing the success of the newcomers, big media companies try to imitate what the challengers do; a case in point is online streaming. After finding these technology companies cannot be beaten, media companies look for partnerships among the newcomers. Therefore, technology companies are not always competing with media companies; there may be more collaboration between media and technology companies.

We also need to be aware that these technology companies compete and collaborate with each other because they do not dominate the same markets: Apple is the strongest in hardware, software, music, and apps retail; Google is the strongest in selling online advertisements in exchange for search results and other "free" services; Amazon.com is an online retailer; and Netflix is in online streaming. Very often, they feed on each other's strengths. For example, watching media content online or ordering goods online require hardware (Apple's products) and software (Apple, Google's Chrome, and Android). None of them could become major companies without each other.

The modern history of media technologies may reveal that new technologies often disrupted the industry: from network television displacing movie theaters, to cable television competing with network television, to the Internet endangering the health of print media.

At every turn, consumers were promised more choices, more convenience, and perhaps a lower cost. However, if we look at the broader political economic picture, we will notice media technologies are no longer invented and fine-tuned by amateur inventors or a few scientists in a laboratory. Media technologies are invented by huge, very often transnational corporations who not only invest in research and development, but also in intellectual property and marketing. As a result, technology and media companies are not only more combined than before, but they also occupy a more concentrated market than before.

Technology: Change Agent, Power Consolidator, or a Curse?

History shows that technology has challenged the domination of major media companies (such as Warner Bros. becoming a major studio after making films with sound) and could be a force of creative destruction (such as the case of Netflix challenging Hollywood distributors, as previously discussed). The same kind of creative destructive force can also be found in tech companies, such as Apple challenging the domination of IBM and Microsoft; Google's search engine making Yahoo obsolete; and Facebook replacing the former social media giant Myspace. The list goes on. However, some tech companies that began as challengers of established companies soon follow market behaviors exhibited by large media corporations (such as consolidation, lobbying governmental bodies, and global expansion) and ultimately became dominant global leaders in their fields.

Media convergence is a strategy adopted by old media and new media firms alike. The biggest global media companies have taken advantage of digitization. If not for media convergence, some media corporations may not be as big as they are today: the digital platform has allowed content to be repurposed in different media that used to be separate entities, such as film, television, and newspapers. If not for media convergence, companies such as Google, Facebook, Amazon. com, and Netflix would not exist at all.

According to Schiller (2007), contemporary media convergence has been fueled by increasingly pervasive digital technologies, and SNSs have become a new target for many media corporations. For companies in the old media industries, media convergence provided an opportunity for these industries to integrate with the new media sector. As a result, there is a new trend of acquiring multimedia and multifunctional networks that can be called industrial convergence—the integration of digital hardware, software, and content (Jin, 2013; Noll, 2003).

Technology companies want to create synergy through merging and acquisitions. Social media and/or digital platform corporations have substantially expanded their business areas, and these new media firms have become the largest segment in the global media and ICT industries. For example, Google purchased YouTube in 2006 for $1.65 billion (Google, 2006). As Google announced, the acquisition combined one of the fastest growing online video entertainment communities with Google's expertise in organizing information and creating new models for advertising on the Internet. Google and YouTube are consistently two of the most-visited sites around the world. They also dominate the traffic of online ads. Another new tech darling, Facebook, purchased WhatsApp, one of the largest mobile instant messaging apps, for $22 billion. Facebook announced that "the acquisition supports Facebook and WhatsApp's shared mission to bring more connectivity and utility to the world by delivering core internet services efficiently and affordably" (Zolfagharifard, 2014, para. 5). However, acquisition does not always work. For example, News Corporation purchased Myspace for $580 million because of its desire to be engaged in the Internet business. But Myspace had become obsolete as a social network. In 2011, News Corporation sold Myspace to the advertising network Specific Media for around $35 million (Steller, 2011).

However, expansion sometimes did not add value to the corporations. In cases such as AOL-Time Warner, News Corporation, and CBS-Viacom, media convergence had become media juggernauts. They had to de-converge their media corporations, because the much-expected synergy did not work. In the case of News Corporation, it was split into two companies: one newspapers (*The Wall Street Journal*, *New York Post*, and *The Times* of London) and the other a fast-growing entertainment unit. News Corporation did not enjoy the expected result of synergy. It believed that a separation of the businesses into distinct public corporations would enhance overall shareholder value. Not only does each individual business have its own identity and strategies, but each could also focus on and pursue distinct strategic priorities and industry-specific opportunities. In this way, de-convergence would maximize each entity's long-term potential (News Corporation, 2012). The case of News Corporation implies that digital technologies sometimes play a major role in driving growth, but at other times do not meet shareholders' expectations. While new media technologies have certainly made the business of media more fluid, in many cases acquiring tech companies alone has not boosted revenues and profits, resulting in the break-up of a conglomerate into different business units. The implication of the case of News Corporation is that technology has acted as a double-edged sword for the business of media: on the one hand, technology has contributed to the growth of media because existing media corporations acquired more companies to become a mega giant. On the other hand, technology could be a threat to existing media corporations when they adopt it without the correct strategy.

Not all hi-tech corporations that invested in digital media have become global leaders. For example, Motorola of the US and Samsung of South Korea could have become global leaders, but they did not take full advantage of digitization, failing to constantly innovate and make correct business decisions. One of the most interesting examples of a failing hi-tech corporation is Motorola, which until the early 21st century was one of the largest global mobile corporations. But its global leader status quickly slipped away, because it did not foresee the coming of the smartphone era. If Motorola had been more determined to become the innovator of the smartphone, Apple may not have its current dominant position in the smartphone market.

The first smartphone, known as IBM Simon, was designed by IBM in 1993, marketed by BellSouth, and built by Japanese Mitsubishi Consumer Electronics of America (Johnson & Fitzgerald, 1994). Motorola, a supplier of the cellular smarts for the prototype, could have built the product instead of Mitsubishi, but it passed on the opportunity to build the product because it was concerned that it would make IBM become its future competitor (Jin, 2017; Sager, 2012). Two other mobile device companies that failed to catch up with the smartphone technology are Nokia of Finland and BlackBerry of Canada.

Andy Rubin, who created Android, went to Asia to sell the idea to handset manufacturers. Even though he was offering something for free, it was a tough sell, because the mobile phone business was so profitable that executives hated to consider new schemes that could be disruptive to existing technologies (Levy, 2011). Rubin vividly recalled the trip he took to meet Samsung executives. During the presentation to about 20 executives, the division head rocked with laughter and said, "you have eight people in your company, but I have two thousand people working on something that's not as ambitious" (Levy, 2011, p. 214). In Samsung's official account, Lee Ki-tae (the former director of the mobile division of Samsung) said the meeting with Rubin was not about Android (Park & Moon, 2012). Regardless of the hearsay, Samsung did not recognize the significance of Android and missed its opportunity to use it on their cell phones.

Both cases imply that technology experts and business executives do not always understand the potential of emerging technologies. If Motorola and Samsung had seized the opportunities presented to them, they could have become global leaders in the smartphone and mobile operating system markets, arguably the two most significant technologies in the early 21st century.

How Can Information Be Commodified?

The rise of digital economy has engaged political economists to pay attention to information, in particular how information is "commodified" in the economy. Business executives and policy makers argue that an information economy is different from an industrial-based economy in the way that what is valued is not physical goods, such as raw resources or manufactured goods, but information—something that cannot be seen or touched. As such, information—in particular consumer information—has "sale-able" values. Some of the largest technology companies, such as Netflix and Google, do not sell physical products, but information. The value of these companies does not come from the physical assets that it owns or the value that their physical goods produce, but the value of information. Value come from two types of information: intellectual property (such as their logos and patents) and information that they license (such as the rights to use their algorithms).

Social media (Facebook, YouTube) are also companies in the information market. They aggressively garner aggregated information from users and sell it to advertisers. Value is created when users share information and produce digital content (Cohen, 2008; Ritzer & Jurgenson, 2010). By spending their time and energy with a click on the keyboard and mouse, Facebook and YouTube users build friendships, acquire information, and entertain themselves. However, as will be explained more in Chapter 9, "Labor," social media users are exploited by social media corporations, because the time spent creating content is not rewarded.

Traditionally, the audience measurement firm Nielsen pays viewers to inform them on how the audience consumes media. As Smythe already argued (1977), "several media research corporations and media corporations themselves as well as AC Nielsen quantified audience participation in order to assure that advertisers get what they pay for when they buy audiences" (pp. 4–5). But social media companies have a more direct way to collect information and they collect them in a "real-time" online environment. Not only do they not pay the viewers, but they also have objective information of users' online activities. As Fuchs (2010) argues, the dominant capital accumulation model of contemporary corporate digital platforms is based on the exploitation of users' unpaid labor, who engage in the creation of content of blogs, SNSs, and content sharing sites. As for the nature of the exchange value, Lee (2011) argues, "the audience in a capitalist media system is best represented as a commodity of exchange value" (p. 445). In the case of Facebook, the company makes money by exploiting the endless time and energy of young users (Jin, 2015b). Once the information is collected through social media and digital platforms, analysts use algorithms to segment acquired information into several sub-categories to target advertising agencies and corporations.

While social media may appear to be free to users, they do not give users the freedom to opt out from being monitored and shown ads. Advertising is the main source of revenue for Facebook. Its revenue has been soaring because the more users it has, the more advertising money it collects. As of June 30, 2016, there were 1.71 billion monthly active users around the world (Facebook, 2016). However, several social media, including Facebook, also risk losing users because of growing concerns over ownership and privacy (van Dijck & Poell, 2013).

Case Study: Are Smartphones Connecting Africa?

The case study presents how smartphones have changed the business of telecommunications in Africa. New technologies are usually associated with developed economies, such as those in North America, Europe, and East Asia. The developing world is seen as the laggard in adopting new technologies. The case in Africa shows something very different: the growth of smartphone use and ownership in Africa is much faster than that in the developed world. Policy makers and global business leaders believe that new media technologies play a paramount role in transforming the economy in Africa and in connecting the continent to the rest of the world.

Cell phone adoption in Africa is said to be a case of leapfrogging. Technological leapfrogging describes how users skip one stage of technological development. Instead of moving from A to B to C, they "leapfrog" from A to C. For example, users who type with a manual typewriter skip the stage of an electronic typewriter to word processing on a computer. In the context of connectivity in Africa, Africans who do not have landline phones are quickly adopting cell phone and Internet technology. Because of the vast geographical area of the continent and the lack of evenly distributed massive city centers, laying phone lines had been an economic and engineering challenge. Cell phones and Wi-Fi connection that rely on towers to transmit signals are then very promising for consumers. As shown in Figure 6.1, landline subscriptions in Africa remained flat from 2006 to 2016, but cell phone subscriptions steadily increased in the same decade. Not only do Africans use the phones for connection, but they also pioneer money transfer and payment on their phones because the density of banks is low. In addition, "Wi-Fi hotspots" in Africa differ from those in developed countries. By drawing on the theories and key questions introduced in this chapter, we guide students to consider if the cell

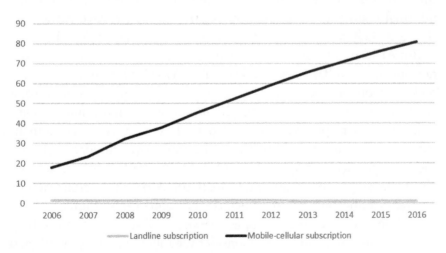

Figure 6.1 *Telephone leapfrogging: Africa (2006–2016)*
Source: ITU

phone was a change agent or a power consolidator in the context of telecommunications industries in developing countries.

Cell Phone as a Change Agent

Africa has some of the lowest levels of telecommunications infrastructure investment in the entire world. There are fewer than two landlines per 100 people. There was even a regression in the growth of landlines: from 1.5 per 100 people in 2005 to 1.1 in 2015 (International Telecommunication Union, 2016). Yet, access to and the use of mobile telephony has substantially increased over the past decade. The number of mobile cellphone subscriptions has soared from 12.4 per 100 inhabitants in 2005 to 76.2 in 2015 (International Telecommunication Union, 2016). As expected, Africa's mobile telecommunications system has brought new possibilities to people and trade in the continent.

Empirical evidence shows that mobile phones have the potential to benefit consumers and producers, as well as to facilitate broader economic development. The challenge is to ensure complementary access to public goods and the development of appropriate policies to evaluate and propagate the benefits of mobile phones throughout the continent (Aker & Mbiti, 2010). A case study of Kenyan mobile banking shows that the ease of physically depositing and withdrawing money has reduced women's poverty and increased children's education. The reason is that mobile banking allows poor women to make informal loans and share investments. When women have extra cash, they are likely to send their children to school (Konner, 2017).

But Africans also use Wi-Fi hotspots differently from people in the developed world. They usually do not have Wi-Fi at home; instead, they seek hotspots in cafes, hotels, airports, and even minibuses because of cheaper and faster access. Song (2014) suggested that point-to-point links are underreported in official data. Low-cost Wi-Fi equipment extends connectivity in hundreds of megabits over hundreds of kilometers. Even with that, some countries embrace this low-tech, low-cost technology more than others do: South Africa is the front-runner, whereas Zimbabwe requires a license for point-to-point links.

Mobile phones connect people, markets, and services because they provide constant information. Consider the following cases, mentioned in Aker and Mbiti (2010): residents in a small place in Mali can call their relatives living in the country's capital as easily as their relatives in France. Farmers in rural areas can send a text message to learn about produce prices in the closest market place, which takes hours to visit. Day laborers can ask about the demand in a town that costs $40 in transportation to get to. Smartphones also remind those affected by HIV and AIDS to take medicines on schedule and to report violent incidents to the international press (also see Chapter 7, "Civil Societies," on the use of new technologies in protests).

Power Consolidator: Liberalization and Privatization

Privatization and liberalization are two trends to characterize the mobile telecommunications industry in Africa. Collaboration between African firms is often global as well, even though the largest telecommunications companies in North America do not play a role in the dual processes. According to Sutherland (2015), the South Africa–based MTN Group is a multinational enterprise that operates mobile telecommunications networks in Asia and Africa. The growth of its business in Asia, Africa, and the Middle East arose from the liberalization of different national markets and the financialization of the sector. The Syrian and Nigerian governments offer licenses to MTN: "to which it pays taxes, provides wire-tapping, collects metadata and censors content" (Sutherland, 2015, p. 471).

By the late 1990s, the major operator groups in Africa were owned by companies based in Europe (such as Celtel of the Netherlands, Millicom of Sweden, Portugal Telecom, Vodafone of the UK), the Middle East (such as Investcom of Lebanon), and Africa (such as Econet of Zimbabwe and Orascom Telecom of Egypt). MTN did a few things to secure its later dominant position in Africa. One of the first business moves of MTN was to enter the Swaziland market—a land-locked microstate—with which the South African government had strong economic and political connections (Sutherland, 2015). MTN beat its South African rival Vodacom to be the sole mobile licensee in Swaziland and formed a joint venture with SPTC. Then MTN entered the markets of Cameroon and Nigeria as well:

> MTN subsidiaries had no need to raise local funds, since the group had access to the large and efficient capital markets in Johannesburg and, once operational, cellular networks quickly generated cash, in addition to having ready finance from equipment vendors.
>
> (Sutherland, 2015, p. 479)

149

From the above example of MTN, African mobile industries thus show a similar trend in other parts of the world: while mobile technologies provide new opportunities for both corporations and people, the nature of business consolidation and conglomeration has not been too different either. The only significant difference between mobile phone companies in Africa and in developed economies is that they have to balance the economic growth of the telecommunications sector with benefits to the general population.

Conclusion

Digital technology provides a backdrop to the book because it has transformed how the industry produces and distributes content as well as how consumers receive content. In this chapter, we specifically discuss the relations between hi-tech companies and media companies. Technology has blurred the boundary between companies that sell technology and those that sell media. Household names such as Apple, Amazon.com, Google, and Netflix may be technology companies, but they also produce and distribute media content. As a result, these companies are sometimes seen as a disruptive force in the industry: not only do they challenge established businesses, but they also take over older, "traditional" media companies. However, the picture of technology taking over media companies is too simplistic; there were also failing cases of media acquiring technology companies and technology companies becoming obsolete. We briefly discuss how technology companies make money by commodifying users' data. The discussion of the commodification of information will continue in Chapter 9, "Labor." We conclude the chapter by discussing how the cell phone is used in Africa: it helps connect one of the least connected continents, but cell phone companies are also quickly consolidated to become conglomerates.

References

Aker, J. C., & Mbiti, I. M. (2010). Mobile phones and economic development in Africa. *Journal of Economic Perspective, 24*(3), 207–232.

Albarran, A. B. (2002). *Media economics: Understanding markets, industries, and concepts* (2nd ed.). Ames, Iowa: Iowa State Press.

Benkler, Y. (2006). *The wealth of networks*. New Haven, CT: Yale University Press.

Boyd, D. (2007). Why youth (heart) social network sites: The role of networked publics in teenage social life. In D. Buckingham (Ed.), *Youth, identity, and digital media* (pp. 119–142). Cambridge, MA: MIT Press.

Cohen, N. S. (2008). The valorization of surveillance: Towards a political economy of Facebook. *Democratic Communiqué, 22*(1), 5–22.

Computer Industry Almanac. (2002, December 16). *USA tops 160M Internet users* [press release].

Davies, M. (2006). Production studies. *Critical Studies in Television: The International Journal of Television Studies, 1*(1), 21–30.

Ellison, N. B., Steinfield, C., & Lampe, C. (2007). The benefits of Facebook "friends:" Social capital and college students' use of online social network sites. *Journal of Computer-mediated Communication, 12*(4), 1143–1168.

Facebook. (2016). *Facebook newsroom*. Retrieved from http://newsroom.fb.com/company-info/

Facebook. (2017, February 1). *Facebook reports fourth quarter and full year 2016 results* [news release]. Retrieved from https://newsroom.fb.com/news/2017/02/facebook-reports-fourth-quarter-and-full-year-2016-results/

Frieden, R. (2001). *Managing Internet driven change in international telecommunications*. Boston: Artech House.

Fuchs, C. (2010). Labor in informational capitalism and on the Internet. *The Information Society, 26*(3), 179–196.

Garnham, N. (2000). *Emancipation, the media, and modernity*. Oxford: Oxford University Press.

Google. (2006, October 9). *Google to acquire YouTube for $1.65 billion in stock* [press release.] Retrieved from http://googlepress.blogspot.com/2006/10/google-to-acquire-youtube-for-165_09.html

Greg, S. (2014, September 5). A look back at why Blockbuster really failed and why it didn't have to. *Forbes*. Retrieved from www.forbes.com/sites/gregsatell/2014/09/05/a-look-back-at-why-blockbuster-really-failed-and-why-it-didnt-have-to/#5d72551b261a

Hargittai, E. (2007). Whose space? Differences among users and non-users of social network sites. *Journal of Computer-Mediated Communication, 13*(1), 276–297.

International Telecommunication Union. (2000). *1999 Annual report*. Geneva: ITU.

International Telecommunication Union. (2016). *Key ICT indicators for developed and developing countries and the world (totals and penetration rates)*. Geneva: ITU.

Internet World Stats. (2016). *World Internet users and 2016 population stats*. Retrieved from www.internetworldstats.com/stats.htm

Investopedia. (2015, November 3). *How Netflix is changing the TV industry*. Retrieved from www.investopedia.com/articles/investing/060815/how-netflix-changing-tv-industry.asp

Jin, D. Y. (2013). *De-convergence of global media industries*. New York: Routledge.

Jin, D. Y. (2015a). Critical analysis of user commodities as free labor in social networking sites: A case study of Cyworld. *Continuum, 29*(6), 938–950.

Jin, D. Y. (2015b). *Digital platforms, imperialism and political culture*. London: Routledge.

Jin, D. Y. (2017). *Smartland Korea: Mobile communication, culture, and society*. Ann Arbor, MI: The University of Michigan Press.

Johnson, B., & Fitzgerald, K. (1994, February 7–8). BellSouth puts smarts in Simon cellular phone. *Advertising Age*. Retrieved from http://adage.com/article/news/bellsouth-puts-smarts-simon-cellular-phone/88511/

Johnson, L., & Lamb, A. (1990). Applying computer graphics technology in media production. *Tech Trends, 35*(2), 8–12.

Konner, M. (2017, January 14–15). Mobile banking gives a big boost to Kenya's poor. *Wall Street Journal*, p. C2.

Lee, M. (2011). Google ads and the blindspot debate. *Media, Culture, and Society, 33*(3), 433–448.

Levy, S. (2011). *In the plex: How Google thinks, works, and shapes our lives*. New York: Simon & Schuster.

Livingstone, S. (2008). Taking risky opportunities in youthful content creation: Teenagers' use of social networking sites for intimacy, privacy and self-expression. *New Media and Society, 10*(3), 393–411.

Mansell, R. (2004). Political economy, power and new media. *New Media & Society, 6*(1), 96–105.

Mansell, R., Samarajiva, R., & Mahan, A. (Eds.). (2002). *Networking knowledge for information societies: Institutions and intervention*. Delft, the Netherlands: Delft University Press.

Mason, P. (2015, July 17). The end of capitalism has begun. *The Guardian*. Retrieved from www.theguardian.com/books/2015/jul/17/postcapitalism-end-of-capitalism-begun

Mayer, V., Banks, M. J., & Caldwell, J. (2009). *Production studies: Cultural studies of media industries*. New York: Routledge.

McChesney, R., Wood, E. M., & Foster, J. B. (1998), *Capitalism and the information age: The political economy of the global communication revolution*. New York: Monthly Review Press.

Nielsen. (2015). *The total audience report Q4 2014*. New York: Nielsen.

News Corporation. (2012, June 28). *Separation would create two category-leading public companies* [press release]. Retrieved from http://newscorp.com/2012/06/28/news-corporation-announces-intent-to-pursue-separation-of-businesses-to-enhance-strategic-alignment-and-increase-operational-flexibility/

Noll, M. (2003). The myth of convergence. *The International Journal of Media Management, 5*(1), 12–13.

O'Neil, M. (2011, November 3). How Netflix bankrupted and destroyed Blockbuster. *Business Insider*. Retrieved from www.businessinsider.com/how-netflix-bankrupted-and-destroyed-blockbuster-infographic-2011-3

Park, Y. H., & Moon, Y. K. (2012, February 9). An icon of unlimited imagination, Lee Ki-tae. *Herald Economy*.

Ritzer, G., & Jurgenson, N. (2010). Production, consumption, prosumption: The nature of capitalism in the age of the digital "prosumer". *Journal of Consumer Culture, 10*(1), 13–36.

Ross, P. (2010). Is there an expertise of production? The case of new media producers. *New Media & Society, 13*(6), 912–928.

Sager, I. (2012, June 29). Before iPhone and Android came Simon, the first smartphone. *Bloomberg Businessweek*. Retrieved from www.bloomberg.com/news/articles/2012-06-29/before-iphone-and-android-came-simon-the-first-smartphone

Schiller, D. (2007). *How to understand information*. Urbana, IL: The University of Illinois Press.

Smythe, D. (1977). Communications: Blindspot of Western Marxism. *Canadian Journal of Political and Social Theory, 1*(3), 1–28.

Song, S. (2014, March 31). A look at spectrum in four African countries. *Many Possibilities* Retrieved from https://manypossibilities.net/2014/03/a-look-at-spectrum-in-four-african-countries/

Steller, B. (2011, June 29). News Corporation sells Myspace for $35 million. *The New York Times*. Retrieved from http://mediadecoder.blogs.nytimes.com/2011/06/29/news-corp-sells-myspace-to-specific-media-for-35-million/?_r=0

Sutherland, E. (2015). MTN: A South African mobile telecommunications group in Africa and Asia. *Communication, 41*(4), 471–505.

Terranova, T. (2004). *Network culture: politics for the information age*. New York: Pluto Press.

Van Dijck, J., & Poell, T. (2013). Understanding social media logic. *Media and Communication, 1*(1), 2–24. Retrieved from www.cogitatiopress.com/mediaandcommunication/article/view/70

Zolfagharifard, E. (2014, October 6). Facebook completes its $22 billion acquisition of WhatsApp after European regulators give the green light. *Dailymail*. Retrieved from www.dailymail.co.uk/sciencetech/article-2782370/Facebook-completes-19-billion-acquisition-WhatsApp-European-regulators-green-light.html#ixzz4KFbNotzf

Civil Societies

At the end of the chapter, students will be able to:

- define and differentiate the concepts "civil society," "public," and "community";
- define what public media and community media are. Name some criticisms of both kinds of media;
- suggest how the three approaches (media economics, political economy of communication, and production studies) conceptualize the media for civil societies;
- name different funding models for civil society media. Give an example for each of the funding models;
- name some criticisms of the funding models;
- define the concepts "independent media," "anarchist media," and "hacker media";
- summarize what a crowdfunding site does;
- analyze a crowdfunding site and/or a crowdfunded project from the three perspectives.

In 2010, protestors from Tunisia to Egypt took to the street and surprised the world with their demand for democracy. The global media were not familiar with citizen activism in the region, so they called the wave of protests the Arab Spring (Keating, 2011). Some explained the quick spread of social movements from one country to another with the citizens' adaptation of social media: protestors used Facebook and Twitter to inform each other where to gather. The ease of uploading images and texts, the cheap cost of mobile devices, and the possibility of bypassing the states make social media the perfect platform for a revolution. Images uploaded on social media not only inspired Arab citizens around the globe to demand democracy, but they also informed Western media of the rising power of political activism on social media. However, it was revealed later that the protest leaders had spent years planning for the events. In fact, quasi-governmental organizations in the US trained activist leaders to campaign, organize through new media, and monitor elections (Nixon, 2011). These background stories made one ask whether the Arab Spring was as homegrown and spontaneous as it seemed. There is no denying that social media was chosen to be a technology of change. Quite suitably, the Arab Spring is called a social media revolution.

Social media was not the first technology that citizens adopted to show their discontent with the government. Since the 1980s, dissidents in El Salvador's civil war have been using the radio as an alternative media to organize social movements. Radio is an effective means for short-distance communication, particularly among populations that have no reliable electricity. For example, Radio Vancermos ("We Will Overcome") became an international hub to inform listeners about the country's civil war (Fry, 2009).

We have learned in the previous three chapters how the lenses of economies, politics, and technologies could inform the media business. On the surface, social movements such as the Arab Spring seem to have nothing to do with the business of media, because they are bottom-up, grassroots politics that capitalize on new technologies. Nevertheless, in this chapter we want to problematize the relations between civil societies and the business of global media by pointing out that the social media platforms that activists use are huge corporations whose main source of revenue comes from advertising. Will social movements indirectly benefit from commercial platforms? Can social media platforms be sites of struggle for activists? To answer these questions, we will address a few broad questions in this chapter.

- What are meant by civil society, public, and community? How are the concepts similar to or different from each other? What are meant by public media and community media?
- Are civil society media noncommercial? In other words, is making money the primary goal of these media organizations? If not, then what are the goals? Does noncommercial media mean they do not have a business model? What kinds of funding do noncommercial media rely on? What do the varieties of business models of civil society media tell us about the business of media?
- Can civil society and public media be called as such if they run on commercial platforms, such as social media platforms? Are there online platforms that counter the hegemony of commercial online platforms? If yes, then what is the economic model of these platforms?
- What power does the public have in materializing the launching of new media outlets? Is crowdfunding a means to launch such outlets from the public for the public?

Definitions of the Civil Society, Public, and Community

In Chapter 4 and Chapter 5, we learned how the economies and politics lenses provide a perspective on studying the business of media. Businesses and governments are two influential actors in the media industry, but civil societies are also another influential actor in the industry. According to the United Nations, "civil society is the 'third sector' of society, along with government and business. It comprises civil society organizations and non-governmental organizations" (United Nations, 2017). The UN realized at the beginning of 2000 that global issues such as the environment, gender, labor, and so on are not the sole responsibilities of the states or businesses; civil society also plays a paramount role in shaping global issues. Civil society comprises different types of organizations—global and local, big and small, well established and contingent.

Nongovernmental organizations (NGOs), mentioned in the above UN quote, may be seen as a subset of civil society. NGOs are registered organizations that provide services for specific populations and lobby for policy changes. The primary goal of NGOs is not to make a profit. For example, the Red Cross primarily provides emergency

157

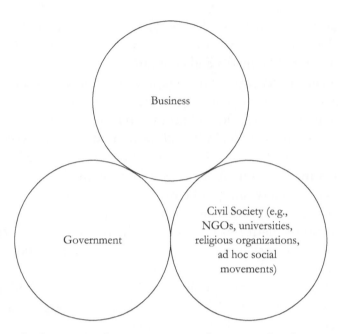

Figure 7.1 *The three sectors of society: government, business, and civil society*

disaster relief and maintains blood banks. Greenpeace lobbies for environmental policy changes and sometimes stages high-profile actions, such as occupying oil drilling sites. In addition to these two global NGOs, there are also many regional and local NGOs.

Although some media organizations are registered NGOs, we usually categorize them as civil society organizations. In contrast to NGOs, the definition of civil society organizations is relatively vague; it includes highly organized nonprofit institutions, such as universities and religious groups, as well as loosely structured ad hoc social movement groups. The UN recognizes a wide range of media organizations as civil society partners, from national public media, such as the Australian Broadcasting Corporation, to regional services, such as the African Woman and Child Feature Service based in Nairobi, Kenya. It also recognizes professional media groups, such as journalists' associations.

Although the UN calls civil society the third pillar of a global society, civil society does not represent everyone's interest. We may have used the services provided by civil society groups, but we may not fully understand their missions and we may not actively partake in their activities. For example, many people benefit from the work of Greenpeace, fewer donate money, and even fewer join their protests.

The concept "public" is then a more encompassing term to refer to a group of people with shared interests. Because this concept emerged with that of the nation-state, the public—in the broadest sense—refers to all citizens in a nation-state, such as the American public. However, this concept is not commonly used for citizens of authoritarian states; therefore, we rarely call the North Korean citizens a public. John Dewey (1927) views the public as situational, because a public arises when a group of people come together and collaboratively solve a problem. For example, the Occupy movements that took place around the globe in the late 2000s showed that the public had a common concern of the domination of financial institutions over other facets of daily life. The case of Occupy Wall Street shows that a public sphere is imperative for the public to meet, discuss social problems, and facilitate dialogue. German sociologist Jürgen Habermas (1989/1962) suggests that private citizens could discuss current affairs to affect political changes in places such as coffeehouses in the 18th century. Many critics who have written about urbanization have pointed out that there is less and less of a public sphere in cities around the globe: not only do real estate developers ask the states to privatize lands, but advertisers and marketers also invade public spaces. An example is displaying company logos as a form of sponsorship in city parks and schools. However, during the Occupy movements, many city streets in financial districts became a public sphere for civic dialogue. The gathering public raises questions, such as who owns the streets in the city: the public or private corporations? The public is also constituted by social media. For example, during the pro-democracy Umbrella Revolution in Hong Kong in 2014, protestors relied on social media to learn where to gather (Lee, So, and Leung, 2015). Even though they gathered in a public space, they connected with each other through the social media as well. Protestors in one place were able to see what others did in other sites. In a way, the public sphere extends to social media platforms as well.

The concept of the public is not without its shortcomings: although this concept is meant to be inclusive, certain populations—namely, educated, middle-class men of the dominant race or ethnicity—have more access to public spaces and are more prepared to engage in a discussion. Uneducated ethnic minorities may feel disfranchised in such a public. Undocumented immigrants may even avoid being in such a public so as not to make themselves visible.

159

The concept of community aims to be inclusive of all populations who share meanings, values, and common interests and—more likely than not—a physical locale. Communication scholar James Carey (1985) proposes the "ritual view of communication" theory to suggest that society is maintained through shared values. This concept of community is less tied to that of a modern nation-state (see Chapter 5, "Politics," for the definition of "nation-state"). Neighborhoods and villages are some examples of physical locales where community forms. The concept of community can also refer to diasporic populations dispersed around the globe, such as the Jewish community, the Armenian community, and so on. Unlike the concept of the public that may imply a top-down decision-making approach, a community's power structure is supposed to be bottom-up. This approach recognizes that every community member has an agency to make changes because every member is a self-reliant, creative problem solver regardless of gender, race, and education level. For example, the community group La Alianza Hispana created in Boston (USA) aims to help Latin American immigrants to strengthen families and communities (La Alianza, 2016).

Despite the fact that community organizing uses a bottom-up approach, realistically not everyone has an equal voice in a community. In a community where cultural tradition is strong and family ties are close, kinship membership may overshadow community membership.

Media for Civil Society

Civil society, NGOs, public, and community are not as discrete as they sound; in reality, most organizations fit into more than one category and they regularly collaborate with each other. For example, in a humanitarian crisis, the Red Cross relies on civil society organizations (such as medical professionals), the public, and local communities to assist with recovery. Because interactions within a civil society are dynamic and fluid, it is hard to neatly lay out the types of media that civil society organizations use to communicate with the public; at any rate, this goes beyond the scope of the book. Instead, the focus of this chapter is to examine organizations that are in the business of public media and community media.

Public media organizations offer outlets to inform, educate, and entertain a general public. Historically, these organizations began as the sole radio and television broadcasters in a country, but they have broadened their scope into other businesses of the media, such as print, film, and online. Europe is the cradle of public broadcasting, which, beginning in the 20th century, has been playing a vital role in shaping a European identity and instilling a sense of citizenship. The British Broadcasting Corporation (BBC) is perhaps the most well-known public broadcaster in the world: not only does it export news content and television programs around the world, but it also exports its operation model to current and former Commonwealth countries, such as Australia, Canada, Hong Kong, and so on. In contrast to Europe, public media in the US was a latecomer. It began in the late 1960s during the civil rights movement to provide free education and information programs to the general public. Because the European model has a longer history, most public media in the rest of the world is modeled after the European framework than the US one. In Latin America, anti-colonialism movements have brought along national media. For example, Peru's national television station aims to promote national politics so that an average citizen would be informed (Fuentes, Juárez, Mejía, Romero, & Vizárraga, 2016, p. 38).

Public media are not the same as state media: the former enjoy independence in editorial content, whereas the latter do not. However, the state may fund both public and state media. Public media are more common in countries with open democracy such as Europe, some African countries (such as South Africa), and some Asian countries (such as South Korea and Japan). "Public" media in countries without open democracy are generally called state media. The state owns the media and may intervene in editorial content. Some notable examples are Chinese Central Television, Russian TV, and the Cuban media. Some may call state media propaganda, because the media are supposed to publicize state policies and ideologies while dismissing oppositional viewpoints. Taking Cuba as an example, former President Fidel Castro used propaganda to win his victory in revolution (CIA, 1984, p. 1). State propaganda can also be done through direct funding: while the US government does not own any media, the "independent," tax-funded Voice of America broadcast US propaganda to rogue countries during the Cold War period.

Public broadcasters are sometimes criticized for being elitists who only cater to an educated and affluent audience. For example, public media newscasters tend to speak in a perceived "refined" accent, such as the received pronunciation accent of BBC newscasters. In another example, public media television shows and films may be adapted from classics and literature. It may produce less sensational content, such as reality shows and entertainment news. In addition, public broadcasting tends to adopt a top-down content management model, in which producers make decisions on what the public might find informative, educational, and entertaining. The audience members may be able to influence the content through advertisers and lobbyists, but they cannot directly shape the content.

In contrast, community media offer media outlets to a smaller audience, sometimes as small as a town or village. For example, a city named Governador Valadares in Minas Gerais, Brazil, offers community radio stations that broadcast religious programs and music. Another example of community radio is the Cultural Survival–sponsored radio programs in Guatemala. The program aims to publicize indigenous people's issues and rights (Cultural Survival, 2016). When compared to public media, community media emphasizes a bottom-up approach to content management. The audience are also the producers who actively shape what is broadcast and printed. Community media also emphasizes social change through education: community members produce media content through learning the technology, be it radio programming or video editing. Because community media outlets favor content that matters to the community, the content may not be widely circulated outside the community.

The above discussion of public and community media shows that public media is usually a top-down organization where the audiences are not involved in decision-making. The cost to establish a public media organization is still considerably high. In contrast, community media is a bottom-up organization where the audiences are usually involved in decision-making. The cost to establish a community media organization is low. Social media play a paramount role in distributing content of community media.

Other than public and community media, there are also online media outlets that aim to foster a global civil society. A good example is Wikipedia. It relies on a large number of volunteers from around the world to provide content in close to 300 languages. Because of the large number of volunteers, Wikipedia employees do not write, edit, or remove content. Instead, the website relies on volunteers to flag offensive and biased content. The example of Wikipedia as a civil society media begs the question: can all online platforms that provide free content be considered a civil society media? If not, why? Is it because of the business models? If it is, then how are the business models of civil society media different from those of commercial media? The three approaches introduced in the book—media economics, a political economy of communication, and production studies—have different takes on this issue.

How the Three Approaches Conceptualize Civil Societies

Among the three approaches, political economists have written the most about the media for and by civil society. Most political economists are in favor of public and community media and lament the shrinking of public funding for both. They argue for publicly funded media on the principle of their provision of public goods. On the other hand, media economists are more interested in understanding the economy of publicly funded media and in comparing how it differs from privately funded media. Production studies scholars examine how public media producers negotiate their identity in an increasingly privatized industry.

Media Economics

Media economists have paid more attention to public *broadcasting* than other forms of public media (such as print and online publications) because of two reasons: first, broadcasting has an inherent problem of scarcity; second, the barrier of entry to broadcasting (in particular television) is high. Because of both reasons, media economists argue that a market-driven approach to allocate resources may not be the most efficient, thus they acknowledge that the broadcasting market has failures (Doyle, 2002). Let's consider the first reason: before the digital age, there used to be a limited number of broadcasting spectra, so there were only a few television channels. We may have heard from an older generation that before cable television, they could only choose from two or three television channels. If all channels are owned by private companies, they may broadcast content that is deemed popular, such as television dramas and sports. Commercial broadcasters may not be interested in producing content that has less market demand, such as educational programs for children and the elderly, government information, or politics (such as debates in law-making bodies). Based on this argument, the broadcasting spectrum and media content should be treated as public goods, similar to public education and infrastructure. Public goods benefit all: no matter how rich or poor one is, everyone has a right to walk in a city-owned street. In the same vein, no matter how rich or poor one is, everyone has a right to enjoy high-quality educational and informational television.

The second reason that media economists use to explain why a market-driven broadcasting industry is not the most efficient is because of high entry cost. Broadcast media, unlike print and online media, require a high upfront cost (such as studio space and equipment), so private investors may not be interested in launching a television station that provides content with little market demand. In a digital age, some critics question how relevant supply and demand theory is. We will explore the "post-scarcity" argument later in the chapter when we discuss the criticism of public funding.

A Political Economy of Communication

Critical political economists are strong advocates of public and community media for a few reasons: the media cannot be reduced to economic institutions; capitalist media are incapable of providing public goods; and the media can be a site of resistance. As mentioned in Chapter 3, political economists do not see the media as merely an ahistorical, economic institution; they see the media as a historical outcome of contesting political, economic, and cultural circumstances. For example, some newspaper owners may want to sway public opinion of political issues and to promote a particular agenda more than make money.

The second reason why political economists advocate for public media is the belief that the market alone cannot provide public goods. As mentioned in the previous section, because media can be public goods, quality content should be evenly and fairly distributed in a population regardless of one's socioeconomic status. If public goods such as the media are seen as private services, only those who have disposable income would pay for the content.

The third reason why political economists advocate for public media is that they believe the media can be a site of resistance. They believe that if a disfranchised population is mobilized to produce and distribute media content, community members will be empowered to become active citizens. Participation in community media will help community members to be aware of news that matter to their daily lives. They will also be able to solve daily life problems without relying on the state or business. In addition, community media allow for an alternative production and distribution of media goods; thus, they allow users to imagine a way to organize social life beyond a capitalist logic.

Production Studies

Production studies scholars do not treat civil society media as an object of study; instead, they see public media production as a case study of production culture. Production studies scholars want to know how public media producers see their roles in an increasingly privatized media industry. Some see themselves as producer-citizens who create quality programs for the greater good of society (Bennett, 2016). At the same time, they are aware of the audience's tastes, so they need to produce content that sells (Zoellner, 2016).

Business Models of Civil Society Media

It is misleading to call public and community media noncommercial, because they also have to worry about market demands and funding. However, the term noncommercial media may conveniently mean two things: first, the primary goal of noncommercial media organizations is not to make money; second, they do not produce content that aims to please the most audience members. We suggest in this section

Table 7.1 *How the three approaches conceptualize civil societies*

	Media Economics	Political Economy of Communication	Production Studies
What kinds of issues are the most discussed	Economic efficiency of public broadcasting.	Whether public media can provide an alternative space and/or a site of resistance.	As a case study of media production.
Whether public media should exist	Only if it is economically efficient.	As long as it provides public goods.	Ambivalent.

that the term noncommercial media is vague for a few reasons. First, public and community media organizations have to balance their account books as much as privately owned media organizations do. Public and community media organizations may not report to business owners and shareholders, but it does not mean that they do not need to be concerned about the market. For example, religious leaders are stakeholders of media funded by religious organizations. They may not worry too much if their media are not making enough money, but they would worry if they don't reach enough people. Second, because of market pressure, public and community media also have to produce content that caters to their audience's taste and, in some cases, advertisers. Third, public and community media borrow strategies from business organizations to expand the market and audience reach. In the following discussion, we consider a few funding models of public and community media. By no means is the list exhaustive, nor does any organization rely on only one kind of funding.

Funding Models of Civil Society Media

1. **License.** Most European public broadcasters require the audience to have a license to receive television broadcast signals. The BBC was the first public broadcaster that adopted this business model. It justifies the license by arguing that this model would provide the best common goods for all; keep the license cost low because of the large audience size; provide creative and diverse content that serves the largest audience possible; and be able to stay independent and impartial (Heath, 2014). The rationale of a television license, as the BBC suggested, is both economic and cultural. The BBC thinks the most efficient resource allocation can be achieved when media products can reach the largest number of people. Hence, the BBC thinks the provision of high-quality cultural goods is a direct result of economic efficiency. High-quality cultural goods are also economically efficient because they have a good chance to be exported overseas, thus expanding the source of funding.

2. **Government funding.** As previously stated, some state-funded media are mouthpieces of the government, but others are independent of the state's influence. In the former, the government usually appoints the chief editorial staff who ensures the content is not politically sensitive; in the latter, an independent board

oversees the editorial direction. The US public television station network PBS and radio network NPR receive government funding, money from foundations, and donations from private citizens. As a result, all television viewers and radio listeners have the right to receive public broadcast signals without paying. In this case, public broadcasting is treated like public infrastructure, such as roads and education. The government collects taxes from citizens and reallocates the money to public services; granted, the US government only allocates 0.012% of its annual budget to both PBS and NPR (Flock, 2012).

In addition to national governments, development aid agencies (such as the Swedish International Development Cooperation Agency) and international government organizations (such as the United Nations Educational, Scientific and Cultural Organization [UNESCO]) also fund community media in developing countries in the name of international development. After WWII, foreign aid and international organizations allocated money to assist developing countries to "catch up" with the developed world. In the 1960s, the mass media was believed to be a vehicle to modernize developing countries through educating the public. Since the 1990s, international organizations and foreign aid agencies realized that a bottom-up approach is more empowering for the local population. Funding agencies are less worried about the immediate economic return of the grant and more about how local people (especially women, children, minorities, and the disfranchised) learn about information through exposure to the media, as well as acquire a skill through producing media products. The economic gain then is more about increasing human capital in developing countries than making a profit by selling media products.

3. **Funding from private entities.** Foundations, private universities, and religious organizations also fund public and community media. These funds usually sponsor individuals and organizations in the form of salary and production costs. While these funds rarely contribute to fixed costs, such as launching a new broadcasting station or a television studio, they do fund alternative outlets, such as small-scale film festivals and online outlets. Some foundations and universities prefer to give money to established individual artists. For example, the Guggenheim Memorial Foundation offers fellowships to citizens in the Americas to pursue arts projects, including

making films. Harvard University also offers fellowships to artists through the Radcliffe Institute for Advanced Study. However, film-makers still need to find an outlet to show their work; the most viable venues are public television and film festivals. These private grant-giving bodies may not look for immediate economic return, but some tend to fund projects that can reach a wider audience and can secure more funds. In this sense, the grant applicants need to consider the economic implications of the proposed projects.

Religious institutions are another type of private entity that fund public and community media. Unlike grants, religious institutions often produce their own media. For example, the Boston-based *Christian Science Monitor* is owned by the First Church of Christ, Scientist. The newspaper was founded in the early 20th century by a wealthy patron who felt that US newspapers induced fear rather than fostered a sense of care among the readers. The newspaper is overseen by the church, but the clergy does not edit its content. In this sense, the newspaper is independent of religious influence (*Christian Science Monitor*, 2017). However, even though it has financial backing from a church, the publication also has to care about its finances. Like many newspapers, it faced the problem of dwindling newspaper readers, so it had to discontinue its print edition. The Vatican has its own official network to inform Catholics around the world of any upcoming events, current news, and videos. News from the Holy See Press Office are written in English, Spanish, French, and Italian. The Vatican and the Pope have their own Twitter accounts, respectively @news_va_en and @Pontifex.

4. **Advertising.** Not all public and noncommercial media are void of advertisements. In fact, because public media tend to attract a more educated, affluent, and older audience, advertisers for high-value goods, such as luxury cars, household appliances, and international packaged tours, may find public media audiences the ideal consumers. Public media can sell their content to commercial media overseas. The BBC runs commercial television outside the UK and is permitted to run advertisements because—unlike the domestic audience—the international audience does not pay a license fee (BBC, 2017). As a result, non-UK viewers that watch BBC World on cable television will have commercial breaks. In another example, Japanese laws do not permit the public broadcaster NHK (Japan Broadcasting Corporation) to show advertisements,

but the laws permit the NHK to form subsidies that make profits. In contrast to both the BBC and the NHK, the partially US government-funded PBS and NPR welcome advertisements and sponsorship. On its page for sponsors, it states its competitiveness against other channels by listing its audience reach, including children (PBS, 2017).

5. **Others.** Public and community media are also funded through licensing rights, subsidies, merchandise sales, membership, and donation. Licensing rights are broadcasting rights bought by overseas television channels to broadcast domestic public media. For example, a number of BBC television shows are licensed in the US and broadcast on PBS. In another example, news channels of public broadcasters are licensed to foreign cable providers that are subscribed to by the international audience. Another means to raise funds is to establish subsidies that are not directly related to broadcasting. Public media organizations may not aim to make money through broadcasting, but they can launch subsidies, such as book publishing and filmmaking, to make a profit. Public and community media can also capitalize on popular media content by licensing characters and images for merchandising. For example, the popularity of the period drama *Downton Abbey* in the 2010s has spawned a wide range of merchandise, from DVDs to teabags to household items. Community media organizations also may offer membership for local residents to use the studio facilities. For example, members may enjoy benefits such as taking media production classes and renting the studio for birthday parties. In addition, public and community media welcome donations from the public.

The above discussion shows that civil society media rely on a range of funding. Like the commercial media, some civil society organizations rely on selling content and advertising money; others rely on membership fees, donations, and public funding.

Criticism of the Funding Sources of Public and Community Media

Critics such as citizens, lobbyists, and academics scrutinize the funding models of public and community media even though these media do not primarily aim to make a profit. In addition to the pro-market and anti-market criticism, there are also criticisms about how some funding sources exercise political influence through public and community media.

To begin with, we examine the pro-market stance. Pro-market proponents criticize both license-based and state-funded approaches to public broadcasting. They believe that public broadcasters should compete at the same level with private broadcasters, and they should let the market decide their survival. Pro-market proponents think that broadcast spectrum scarcity is not an issue anymore, because the switch from analog to digital broadcasting is supposed to create a "post-scarcity" economy. Digitization allows for more than a few television channels; therefore, no broadcaster should be "protected" from competing in the market. Pro-market proponents further suggest that the audience should be given a choice to choose media content, so it is unfair to taxpayers if their money is used to fund public media.

The anti-market proponents, on the other hand, feel that even though public broadcasters aim to provide high-quality content, the gradual reliance on advertising and marketing would erode a public media sphere. As revealed in the previous section on funding, civil society is not devoid of commercial interests. For example, although PBS is proud of its children's programs promoting school readiness, it sells ad space on its website. Advertising on PBS seems to go against the stated mission of education, because research has shown that young children cannot differentiate advertising from editorial content. Therefore, PBS may do children a disservice by asking them to watch educational television as well as advertisements. In addition, in 2015 a private US cable company and content producer HBO had the first-run right to *Sesame Street* shows. For children whose parents could afford a subscription to this cable channel, they would enjoy timely new content on a cable network. For those who could not afford the subscription, they would need to wait for nine months to watch the shows on public television. Playground conversations may show who come from a more comfortable economic background and who don't.

Critics (see Krugler, 2000) also state that foreign funding of community media may be a strategy for one country to exert political influence on others. This was particularly the case during the Cold War, when the US government actively funded media in developing countries to promote its political agenda so as to recruit allies. The Arab Spring example that opens the chapter illustrates that the CIA trains citizens in nondemocratic countries to use social media for opposition movements. Even though foreign aid agencies nowadays rarely sway international politics through media funding, recipient countries have to agree with donor countries' viewpoints on a number of subjects, from democracy to indigenous culture; this is especially the case with bilateral aid, where recipient countries directly receive money from donor countries. Therefore, community media projects may not empower local populations so much as please the donors.

Lastly, even though Wikipedia may appear to be a public goods site that deserves donation, critics argue that the site has more money than it claims. Wikipedia users regularly find a yellow banner asking for a small donation to keep the page running. The founder states that Wikipedia has few staff members and no direct revenue, so every donation will help prevent it from shutting down. However, it has been revealed that Wikipedia has more cash than it claims. Its money is used to pay staff members whose work is peripheral to the maintenance of the online encyclopedia (Orlowski, 2012).

Alternative Media and Platforms

So far, we have shown in this chapter that there are different economically sustainable business models for civil society media. We have considered a number of public and community media examples to illustrate that they have heterogeneous missions—from providing high-quality content and serving a niche audience to promoting an alternative worldview. However, none of the media organizations we have mentioned has an "anti-capitalist" or "anti-transnational corporations" stance. In other words, they were not launched to critique mainstream media owned by transnational corporations. In some ways, these public and community media organizations coexist with commercial and transnational media organizations, and they do not seek to challenge their domination in the global media landscape. In fact, public media and mainstream media mutually benefit each other. A good example is that many public news channels (such as BBC World, NHK World) are licensed to cable providers owned by transnational media companies (such as SkyTV). Public television shows also may be franchised to commercial television channels. An example is the British mockumentary *The Office*, which became an NBC show in the United States. On the other end, community media may adopt mainstream television and radio formats (such as political talk shows, news reports, radio drama) for a local audience. The fact that the Vatican has a Twitter account and is constrained to the word limit shows that even the Pope is not exempt from character limit. In this section, we look at media organizations that aim to provide an alternative to commercial media and platforms: some produce media content that is explicitly against capitalism and/or transnational media corporations; others seek to provide the public with an alternative media platform to a commercial one.

The Alternative: Independent, Anarchist, and Hacker Media

Fuchs (2011) suggested two things that differentiate alternative media from mainstream media: first, the practices of production and reception; second, the structures of production and distribution. Alternative media emphasize the "do-it-yourself" practice of grassroots media production; the consumers are often the producers. The production structure is characterized with consensus-building and symmetric power distribution. Further, little money is spent on marketing and advertising the products. It should be noted that Fuchs's definition of alternative media is normative rather than descriptive; real-life examples show that some independent, anarchist, and hacker media may only partially fit the characteristics of alternative media.

In a broad sense, independent media refer to organizations that are not owned by media conglomerates. Clearly, public media could be a type of independent media, but there are other types too. There is an assumption that media ownership influences the content produced. However, what is counted as "independent" varies across industries and countries. For example, in the US context, independent media may be organizations not owned by one of the largest media conglomerates (such as Disney, Viacom, Time Warner, Bertelsmann, Comcast Universal, New York Times, News Corporation, Condé Nast), but some of the independent media organizations are large in scale and their business model is similar to the one used by media conglomerates. For example, the US independent film industry may appear to stand apart from Hollywood, but it also follows the studio-distributor-exhibitor business model and is very organized (Wasko, 2003). In fact, some of the "independent" studios are large in scale when compared to studios in other major film industries, such as Bollywood and the Greater Chinese cinema, even though Bollywood produces more films than Hollywood does. For example, the largest independent US film studio, Lionsgate, co-produces an average of ten films and distributes a few more in a year. Moreover, some of the US theaters that show independent films are national chains. For example, Landmark Theatres owns more than 50 theaters and 200 screens across the country. Another example to show how the US independent film industry is an extension of Hollywood is that big studios have their own divisions to produce "arty," independent-like films; some examples are Fox Searchlight (owned by 20th Century Fox) and Paramount Vantage (owned by Paramount).

In comparison to the US independent film industry, the independent magazine industry is less organized. Because readers can subscribe directly to the magazines from publishers/creators, they can bypass the control of distributors and retailers. In addition to magazines that are circulated nationally and regionally, many local creators produce "zines" sold online, in local bookstores, and at conventions. Needless to say, there is a plethora of independent media content online. One only has to go to YouTube channels or Vimeo to find many individuals producing content with their own funds. In a sense, they are all independent media producers, because they do not work for a media conglomerate. However, if media producers use social media as a platform to showcase their work for potential employment, will it make them less independent? If producers emulate content produced by media conglomerates, will it make them less independent? In addition, if the social media platforms they use are profit driven, will it make them less independent? All these questions point to the difficulty of defining "independent" media on a digital platform. Should "independent" media be defined as those that are independently funded? Or those that have content not found in the "mainstream" media? Or those intended to be "independent"?

Anarchist media, in contrast to alternative media, are explicit at stating their political stance of being anti-mainstream, anti-transnational corporations, and in some cases anti-capitalism. Because of their political stance, the owners of anarchist media are conscious of how the media are funded. Not only do they believe independent funding would produce content that is critical of the mainstream media, but they also believe that independent funding is imperative to show how an alternative economic arrangement is feasible—if not more sustainable—than a capitalist one. In this sense, anarchist media are more like social activism and social movements, through which the producers aim to raise awareness among media users about the domination of corporations over social lives. Anarchist media also aim to transform passive consumers into active agents. Agency is constituted by social consciousness and a belief in transformative power.

In the following, we look at three kinds of anarchist media: first, the anarchist publication *Adbusters* and anti-capitalist campaigns; second, the open-access license organization Creative Commons; and third, a community of programmers who write open/free source software. An average media consumer may not have heard of these organizations and movements, but their impact has wider implications: from how factory workers are treated, to how Google is run, to how the White House licenses its images.

Based in Canada, *Adbusters* aims to "[fight] back against the hostile takeover of our psychological, physical and cultural environments by commercial forces." Because it defines itself as "the unwavering voice of dissent in a media landscape" (*Adbusters*, 2017a), it does not carry advertisements at all. Funding comes from subscriptions to its print and online editions, as well as donations. It aims to bring along a radical transformation for a collective future by offering "critical perspectives on the fate of modernity, the spell of reason and mental environmentalism" (*Adbusters*, 2017b). Unlike some anarchist magazines that favor amateurish low-tech production and reproduction, *Adbusters* is a high-end glossy magazine with eye-catching, provocative cover images that appear to mock the superficiality and absurdity of modern advertising images. In addition to magazine content that critiques consumerism, it also works with global affiliates to organize Buy Nothing Day and Buy Nothing Xmas. (See Chapter 8, "Cultures," about the arguments against the commercialization of cultures such as religious holidays.). It also advises activists to organize visible protests against consumption; some suggestions are offering a credit card–cutting service for shoppers inside malls and pushing empty carts with friends in shops. It also offers "spoof ads" for activists to download. The ads are parodies of advertisements, such as Joe Camel of Camel cigarettes and Uncle Ronald McDonald. One of the most memorable parodies is a US flag with corporate logos replacing the white stars. Activists are invited to hang those posters in public spaces as an act of "culture jamming." Ironically, *Adbusters* also has a "culture shop" that sells the Corporate America flag in case activists prefer a cloth one, not a paper copy.

Some anarchists challenge the copyright laws of media content; one example is Creative Commons. It was founded to offer free copyright licenses for creators who wish to share their work without being constrained by existing copyright laws. Intellectual property laws are supposed to protect copyright holders from content violations; however, some content creators have found current laws to be too restrictive. Book printers used to be the ones who held copyrights of published work because they were the ones who prepared the typeset. However, the laws that were written to protect individual interests have come to protect big corporations. Content creators have found that they could not use their own creation in whatever way they like. For example, musicians have to request permission from record companies to reprint lyrics on record sleeves and to perform their own songs, and writers have to request permission from publishers to reprint their works in another venue.

The founders of Creative Commons (Hal Abelson, James Boyle, and Lawrence Lessig) believe digital technology has allowed possibilities for content sharing. In fact, the ease of reproducing and sharing digital copies means both creators and readers can benefit from a "common" of knowledge. In this common, users don't have to pay a hefty price to acquire copyrighted content; creators can directly share their work with users without being constrained by copyright laws. Open access licenses have a few positive impacts. For example, students in developing countries can access high-quality teaching materials without paying a lot of money; creators may build their work upon previous ones without infringing copyright. Documentary filmmakers and music DJs benefit from using shared files in the common.

Although an average media consumer may not know of Creative Commons, they have directly benefited from it. For example, content sharing sites, such as Wikipedia and Flickr, allow users to license their content under Creative Commons. In addition, content on the White House website are licensed with Creative Commons; users are free to share and adapt the content for any purpose, including commercial ones.

The concept of Creative Commons built on others' work as well. It was inspired by the Open/Free Source Software movement. Most of the software preinstalled in personal computers is proprietary. Proprietary-owned software means software has closed-source code. Users cannot view the code of closed source, let alone improve it. Computer users may be frustrated when software crashes and the most they can do is to report the errors to the company. Even if users have the knowledge to fix the bugs, they are not allowed to do so. For this reason, free source software advocate and hacker Richard Stallman believes closed source software stifles creativity and discourages improvement. Like the founders of Creative Commons, he believes sharing code and collaborating authorship are imperative to building a knowledge commons. Stallman has famously said that the free in free software is the same free as in freedom, not the free as in free beer. Free source software is like freedom, it can be equally shared among people without reducing the quality and quantity of freedom. The fact that one enjoys freedom does not prevent the next person from enjoying it. However, copyright owners see software as private property. They see free source software as free beer. Free beer to one means another person needs to pay for it.

An average computer user may find hacker culture a fringe culture, but most computer users have benefited from hacker culture without knowing it. Google—the most popular site in many countries—runs on the free source software Linux. Linux, together with Microsoft Windows and Apple OS, are three dominant operating systems, even though only the most enthusiastic computer users may install Linux for personal use. However, choosing Linux is sometimes a conscious choice for those who want to counter the domination of Microsoft and Apple in the operating system market. Competent coders can voluntarily contribute their code to the ongoing Linux project. Programmers offer their service and expertise to the project for free, much like Wikipedia contributors. Although some programmers contribute to Linux to enhance their credentials for career advancement, economic reasons alone cannot explain their motivations to join the Linux community. Some noneconomic motivations are to establish a sense of community, to improve upon existing code, and to show resistance towards big computing corporations (Ghosh, 2005). (We will review the discussion on free labor in Chapter 9, "Labor.")

Case Study: Crowdfunding—for the People, from the People?

Earlier in the chapter, we raised a few questions of what is meant by independent media in the digital age. We asked, are independent media produced by people who don't work for a media conglomerate?

Or is the content unlike that in the commercial media? Or should the production be independently funded? Or should the producers have an "independent" mind? Fundraising campaigns on crowdfunding sites seem to exhibit all the above features of independent media.

Amateur media producers may have always sought monetary support from family, friends, and fans to realize their dreams. In return, supporters would have a chance to preview the finished work and receive a copy of the product. How have crowdfunding sites changed this informal way of fundraising? On the one hand, crowdfunding appears to be as simple as moving offline fundraising online so as to simplify the process and to attract a wider circle of supporters. On the other hand, crowdfunding sites formalize the procedure of fundraising, making fundraising more like a business proposal. In this procedure, both the fundraisers and donors are subjugated to a specific social relation. So is crowdfunding a platform for the people from the people? Or is it a business enterprise that monetizes creativity and social relations?

In order to determine whether fundraising on crowdfunding sites helps achieve the goals of public and community media, we examine in this section the site Kickstarter by asking a few broad questions: (1) how does this site conceptualize the relations between the fundraisers and donors? (2) How does this site make money? (3) What kinds of projects are likely to be successfully funded? After answering the three broad questions, we guide readers to think about how a crowdfunding site can be understood from the perspectives of media economics, political economy, and production studies.

Kickstarter, along with Indiegogo, Rockethub, and Crowdrise, are some popular donation-based crowdfunding sites. They are different from investment-based crowdfunding sites. Donation-based crowdfunding raises money from supporters who in turn may get a reward (such as a copy of the finished work). Investment-based crowdfunding sites recruit stockholders who give money hoping to make a subsequent profit. Among all donation-based crowdfunding sites, Kickstarter is specifically designed for funding creative work from the arts to music to film. It only funds individuals, not companies or charities.

Social Relations: Fundraisers and Donors

Launched in 2009 in New York City, Kickstarter's mission is "to help bring creative projects to life." Kickstarter calls its fundraisers and donors "a global community" of over 10 million people. Some artists are said to be well known, but most aren't; regardless, fundraisers are fully responsible for their projects. Kickstarter is not involved in developing projects for artists; it lets donors decide which projects are worthwhile to fund. It recognizes that fundraising is a "public" act and that the artists risk ruining their reputation if they do not complete the project (even though Kickstarter cannot refund the contributions of donors). Therefore, artists are advised to list their past experiences and accomplishments to lend credibility to the proposed project. In case a funded project fails to come to fruition, artists should refund backers or offer alternatives.

The artists are responsible for making contact with donors. Kickstarter suggests that artists spread the word about their projects through social media, such as blogs, Facebook, and Twitter. Artists also need to constantly update donors concerning the progress of the project and to make the donors feel that they have pledged for a viable project. In addition to e-mailing acquaintances, artists also may get exposure if someone searches projects on the Kickstarter site. The site states a few reasons why backers would like to support a project: supporting friends and family members (relational); wanting the rewards (material); and liking an idea (ideological). But it stresses that donating to a project is more than just giving money; it is about making the dream of the artists and supporters come true.

The employees of Kickstarter are also artists whose projects were successfully funded on Kickstarter, but they are not supposed to advocate one project over others, even though there are "highlights" on the sites. Kickstarter sees itself as a neutral "broker" that facilitates exchange between the fundraisers and the donors.

How a Crowdfunding Site Makes Money

Kickstarter stated that its success is measured by how many creative projects are successfully funded, not by the size of profits. In 2015, it became a benefit corporation that is obligated to measure how it makes a positive impact on society. Benefit corporations are private entities like corporations, but they also vow to make a positive impact on workers, society, and the environment. They can be incorporated in a number of states in the US. Some of the missions of Kickstarter are:

- connecting people around projects;
- engaging in conversations affecting artists and creators;
- not lobbying or campaigning for public policies;

- donating profits to support arts and education, especially to students in underprivileged urban areas;
- committing to the arts, especially those working in less commercial areas;
- providing opportunities for employees to work with the under-privileged community.

Kickstarter makes money by keeping a percentage of the funds of successful projects. First, artists estimate how much a project will cost and suggest how the raised funds will be used. Usually, they will offer incentives for donors, such as giving out t-shirts or pins. Backers will pledge an amount, but their credit cards will only be charged if the project reaches its initial fundraising goal. If the project fails to reach the goal, donors will not be charged. If a project has reached the fundraising goal before the deadline, artists are welcome to increase the goal. For successful projects, Kickstarter will take 5% of the total funds raised and 3% of the payment processing fee, as well as a few cents of every pledge. For unsuccessful projects, Kickstarter does not charge anything. Therefore, projects that seek considerable money and with a lot of backers benefit Kickstarter more. However, the maximum amount that an artist could initially ask for is US$10,000 as of 2016. To maximize the success rate of the projects, Kickstarter offers a creator handbook that teaches artists how to promote the project and to narrate their story. It also builds a community of fundraisers by organizing an online forum for questions and answers.

What Kinds of Projects Are More Likely to Be Funded?

As of July 2016, about 36% of projects launched on Kickstarter have been successfully funded. Projects in dance and theater were the most likely to be funded (over 60%); those in technology were the least likely to be funded (below 20%). The majority of successfully funded projects raised between US$1,000 and US$10,000 (58%), but a minority have raised over US$1 million (0.16%). The projects that have raised over US$1 million are concentrated in the categories of film and video, games, technology, and design. The failure rate is 64%, with about 14% of projects receiving no pledges. However, most projects that raised more than 20% eventually succeeded. Kickstarter also found that projects with videos and a shorter funding period (one month) are more likely to be successful.

One of the most hyped projects is an American man's project to make potato salad. He asked for ten dollars and easily reached his goal. Donors who pledged ten dollars could watch a video of the man making potato salad, choose an ingredient for the dish, sample the salad, and receive a verbal thank you. Eventually the project received over $55,000 from close to 7,000 backers, with an average of eight dollars per donor and the majority of donors contributing a dollar. This project may provide much humor to how Kickstarter can be exploited, but it also raises a question: is making potato salad a creative project? Is the public act of making salad a community action? How did a man making potato salad positively impact society?

Analysis of a Crowdfunding Service

In order to analyze whether Kickstarter is an appropriate tool for raising funds for civil society media, we have to first decide on a definition of public or community media. As shown in this chapter, media for civil societies encompass a wide range of organizations with different histories, funding models, missions, and ideologies. However, most of them do not prioritize profits above other goals. From the fundraising site, one may select a proposed media project that aims to provide greater goods for the public/community. The Kickstarter site allows users to search for projects by using keywords. For example, the keywords "documentary" and "social justice" show a few films that were produced after successful fundraising. The keywords "refugees" and "writings" show projects that fund the publishing of refugees' writings. After arriving at a working definition of public/community media and choosing a project, we can understand the relation between the crowdfunding site and the proposed project from three different perspectives.

First, from a media economic perspective:

- What is the business model of the project? In addition to fundraising on Kickstarter, is the project funded in other ways? For example, subscription, personal funds, or public and private grants.
- Does this project have a market? That is, if it were to be funded in other ways (such as by subscription), would there be a market for it? If not, why not? Is it because the subject matter is not appealing to most audience members? Is it because the potential audience is too small?

- What is the business model of the crowdfunding site? Does it have a viable market with enough buyers (i.e., artists and donors)?
- Does the business model of this crowdfunding site correct market failures? Is there a sustainable economic model of fundraising?

Second, from a political economic perspective:

- Does the project benefit the public/community? For example, does it talk about issues that commercial media tend to avoid? Does it involve community participation?
- What is the relation between artists and donors? What kinds of incentives does the artist give to donors? Did the donors explain why they gave money to the project?
- What are the artists' motivations for launching the project? Are these motivations economic, cultural, social, or political?
- What is the relationship between the artists and the crowdfunding site? What is the relationship between the donors and the crowdfunding site?
- How does the site make money? What has been commodified for profit making? For example, is the social relation between artists and donors commodified? Are friends and family members obligated to commit to the project, especially when their names may be publicly displayed?

Third, from a production studies perspective:

- What kinds of language do artists use to show they are media practitioners?
- What kinds of previous projects and experiences are mentioned to illustrate membership in a media community?
- Do the artists talk about the importance of being a media producer-citizen?
- How can donors help so that they can claim membership in a media community?
- What kinds of guidelines does the site give to artists for them to have a professional-looking page?
- What kinds of advice do community members give to each other for best practices?

The above list shows that the three approaches ask different questions about crowdfunding sites and projects. A media economic perspective would like to understand the market supply and demand of such sites; a political economic perspective would like to know how social relations are formed between the sites and the artists, the artists and the donors; a production studies perspective would like to know how amateur producers develop a professional identity through fundraising efforts.

Conclusion

Civil society has used low-tech, such as the radio and fax machine, to distribute their messages, but images on social media help catch the attention of the global media. However, the term "civil society" is problematic because it includes all nongovernmental and noncommercial entities, ranging from universities to neighborhood associations to loosely organized, ad hoc citizen groups. Therefore, the business models of civil society media vary greatly: some gladly accept advertising money, some vehemently refuse it; some need to be responsive to the audience, some to the overseeing board. There also exist alternative media that have an anti-capitalist and anti-corporation tenor. These media tend not to rely on advertising money, but on subscriptions and donations. We conclude the chapter by looking at crowdfunding as a case study: we question using the three approaches whether a crowdfunding site is for the public by the public.

References

Adbusters. (2017a). *Donate to Adbusters Media Foundation*. Retrieved from https://subscribe.adbusters.org/pages/donate

Adbusters. (2017b). *Submission guidelines*. Retrieved from www.adbusters.org/submissions/

La Alianza Hispana. (2016). *Mission*. Retrieved from www.laalianza.org/index.php?option=com_content&view=article&id=5:our-mission&catid=29:mission-and-history&Itemid=57

Bennett, J. (2016). Public service as production cultures: A contingent, conjunctural compact. In M. Banks, B. Conor, & V. Mayer (Eds.), *Production studies the sequel: Cultural studies of global media industries* (pp. 123–137). New York: Routledge.

BBC. (2017). *Inside BBC*. Retrieved from www.bbc.co.uk/corporate2/insidethebbc/howwework/policiesandguidelines/advertising.html

Carey, J. (1985). *Communication as culture: Essays on media and society*. Boston: Unwin Hyman.

Christian Science Monitor. (2017). *About the Christian Science Monitor*. Retrieved from www.csmonitor.com/About

Cultural Survival. (2016). *Indigenous rights radio*. Retrieved from http://rights.culturalsurvival.org/

CIA. (1984, November). *Cuba: Castro's propaganda apparatus and foreign policy*. Washington, DC: CIA. Retrieved from www.cia.gov/library/readingroom/docs/DOC_0000972183.pdf

Dewey, J. (1927). *The public and its problems*. New York: Henry Holt & Co.

Doyle, G. (2002). *Understanding media economics*. London: Sage.

Flock, E. (2012, October 4). Five things the government spends more on than PBS. *US News and World Report*. Retrieved from www.usnews.com/news/blogs/washington-whispers/2012/10/04/5-things-the-government-spends-more-on-than-pbs

Fry, W. (2009). El Salvador: Alternative media giving a voice to the voiceless. *Green Left Weekly*. Retrieved from www.greenleft.org.au/content/el-salvador-alternative-media-giving-voice-voiceless

Fuchs, C. (2011). *Foundations of critical media and information studies*. New York: Routledge.

Fuentes, C., Juárez, L., Mejía, M., Romero, K., & Vizárraga, R. (2016, June). *Lineaminetos para el desarrollo de la televisión pública en el Perú*. Lima: ESAN adiciones.

Ghosh, R. (2005). *CODE: Collaborative ownership and digital economy*. Cambridge, MA: MIT Press.

Habermas, J. (1989). *The structural transformation of the public sphere: An inquiry into a category of bourgeois society* (T. Burger trans.). Cambridge, MA: The MIT Press. (Original work published in 1962)

Heath, J. (2014, July 14). Why the licence fee is the best way to fund the BBC. *About the BBC Blog*. Retrieved from www.bbc.co.uk/blogs/aboutthebbc/entries/9637e45d-c96c-36c6-9e3f-af141e81cab4

Keating, J. (2011, November 4). Who first used the term Arab Spring? *Foreign Policy*. Retrieved from http://foreignpolicy.com/2011/11/04/who-first-used-the-term-arab-spring/

Krugler, D. (2000). *The voice of America and the domestic propaganda battles, 1945–1953*. Columbia: University of Missouri Press.

Lee, P. S. N., So, C. Y. K., & Leung, L. (2015). Social media and Umbrella Movement: Insurgent public sphere in formation. *Chinese Journal of Communication*, 8(4), 356–375.

Nixon, R. (2011, April 14). US groups helped nurture Arab uprisings. *New York Times*. Retrieved from www.nytimes.com/2011/04/15/world/15aid.html

Official Vatican Network. (2016). *News*. Retrieved from www.news.va/en

Orlowski, A. (2012, December 20). Wikipedia doesn't need your money—so why does it keep pestering you? *The Register*. Retrieved from www.theregister.co.uk/2012/12/20/cash_rich_wikipedia_chugging/

PBS. (2017). *PBS infographic*. Retrieved from www.pbs.org/about/about-pbs/overview/pbs-infographic/

Streema. (2017). *Governador valadares radio stations*. Retrieved from http://streema.com/radios/Governador_Valadares

United Nations. (2017). *Civil society*. Retrieved from www.un.org/en/sections/resources/civil-society/index.html

Wasko, J. (2003). *How Hollywood works*. London: Sage.

Zoellner, A. (2016). Detachment, pride, critique: Professional identity in independent factual television production in Great Britain and Germany. In M. Banks, B. Conor, & V. Mayer (Eds.), *Production studies the sequel: Cultural studies of global media industries* (pp. 150–163). New York: Routledge.

Cultures

8

At the end of the chapter, students will be able to:

- explain why and how cultures and markets interact with each other in daily lives;
- suggest how the three approaches (media economics, political economy of communication, and production studies) conceptualize cultures in the business of media;
- define the concept "cultural industry" and explain why the cultures of media industry are seen to constitute a viable economic sector;
- define the concept "cultural capital" and explain why it reinforces middle-class interests;
- explain why the concept "the audience" is abstract;
- define the concept "media participant";
- explain why fan culture can be commercialized by the media industry;
- explain what a production culture is and why professionalism is a culture that is acquired, not given;
- name some positive and negative implications of the global expansion of media corporations on local cultures and practices;
- explain how a global product is made relevant to a local audience.

In a digital age in which audiences have multiple screens and channels to choose from, few events attract television audiences around the world to watch in real time. The Olympic Games is one such event. The London Olympics in 2012 attracted 3.64 billion television viewers worldwide ("Olympic Summer Games," n/a); one in two people in the world watched the games on television at some point during the two weeks.

The Olympics has not always been an international event. In fact, when it took place in Ancient Greece in 700 BC, it was a local event. It could only be attended by people who would travel to the competition venues. The Olympics also has not always been televised; the first one broadcast was the Berlin Olympics in 1936. It was not the kind of television broadcasting we know of today. It was broadcast on closed circuit television, where people in Berlin gathered in public halls to view the games. The first games in which broadcast rights were sold were the Melbourne Olympics in 1956. Television stations in the UK, the US, and Europe bought the rights to the games and showed it to domestic audiences.

Since then, the number of television channels on which the games were broadcast skyrocketed, as did the price for the broadcast rights. NBC, the US broadcaster of the Rio Olympics in 2016, paid US$1.23 billion to the International Olympic Committee (IOC) to secure the exclusive right to broadcast the games to the domestic audience (Vranica & Flint, 2016). What did the television channel receive in return? Audience and advertisers. Twenty-six-and-a-half million US viewers (or 8.3% of the population) tuned in to NBC to watch the opening ceremony of the Rio games. Because the games were widely watched, advertisers competed fiercely to secure commercial spots. Even before the games began and the audience tuned in, the broadcaster had already broken even with the IOC by selling advertising spots. A 30-second primetime spot cost US$1 million and an ad package cost US$10 million. In Brazil, the local network prepared for their largest audience ever, even before the games began. There were a total of 2,680 commercial spots, each of them costing 255 million Brazilian reais (approximately US$81 million) (Macedo, 2015).

Broadcast rights are not the only big business in the games; sponsorship is another. IOC also named a number of corporations as the official Worldwide Olympic Partners of the 2016 games; the majority are American (such as Coca-Cola, General Electric), but there are also Japanese (Toyota), Korean (Samsung), and Swiss (Omega). Even though the games took place in Brazil, none of the top sponsors came from the country or even from South America. Moreover, none of the brands is in the sports business. In fact, two of them—Coca-Cola and McDonalds—are known for making high-fat, high-sugar food products that may harm athletic performance. Rede Globo—the Brazilian station that broadcast the games—had six deals with sponsors such as Bradesco (a Brazilian bank), Coca-Cola, P&G, Fiat, Nestle, and Claro (a subdivision of America Móvil owned by Mexican businessman Carlos Slim).

The IOC is not the only party that benefits from sponsorship—athletes can also make money by endorsing brands. Globally known gold medalists can expect to sign million-dollar deals with corporations. For example, Jamaican track and fielder Usain Bolt has deals with beverage company Gatorade, watchmaker Hublot, Virgin Media, and Visa (Badenhausen, 2012). Michael Phelps—the most decorated gold medalist of all time—has deals with sporting companies Speedo and Under Armour, food and beverage company Kellogg and Subway sandwich, hotel chain Hilton, and luxury goods brand Louis Vuitton. It is estimated that almost all of Phelps's $96 million net worth came from brand endorsements (Gerencer, 2016). Brazil's top soccer player, Neymar Jr., has multiple endorsement deals with brands such as Nike, Red Bull, Panasonic, Konami (video game company based in Japan), and Gillette. In 2016, Neymar made US$23 million from endorsements alone (Forbes, 2016). While the commercials with Neymar are usually broadcast in Brazil, he was featured in a Nike commercial made for the Rio Olympics along with American athletes, such as Serena Williams and Kevin Durant (Tsuji, 2016).

Some criticize that the staggering costs of broadcast rights, commercial spots, and sponsor deals have little to do with the original meaning of the games, which were a religious gathering for Greeks to honor Zeus, the king of all gods. The staggering costs also have little to do with the goal of the Olympic Movement that marked the first modern Olympics in 1896, which was "to contribute to building a peaceful and better world by educating youth through sport practiced without discrimination or any kind, in a spirit of friendship, solidarity and fair play" (The International Olympic Committee, n/a). Instead, the modern Olympic Games are a major global media event, where big money changes hands—from television stations to the International Olympic Committee, from advertisers to television stations, from corporations to advertisers, and from consumers/viewers to corporations. Have the games lost their religious and educational meaning, because the highly commercialized event is dominated by major news networks, transnational corporations, and wealthy athletes? Can we trust that athletes compete because of friendship and fair play, not because of fame and money? Can an international sporting event still be an authentic culture despite commercial interests?

The criticism of the modern commercialized Olympics seems to imply that culture and market belong to two separate spheres that can't be merged. Digital technology may have blended the two spheres by expanding the global market, so that the same cultural products can be consumed over national boundaries. At the same time, a digital age may have created a more fragmented audience, because they have more choices of what to watch in their spare time. This begs the question: how has the relation between culture and market changed because of the digital age? Relating to this question, we ask in this chapter, can "real" culture exist in a market? Can all cultures be marketable goods? If not, why are some cultures hard to be marketed outside the place of origin even though advanced technologies could bring them across borders? Last, we ask a less obvious question: what is the culture of the media industry? How do global conglomerates, in particular hi-tech companies, introduce work cultures to other regions?

Culture adds to an understanding of the business of media, because culture is embedded in media content and technologies. Not only are entertainment media content about culture, but political and sports media are about content as well.

Business vs. Culture?

Many aspiring students want to study media and film because they plan to do something creative and socially meaningful. Some may think that learning about the business aspect of media is boring and irrelevant, because they do not intend to get rich by making art. However, many students get discouraged when they look for internships or their first job because media internships are typically unpaid; students find themselves working for free to gain experience. Their frustration does not end there. Even with substantial internship experience, it is difficult to get a first full-time job with good benefits in the media industry. Also, students may come to accept that one either sells out to the business of media or remains true to the artistic self. This revelation implies that business is antagonistic to culture, because culture is seen as something that should not be commercialized. As shown in the Olympics example, it is believed that once culture is commodified for commercial gains, it loses authenticity and real meaning. The argument that culture should not be mixed with business has two assumptions: first, culture should not be assigned a market value; second, the demand for cultural goods should not be driven by the market alone. While this argument may have validity, it assumes that culture and economy are two separate spheres that do not interact. To show how the spheres of culture and economies are fluid and interact with each other, we look at both the pro-market and pro-culture views of three types of culture in the following: high culture, street culture, and culture as a way of life.

Pro-market proponents argue that high culture (such as opera, ballet, classical music) burdens taxpayers, because the state has to invest a lot of money to create and maintain high culture. The argument is similar to that of reducing state support of public media (see Chapter 7, "Civil Societies"). Therefore, they want cultural organizations to seek independent funding from private endowment. On the other hand, pro-culture proponents argue against a pro-market approach for a number of reasons: first, the audience needs to spend a long time to cultivate an appreciation of high culture, thus the usual cycle of supply and demand does not apply; second, high culture is not meant for the masses, but a small group of selective audiences who have acquired the cultivated taste; and built on the first two reasons, the third reason is that a significant amount of time and money is required to invest in training artists, musicians, and dancers. Modern states usually intervene in the high culture industry to train artists and sustain cultural organizations, because market forces alone cannot justify the investment.

Despite the criticism of high culture having little market value, it has a significant symbolic value because it is a kind of cultural capital: high culture symbolizes a person's good taste and a population's refined culture. High culture serves as a barometer of how "culturally advanced" a country or city is. To illustrate this, tourism boards boast the number of performance groups, and higher education institutions and transnational corporations draw attention to local high culture to attract an educated workforce to move to a region.

The second type of culture seen as something that should not be commercialized is street culture. Pro-culture proponents argue that once street culture becomes mainstream, corporations and enterprising individuals would sell it to a larger crowd who may not understand the roots of this culture. Hardcore street culture fans criticize a dumbed-down commercialized version to be inauthentic and harmful to the identity of street artists. For example, many musical genres, such as hip-hop and rap, were once the music of the oppressed, but when the genres gained acceptance by a larger population, the artists are seen as sell-outs who reflect little of the cultural roots. Mainstream hip-hop music is said to ignore inner city youths' grievances of racial injustice; instead it celebrates money, fame, and a pornographic fantasy. Another example of commercialized street culture is street art. Street art is not confined within museums and galleries; it is displayed on buildings and street fixtures. Often street artists do not seek property owners' consent; the risk of being arrested is part of the reason why street art is seen as "authentic." However, some street art has a market, such as that of Banksy. Banksy allegedly sprayed a print called "I remember when all this was trees" on a concrete wall in a Detroit urban ruin. A nonprofit arts gallery removed it and subsequently sold it to an arts collector for six figures (Stryker, 2015). Another example is the well-known street artist Shepard Fairey: although being an outspoken activist, Fairey has a fashion line OBEY, whose products are sold in high-end department stores.

The last type of culture that is seen as authentic is culture as a way of life. This kind of culture is also believed to be best devoid of commercial interests, because it is supposed to be shared among people of specific cultural, ethnic, and religious groups. Some of the shared histories are national, such as days that celebrate the founding of a nation; others are religious, such as Muslims fasting during Ramadan. Yet some others are shared among diasporas, such as Jews and Armenians connecting to each other through festivities and religious activities. In addition, some shared histories are about a traditional way of life, such as celebrating days of harvest by attending country fairs.

Obviously, religious, cultural, and national holidays have been commercialized in a consumer culture and the media. In particular, Christmas is exploited as a holiday for conspicuous consumption. To show one's love for family and friends, advertisers and marketers encourage consumers to send gifts to each other. In addition, Christmas is both a popular season for blockbuster films and a popular subject matter for many media products. The video game industry releases the most anticipated titles during Christmas because games, like toys, are popular Christmas presents (Nichols, 2008). Even though the religious meanings of Christmas may be irrelevant to non-Christian cultures, such as Asian cultures, its commercial meanings are not lost on those populations. For example, Marling (1992) suggested that Japanese Christmas is always hybrid because the season coincides with the year-end Japanese tradition of gift giving to superiors.

The cases of high culture, street culture, and culture as a way of life show that cultures and economies do not belong to separate spheres. There is nothing called authentic culture that is pure and static. On the other hand, any culture can be commercialized if the associated artifacts and symbols can be commodified. Both pro-market and pro-culture proponents neglect to mention that any culture is created and evolves in a political economic system, and that culture reflects the dominant ideology of that system. For example, religious institutions used to support high culture institutions, which in turn reflected what the dominant class deemed important and aesthetically pleasing. For example, the church commissioned many paintings of saints and biblical teachings; they did not commission paintings to depict the lives of peasants. Buddhist monks commissioned sculptures of Buddhas, but not of themselves. Similarly, national culture reflects how a nation chooses to distribute wealth and resources. Christmas is traditionally a time when the wealthy shared their wealth with the poor, particularly among the gentry class in a class-based society. In both the cases of religious arts and Christmas charity, culture was created and evolved in specific political economic systems; therefore, we should not assume that culture is pure and should be kept as such.

If culture is not devoid of political economic interests, economic and business institutions are not devoid of culture either. We covered in Chapter 4, "Economies," that economics is about the study of how a group of people chooses to distribute wealth and resources among themselves, and culture shapes who should get more and who should get less. An obvious example is how girl children are pervasively given less food than are boy children in many cultures throughout history. Similarly, slaves were treated as private property, thus they could not own property themselves. Cultures also influence how businesses organize themselves. For example, mainstream media in the

US value male workers more than female workers, and this ideology creates a gender inequality in remuneration, career path, and decision-making. Because culture is created in a political economic system and because the media industry has culture, the study of the business of media should therefore include culture.

Based on the above discussion, we ask four questions in this chapter:

- What are a cultural economy and cultural capital? Despite the facts that high culture needs long-term investment and that the value of cultural products cannot be easily measured, no country would claim their cultures are worthless. Why?
- How does the concept of an audience differ from that of a media participant? Most media companies assume audience taste is elusive; hence, they would spend a lot of money on acquiring data on the audience. However, fans and media participants do not shy away from exhibiting their preferences and tastes in the digital landscape. So why should companies spend such money acquiring data?
- How is production a "culture"? Media corporations are seen as powerful players in creating and maintaining popular culture; yet, do all media producers subscribe to the same set of industry practices? In addition, how do media practitioners create industry norms and standards through everyday practices?
- How do local media practices influence global media practice and vice versa? Few cultures are completely insulated from the global media culture, because culture is malleable. How are local cultures influenced by the global media culture and vice versa?

How the Three Approaches Conceptualize Cultures

Among the three approaches, production studies is the most explicit at suggesting why cultures matter to the business of media, because it aims to examine how media workers construct their personal and professional identities, which in term shape media practices. Political economists pay attention to cultures to a certain extent, but they are more interested in analyzing how media corporations wholesale cultures to the audience. Media economists are relatively oblivious to cultures and their relation to the economy.

Media Economics

The media economic approach has little to say about culture. Because this approach tends to see economy as separated from culture, it does not see culture influencing an economy or vice versa. However, it recognizes audience taste as a factor that affects product demand. Price alone cannot predict whether a media product will be popular or not. Therefore, we find that the same type of media products (such as DVDs) cost almost the same. The media economic approach also recognizes that audience taste and preference play a role in determining the success or failure of a media product. Therefore, product differentiation is a major factor in the production and consumption of media products. Product differentiation refers to how different two products are perceived by consumers. Because the same type of media product costs the same, consumers choose one product over another based on how different the products are perceived. For example, consumers who like action films more than animation would choose to see a film with fast cars instead of one with cutesy characters. Even if the ticket price of an animation costs half of that of an action movie, the consumers may not be more willing to see the animation film. Product differentiation may play a lesser role in other consumer goods. For example, if the price of Brand A is half of Brand B, consumers may buy Brand A even though they prefer Brand B to Brand A. As we cover in Chapter 3, food and beverage are necessary for life sustenance, so consumers tend to differentiate brands because of price. In sum, the media economic approach does not see culture as a factor in determining how an economy works, but it acknowledges that objective factors (such as price and market demand) alone cannot explain why some media products are popular while others are not.

A Political Economy of Communication

A critical political economy of communication is not always explicit when describing how culture relates to macroeconomic issues such as market structure, but it recognizes that culture influences resource distribution at the macro level. Mosco (2009) defines a political economy of communication as a study of how power governs the production, distribution, and consumption of resources and goods. He further suggests that power relations are gendered, racialized, and culturally specific. In other words, a group of people may be historically legitimized to control resource allocation, because they have been seen as more capable of managing resources and exercising control. In most cultures at some point, men of the dominant race/ethnicity are legitimized to control resources. In turn, culture plays a role in determining how capability is defined; leadership qualities such as risk-taking and decisiveness are usually associated more with men than with women.

A political economic approach also pays attention to how macro-economic issues influence culture. In Chapter 2, "The History of the Study of the Business of Media," we discuss the ideology of neoliberal capitalism, which privileges the market over other facets of modern life, such as society, religion, and community. A neoliberal capitalism promotes an ideology that everything can be commodified and sold in a market. A neoliberal capitalist ideology has been critiqued to have broken up community relationships by seeing family as a private unit, not part of a community. In the absence of community resources, a family has to turn to paid labor for help. For example, affluent households hire caregivers, private chefs, and landscapers to take care of family members and properties. Ironically, household helpers advertise their services as personal and caring—altruistic qualities that are independent of economic exchange.

Production Studies

Drawing on cultural studies theories and political economy (Mayer, Banks, & Caldwell, 2009), production studies scholars aim to understand the cultures of production, in particular how the gender, race, and class of media producers shape their workplace identities and industry practices. Cultural studies scholarship focuses on consumption, such as how an audience actively makes meanings of media texts, how consumers construct their class, gender, racial, and sexual identities through media texts, and so on. The earliest cultural studies scholarship tended not to pay attention to who produces media goods. Production studies scholarship thus fills in this gap by theorizing media production as a process in which practitioners negotiate their professional and personal identities. Production studies scholars pay attention to the discourses—such as technical language, anecdotes, stories—of media producers as much as the working conditions of the industry. From this approach, the media industry is primarily seen as a constantly changing set of practices rather than a business sector or

Table 8.1 *How the three approaches conceptualize cultures*

	Media Economics	Political Economy of Communication	Production Studies
How cultures are related to an economy	Audience taste and preference influence product demand.	Cultures influence resource allocation at the macro level. Also, macroeconomic structure influences cultures.	Cultures are embedded in media production.

economic organization as viewed by media economists and political economists. In the same vein, this approach does not see media practitioners as primarily economic beings whose main goal is to maximize profits; in fact, practitioners have to negotiate between making money and making arts in the industry (see Chapter 9, "Labor," for details). The production studies approach pays the most attention to a micro level of cultural practices in the context of the media industry.

What Are Cultural Economy and Cultural Capital?

We started the chapter by stating that economies and cultures interact with each other in daily life. The interactions are evident by the fact that some states handpick cultural industries as sectors for expansion, investment, and exports. Digital technology has lowered the entry cost to the media industry, making it a viable economic development. In addition, cultural products can be exported overseas and enhance a country's soft power (Nye, 2009). (We will explain the term "soft power" in the next section). At the beginning of the chapter, we stated that high culture organizations are criticized as cost ineffective, yet few countries would claim their cultures worthless. In fact, high culture is used by national and regional governments to attract an affluent and educated population to move to certain regions to work and live.

The Culture Industry

Creative and cultural industries may appear to be new industries in the context of digital technology, yet the term "culture industry" is not new. In the 1940s, the Frankfurt School coined the term "culture industry" to describe mass culture. Jewish intellectuals, such as

Theodor Adorno and Max Horkheimer, immigrated to the US to escape anti-Semitic sentiments that were brewing in Germany. In the New World, they found a more vibrant and commercialized popular media than in Europe. Film, in particular, was a popular medium for the masses. They coined the term culture industry to refer to "the process of the industrialization of mass-produced culture and the commercial imperatives that drove the system" (Kellner, 2009, p. 96). Frankfurt School scholars were critical of mass culture. They believed media products dupe the audience into passive consumers. As a result, the audience does not question the reality of unequal class relations.

The concept of the culture industry is rejected by contemporary media scholars for a few reasons. First, the Frankfurt School assumed there was an "authentic" culture made up of high culture. High culture audiences were assumed to be more intelligent, hence they could detach themselves from the culture that they enjoy. This assumption reflects a class prejudice: that educated people would naturally be more objective and critical of the culture that they consume. In fact, middle-class culture reflects a dominant ideology. As we stated in Chapter 7, "Civil Societies," public media is criticized as being too highbrow and serving only middle-class interests. The second criticism of the culture industry is that it assumes a dichotomy between high culture and mass culture (Kellner, 2009). For example, all mass audiences are passive while high culture connoisseurs are active. Moreover, the less educated population is likened to be a sponge that absorbs whatever the media tell them, whereas the more educated population is more critical. This approach does not take into consideration that the audience may make different meanings of the texts.

The Industries of Culture

Most contemporary media scholars no longer subscribe to the theory of the culture industry; indeed, the irony is that the study of cultural and creative industries has become a discipline in higher education. For example, Ryerson University (Canada) has a School of Creative Industries, and the Queensland University of Technology (Australia) has a Department of Creative Industries. It seems that the cultural industries are no longer something to be condemned, but to be studied and embraced. Higher education's legitimization of the study of cultural/creative industries may confine the economic value of the industries, such as its impact on national growth, employment, and foreign investment. In Chapter 4, "Economies," we show how some regional and national governments (such as the European Union and the Australian government) calculate the media and cultural economies by collecting data on the labor force in the media, cultural, and creative industries. In Chapter 5, "Politics," we discuss how national governments such as Japan and South Korea strategize their investment in the cultural and media sectors so that they can export media goods to other Asian countries and beyond.

In addition to boosting exports and attracting foreign investment, the cultural/creative industries also help to increase the "soft power" of a country. Joseph Nye (2009) coined this term to describe how much

Table 8.2 *Examples of creative industries programs*

University	Rationale of studying creative industries	Course examples
Bentley University (US)	The creative industries drive global growth.	Web design; visual communication; creative industries and production culture; studios, networks, and media convergence.
Ryerson University (Canada)	The creative industries are the world's most dynamic emerging sectors. An increase in trade in global creative goods and services.	Creative industries overview; imagining the creative city; issues in the digital age; entrepreneurship in creative industries.
Queensland University of Technology (Australia)	The creative industries are innovation led, knowledge intensive, and highly exportable.	Major areas of study: animation; art and design history; creative and professional writing; dance studies; drama; entertainment industries; fashion communication; film, television, and screen; interactive and visual design; journalism; literary studies; media and communication; music.
University of Glasgow (the UK)	The creative industries have been reshaped by policies, business models, and working practices.	Creative industries and cultural policy; creative lives and cultural industries; managing innovation and creativity.

power a country has because of perceived cultural attractiveness. This contrasts with "hard power" lent from military strength and economic prowess. For example, France has a lot of "soft power" because of its cuisine, fashion, and association with romance. The US also has a lot of soft power, because American popular culture such as Hollywood films and music has strong appeal in different cultures. In Asia, Japan has the most soft power, because not only are Japanese cuisine and fashion popular in East Asia, but they also influence cultures in other Asian countries, such as South Korea and China. In recent years, South Korea has become a "hip" country thanks to the Korean Wave (see Chapter 5, "Politics"). In Latin America, Mexico is a top exporter of cultural goods in terms of performance and celebration, such as musical instruments and recorded media (UNESCO, 2016).

To countries that do not yet have much export of cultural goods or an internationally known culture, popular media is a means to boost overseas exports, increase foreign investment, and promote tourism. For example, the New Zealand government has been investing money in the film industry to attract foreign companies in bringing their production to the country (Newman, 2008). The government gives producers tax credits to lower production cost. As will be mentioned in Chapter 9, "Labor," this kind of production is called economic runaway: production that is done outside the country of origin because other countries have cheaper labor and material costs. Canada is a popular runaway location for US films, because English is also the official language and Canadian film labor is less unionized.

In addition to economic runaway, there is also creative runaway, where the production requires locations that are not available domestically. New Zealand wants to tap into its natural scenery for creative runaway. For example, the two fantasy trilogies *The Lord of the Rings* and *The Hobbit*, produced by New Zealand film director Peter Jackson, were filmed in his home country because it provides a natural environment not found elsewhere. The popularity of the two trilogies has increased the soft power of New Zealand because they promote tourism. Fans of the trilogies may travel to New Zealand to experience the Middle Earth envisioned by J.R.R. Tolkien, whose work Peter Jackson adapted. The Mexican film industry is also ideal for creative runaway, thanks to directors and actors such as Iñárritu and Cuarón who have succeeded in Hollywood. The country is hopeful that the popularity of these filmmakers will bring more film production to the country and therefore benefit the economy (Illingworth, 2015).

The above examples show that although the Frankfurt School had condemned the culture industry as a mind-numbing drug for a mass audience, at present some governments embrace the cultural industries because they see cultural goods as profitable foreign exports and boosters of national culture overseas.

Cultural Capital

While soft power refers to a country's perceived attractiveness, cultural capital refers to the cultural taste of the population. An attractive culture not only lures short-term tourists, but it also attracts professionals to move to a region to work. However, not all kinds of culture are used to promote a region, nor are all kinds of workers welcomed. For example, most immigration policies welcome highly skilled workers much more than unskilled workers: the former not only brings skills to the country, but they are also seen to enjoy cultural activities more. French sociologist Pierre Bourdieu (1984) used the term "cultural capital" to refer to the cultural taste of the middle/upper class who enjoys high culture such as opera, classical music, and ballet.

Cultural taste and arts appreciation are acquired from family members or learned through paid lessons. The working class may not find high culture meaningful because they don't have the right social resources, economic means, social network, or leisure time to enjoy it. The new rich may have the economic means but not the social resources to enjoy high culture; therefore, they may pay others to teach them about high culture. The middle class may criticize the new rich for not being refined enough to understand the culture, hence the middle class maintains a distinction between themselves and the new rich by making certain institutions exclusive or developing a language to talk about certain cultures. For example, fine dining establishments commonly toss in French words on the menu; elite schools retain the teaching of Latin and Greek.

Cultural capital is also a factor to attract an educated workforce. Governments attract international talents by highlighting the high culture that a city offers, implying that the most talented professionals would have the cultural capital to appreciate arts. For example, the prestigious Harvard University located in Cambridge, Massachusetts, lists "tak[ing] advantage of unparalleled cultural opportunities" as a reason to work for the university. The stated cultural opportunities are theater, arts museums, musical events, and lectures, as well as a botanical garden. What the website does not mention is that Cambridge also has a vibrant black culture; the absence of such mention implies international talents would not be attracted to black culture as much as high culture. Because high culture is believed to be vital to attract professionals who produce high-value goods and who consume high-end products, some states would invest in maintaining cultural institutions even though they are deemed cost ineffective. In contrast, the working class is rarely lured by regional/city governments for relocation because laborers do not provide specialized skills; therefore, few governments would use working-class culture as a promotional strategy to attract newcomers.

This section has introduced the concepts of "soft power" and "cultural capital." The digital media industry contributes to a country's cultural appeal, while cultural capital is confined to the taste for high culture. The digital media industry is seen as a kind of cultural/creative industry, producing video games, mobile phone apps, transmedia products, and so on. One characteristic of these products is they do not rely heavily on local culture for content. For example, the video game *Angry Birds* is not particularly Finnish, even though the developers are Finns. The game's popularity brought along multiple games, a movie, and merchandise. The digital media industry is seen to be a viable economic sector because the entry cost is low. The industry does not rely on expensive infrastructure or natural resources.

High culture resists being digital. A vibrant digital media industry does not seem to enhance a population's cultural capital. The digital arts may find their way to a contemporary art museum, but they are not seen to be in the same league as old masters' paintings. Watching a recorded play is seen as inferior to seeing it live. Some established performing arts companies try to modernize themselves by inviting younger audience members to live blog/live tweet the events. This attempt has been met with contempt from the usual patrons, because they think the audience should not multitask when enjoying the arts.

What Is "The Audience"?

The second major keyword we cover in this chapter is "the audience." Digital technology is assumed to have done two things to "the audience."

On the one hand, it has fragmented the audience because it offers more choices of what to watch and when to watch. On the other hand, digital technology enables advertisers to have a better understanding of who the audience is and what the audience does with the media. At first glance, this concept seems unproblematic because we understand that the audience consists of those who watch a film, read a magazine, and surf the Internet. However, if the audience concept were *un*problematic, then media companies and research firms would not spend a huge amount of money on knowing and understanding the audience. In addition, the field of communication would not have audience studies as an area of study. The concept of "the audience" is complex, because while research firms prefer to categorize the audience based on gender, age, and income level, audience members are also cultural actors who embed media use in everyday life. In other words, when audience members consume the media (be it newspaper, film, or the Internet), they are in a *habitus* in which they make meanings of the unmediated surroundings (such as the layout of an indoor space) as much as the mediated environment (such as the television, the smartphone). For example, most audience members are aware that watching a film on a smartphone in a subway is not a private activity as other passengers may see the screen. Therefore, subway passengers would wear headphones, watch inoffensive materials, and be aware of which subway stop to get off. Similarly, when television viewers are watching television at home, they may text their friends or go to the bathroom during commercial breaks. Rather than assuming the audience members are "distracted" during commercial breaks, we have to accept that they are cultural actors who organize their lives in both mediated and unmediated environments.

Audience measurement is a big business in the media industry. Nielsen has been a major global player in providing audience data to media companies and advertisers. However, the popularity of watching television shows on a mobile device has allowed other competitors to enter the once monopolized business. Nielsen was founded in 1923 in the US to measure which radio programs telephone subscribers tuned into. At that time, telephone subscription was pricey, whereas radio programs were available to all who owned a radio set. Nielsen was not interested in the media habits of all radio listeners, but only those of a higher socioeconomic status. In addition, Nielsen was not interested in measuring the listening habits of both men and women, but only that of the "master" of the household (Meehan, 1993).

Nielsen television measurement in the 1980s shows the company continued to limit its interest to middle-class males. The company used Peoplemeter to record how household members watch television: who watch which programs and when the viewers switch to another channel. Nielsen's interest in gathering data of primetime television watching implies that the ideal viewer is a full-time employed person who returns home to relax after a long day of work. Past studies, such as by Morley (1980), show the male adult family member controls the remote control in the household, so he is the one who really matters to audience measurement firms. Even though Nielsen favors middle-class families and privileges male viewers, it uses the household as a unit of measurement. This begs the question of whether Nielsen *reflects* the viewing habits of the television audience or *creates* the audience through measurement.

To the above question, Meehan (2005) argues that the audience is an abstract concept created by measurement firms such as Nielsen. The audience did not exist until they were segmented and measured. The abstract audience was then packaged as a product sold to advertisers. In this sense, the audience *is* the consumers: they are expected to watch the advertisements shown during commercial breaks and potentially consume the goods and services. It is no surprise that in the US, the most sought after audience/consumers is males aged 18–34. It is possible that this group has the most disposable income to spend on consumer goods, but it is also possible that the marketable value of this group comes from the fact that it is studied and measured the most. In other words, the tastes and preferences of this most desirable audience/consumer segment are mutually reinforced by measurement firms and advertisers.

Yet, the domination of Nielsen as an audience measurement firm has been threatened by new ways to watch television. A few newcomers entered into the audience measurement market by measuring what viewers watch on a mobile device. For example, comScore is a company that measures audience viewing patterns online, on demand, and through recording devices (Sharma & Stewart, 2014). Another complication of audience measurement is that some television watching activities are impossible to know because the data are kept private. For example, Netflix—an international DVD mailing rental service—and Amazon's Prime Instant Video do not disclose data of the most popular titles. Nielsen is trying to capture that data but could not find a way to measure viewers who stream on mobile devices (Hagey & Vranica, 2014). All these fragmented data show that it is more difficult to have a global sense of audience tastes and preferences in the multi-platform era than in the network era.

Fan Culture

Closely related to the concept of an audience is that of a media participant. Whereas the concept of an audience implies passivity and homogeneity, that of a media participant implies engagement and heterogeneity. Audience measurement firms assume television audience members behave in the same way, in particular how they watch advertisements. In addition, these firms assume audience members who belong to the same demographic segments (such as gender, age, and income level) have similar media tastes and consumer goods preferences. In contrast, the concept of a media participant implies television viewing is only one activity among many that participants do to engage in the mediated and unmediated worlds. Some participants would discuss the shows online and offline reconstruct the narratives through filling in story gaps or suggesting an alternative ending, and create fan arts such as comic books and videos. An example of fan arts is E.L. James' *Fifty Shades of Grey*—a "pornographic" women's novel—inspired by Stephenie Meyer's *Twilight* series on vampires and werewolves. In Japan, manga fans produce their own versions of comic books by imagining the sex lives of the characters (Eng, 2012). These fan-produced comic books are not part of an underground, fringe culture, but a major part of the manga industry.

Henry Jenkins coined the term "participatory culture" (2006) to describe the creativity of media consumers. Participants can be involved in the participatory culture through (1) affiliation, (2) expression, (3) collaborative problem solving, or (4) circulation. Affiliation means participants have a sense of membership (for example, gamers who play a certain game). Expression means consumers would create and appropriate media content (for example, making short videos to comment on a video game). Collaborative problem solving means finding new knowledge with one another (for example, gamers who share resources about a game so that others would know where to find hidden games). Circulation means the flow of participant-initiated projects (such as posting self-made videos online).

Some illustrative examples of participatory culture are events such as Comic Con in major cities around the world. Fans dress in home-made costumes to "cosplay" their favorite characters from video games and comic books in a highly visible fashion. In addition to showing off their devotion to the characters and their stories, dressed-up fans also construct a narrative by interacting with other "characters" at the convention. Another example of participatory culture is the *otaku* culture (obsessive fans of a particular type of popular culture). While the usual perception of an *otaku* is an introverted male who spends most of the time playing video games at home, these fans construct a narrative by using their life experiences by drawing on popular cultures. Children are also active participants in popular culture. Otsuka Eiji (cited in Mōri, 2013) found that Japanese young children who collected Pokémon flash cards do not collect them just because they want to have a complete set, they also construct a narrative from the cards. In another example, the popular and internationally beloved sport of soccer has allowed fans to create media not for commercial purpose. For example, fans will create montage videos of their favorite players scoring the best goals or taking penalty shots. The YouTube channel 442oons creates cartoon parodies of certain players and matches, and is typically very quick in creating videos for their fans to enjoy (www. youtube.com/user/442oons).

Despite the fact that participatory culture seems to be fan driven, fan gathering events can be highly commercialized. For example, Comic Con events have sponsors, such as comic book publishers and automobile companies. They also attract media professionals such as film producers, public relations firms, and agents who want to learn about fan cultures and cultural trends. For example, Hollywood film executives frequent comic conventions to look for the next big ideas for hits. Because Hollywood has been exhausting major comic characters (such as Batman, Superman, Spiderman) in blockbusters, they keep looking for new comic book characters who already have a fan base. Comic artists who aspire to sell licensing rights to Hollywood and television executives also conceptualize their story as a "ready-to-be-adapted" format (Schwartzel, 2016). This once again shows that the boundary between culture and market is malleable.

Fan culture and youth culture are elusive—they are fast-changing and difficult to predict. Fans grow their cultures on both online and offline platforms. Fans' high engagement level means their activities cannot be simply quantitatively "measured," but qualitatively interpreted. Mass advertising and marketing are sometimes found to be inadequate at influencing fans behaviors. Thomas Frank's book *The Conquest of Cool: Business Culture, Counterculture, and the Rise of Hip Consumerism* (1997) discussed how "cool-hunting" firms find out how trendy young people act and behave in city streets. Like what anthropologists do in a field, cool hunters learn the language and culture of trendy youths in order to understand their tastes and preferences. The knowledge that cool hunters learn from the streets is then sold to marketers and advertisers. Frank also showed that young people are very skeptical of advertising and tend to dismiss mass advertising. Advertisers and marketers instead turn to other means such as sponsoring events and paying opinion leaders (such as bloggers) to talk about specific brands and products. Firms like Google and Facebook have looked beyond computer programmers and marketers to tell them about cultures—they regularly hire anthropologists to understand users' behaviors online as if they belonged to an exotic tribe.

Production Culture

Culture is an interplay between a macro-level industry and micro-level social interactions: on the one hand, states see culture as a macro-level industry that can be developed for foreign investment, exports, and tourism; audience measurement firms see the audience as a mass that can be quantified and sold to advertisers. On the other hand, the concept of media participant implies that culture plays a role in micro-level social interactions. Production studies scholars refuse to see that a dichotomy exists; they want to see the industry as a web of social interactions. At the same time, the interactions establish norms for the industry.

Since the 1980s, cultural studies scholars have been paying attention to the identity of media consumers, their gender, racial, and class identities. They do not see identities as *given*, but *negotiated* through consuming media texts. Similarly, production studies scholars see media practitioners as professionals who negotiate their identities at work. Identity negotiation may have resulted from post-Fordist production and flexible labor. As we will explore in Chapter 9, "Labor," Fordist production is characterized by a division of labor, a master-apprentice model of learning, and long-term employment. Golden Hollywood

(1917–1960) exemplified this production model: directors and actors signed long-term contracts with production companies. As a result, actors found themselves starring in more films than do contemporary Hollywood stars. However, they only appeared in one genre, because each studio only specialized in a few. A similar situation can be found in Asian television stations. Directors, producers, and actors sign long-term contracts with the stations. While talents are guaranteed a monthly salary, television executives determine the work prospects of the talents, such as whether they will play the main characters or not. Popular on-screen talents may supplement their salary with endorsements and may finally break away from television contracts by becoming free agents in the film industry. Unpopular on-screen talents have little choice but to earn a meager salary while being underemployed in the stations.

In contrast to a Fordist production, a post-Fordist production emphasizes flexible labor arrangements, making workers take up short-term projects and change jobs frequently. We will suggest in Chapter 9, "Labor," that both above-the-line and below-the-line film industry workers are flexible: some flexible workers are famous movie stars who work on big-budget productions and receive lucrative endorsements, others are production assistants who are paid by the day. Regardless of one's status, a post-Fordist model sees media workers as free agents who control their mode of production, namely time and skills. As free agents, workers are asked to learn the trade by adopting a professional identity before entering the industry. Media students are asked to see themselves as professionals. To learn the trade, they are asked to network with professionals, intern at media organizations, and develop portfolios. In this culture of professionalism, the industry shifts its responsibility of on-the-job training to higher education institutions and individuals. Also, the culture of professionalism demands that media workers continually improve themselves and create opportunities for themselves.

However, what does it mean to be a media professional? In a post-Fordist mode of production, being a professional is not merely about meeting a list of criteria stipulated by the industry, but being cultivated to act and think in a particular way. Mayer (2011) discussed how freelance media producers see themselves as professionals, not as amateurs. Because freelancers may not make more money than amateur producers do, they differentiate themselves by highlighting skills and experiences. Mastering the discourse of a media professional constitutes the identity. However, the fluidity of the meaning of "being a professional" does not mean that everyone can be a professional, because production culture is gender, race, and class specific. In general, women have a harder time seeing themselves as professionals because they are perceived—and in turn perceive themselves—to be less "tough." In other words, women are seen as not being masculine enough and not able to work for long hours. Little consideration has been given to women's status as mothers and caregivers and to their not having as much flexibility to work long hours.

To show that the industry is not a "thing," Havens and Lotz (2012) use the word "practices" to describe what constitute the macrostructure. To them, practices refer to how individual workers see their roles and what their daily routines are. Why the media industry is as such is because of individuals' opinions, perspectives, and decisions. One example that Havens and Lotz use to show how the industry is constituted of practices is how different workers approach the same titles differently. For example, the producer title does not dictate what the person does. Some producers see the film industry as a moneymaking business and only care about the bottom line. Other producers prefer to see the business as art and pick up riskier projects that may not make a lot of money. Some producers may be more involved in the artistic decisions of the film, whereas others leave these decisions to the director.

If the film industry has its own specific culture, we can assume that global media corporations also have their own specific cultures. We will explore how the practices and work cultures of global corporations would impact local practices.

Global Corporations and Local Practices

The last type of culture we discuss in this chapter is transnational corporate culture. Among the three approaches discussed here, a political economic approach pays the most attention to how transnational corporations impose their business models and practices on local businesses. Some negative implications include imposing a certain worldview on local populations, exploiting workers, and destroying natural environments. Political economists do not pay sufficient attention to how corporate culture may bring in positive aspects to a local culture, such as diversity in the workplace, environmental protection, and philanthropy.

We have explored in Chapter 3, "Theories and Approaches to Study the Business of Media," that some political economists are interested in mapping out the ownership and control of the media industry. National boundaries can hardly contain media corporations that expand their operation overseas to search for new markets. Economic motivation leads to other undesirable consequences. For one, political economists believe that the global expansion of media companies would lead to a single worldview. For example, News Corporation has been acquiring many family-owned newspapers around the globe. News Corporation major owner Rupert Murdoch intervenes in how news content should be delivered. After he acquired *The Wall Street Journal*, he expressed his opinions that the newspaper should have shorter articles, more pictures, and less analysis (Vascellaro, Marr, & Schechner, 2008). To some, Murdoch has destroyed the journal's tradition of being independent. The former owner, the Bancroft family, was commended for letting the editors decide the presentation and the content of the newspaper. Thus, the former owners respected the news industry as being the Fourth Estate, not a moneymaking machine.

Transnational media companies that bring entertainment to a global audience are also criticized as negatively affecting local cultures. In the monumental book *The McDonaldization of Society* (2011), sociologist George Ritzer coined the term "globalization of nothing" to refer to the most banal and commercialized kind of globalization. In this kind of cultural globalization, media corporations control how goods are produced and delivered to local audiences. Goods that are produced in this kind of globalization are not meaningful and do not have long-lasting cultural value. These goods are produced to cater to the lowest common denominator; they are discarded once they are consumed.

Disney Co.—with its globally recognizable characters—is often seen as a major exporter of a "globalization of nothing" culture and a leader of imposing American worldview on local cultures. Disney animations and amusement parks have been scrutinized as mass products embedded with national, gender, racial, and political ideology. A common critique is that Disney has fostered a dangerous message underneath the "magical" image. This message legitimizes white men's (or simply American) power on the Other and nature through colonization and capitalism. A lot has been written on local receptions of Disneyland (see Wasko, 2001). For example, some French called Disneyland Paris a cultural Chernobyl, but the Japanese welcomed Tokyo Disneyland and have derived their own meanings for the park. Relatively little is known of the impact that Disney management has on local cultural practices. Wasko (2001) suggested that Disneyland controls the appearance and behaviors of US Disneyland workers; however, little is known whether the same employee handbook was adopted elsewhere. When Hong Kong negotiated with Disney Co. about building the third overseas amusement park, the city-state government was explicit that the locals could learn from Disneyland about American-style management. As it turned out, it was reported that the management has strict requirements for the workers, such as long work hours without a lunch break. In addition, Hong Kong Disneyland management also laid out rules to control tourists' behavior, such as forbidding them to sit on the ground during the parade (Fung & Lee, 2009). The management of Disneyland has changed businesses in the Greater China area in two different ways: first, a Hong Kong amusement park Ocean Park copied Disneyland moneymaking strategies by increasing the number of gift shops and dining options, but it did not adapt Disney characters to the park (probably due to copyright concerns). Second, a Beijing park, Shijingshan Amusement Park (now closed due to probable complaints from Disney), adapted Disney-like characters for its rides and parade, but it did not follow a Disney-style management: employees in costume would take it off partially at work, a practice that is strictly forbidden by Disney. This shows that the management style of transnational corporations do influence local business practices, but local businesses may only adopt what they see fit. On the other hand, Disneyland also attracts more consumers by catering to different markets. For example, it offers birthday party packages for the Latin American coming-of-age celebration, *quinceañera*. Packages can run between $6,000 and $7,000 per girl and include a 12-night stay at Disney, transportation, hotel stays, admission into all four parks, and characters (Amrhein, n/a).

The largest media and hi-tech corporations based in the US (such as Comcast NBCUniversal, Apple, and Microsoft) are all transnational corporations: not only do they have markets in most of the advanced economies, but they also rely on raw materials and cheap labor power in less advanced economies. Political economists tend to focus on how

209

transnational corporations negatively impact local workers, environment, and culture. For example, the much-publicized serial suicides on the Foxconn "campus" in Shenzhen revealed the exploitative and mind-numbing working conditions of migrant workers (Maxwell & Miller, 2012). In order to meet consumer demands for Apple products, factory workers are subjugated to an assembly work culture, such as performing highly specialized mundane work and living a highly structured life in the dormitory. This highly controlling work culture may be very different from manual and farm work, which migrant workers might be more used to. In another example, the manufacturing of audiovisual hardware in Mexican free economic zone *maquiladoras* has created a women-unfriendly work environment: male managers not only sexually harass women workers, but they also control workers' bodily functions, such as limited bathroom breaks and forced abortion.

Despite the highly publicized negative aspects of transnational operation, corporations may bring in a work culture benefiting employees in regional offices. Local employees see working for an American firm as a sign of success, not only because it pays better, but also because it cultivates positive work cultures. For example, two American companies, Google and American Express, are named the best places to work in India. Employees praise the company for pampering workers by giving them spas and massage chairs (Ganguly, 2016).

Hi-tech firms such as Apple, Google, and Microsoft emphasize the importance of diversity and gender equality in the workplace. Local branches of these hi-tech transnational corporations may create more opportunities for employees who may traditionally be disadvantaged in a work environment. Moreover, transnational corporations offer more formal training, overseas exchange opportunities, and longer vacation time than many local companies. Granted, the ones who benefit the most from transnational corporate culture are those who are highly educated and have the most upward mobility. The local elites tend to be more positively impacted than their less skilled counterparts. For example, Thomas Friedman's documentary *The Other Side of Outsourcing* (Friedman, Lewis, & Reverand, 2004) shows that college graduates compete for call center jobs in Bangalore, India. Although Americans look down upon call center jobs as entry-level, dead-end service work, young Indian women enjoy some newfound economic and social freedom by working in call centers. Unlike an older generation, working outside the home gives young women more options than simply waiting to get married. In another example, the work/play culture of Google has introduced collaborative teamwork and lateral management to its global offices.

The double-edged sword of cultures fostered by transnational corporations can be illustrated by the contradictory culture of fast technology and green technology. On the one hand, hi-tech companies need to regularly release new products to create market demands. For example, major cell phone companies such as Apple and Samsung simultaneously introduce new mobile phone models to all markets. This results in consumers constantly upgrading the hardware and dumping electronic waste in developing countries. To discourage consumers from using old models, technology companies usually phase out supporting computer and cell phone models that are older than five years. Maxwell and Miller (2012) have written on the toll that electronic waste brings to the environment and to the scavengers who recycle the dumped waste. On the other hand, the green environment commitments of many hi-tech firms raise consciousness among consumers and governments. For example, because Europe has more advanced technology recycling systems, European-based companies may push local governments to adopt stricter recycling codes. An example is the Finnish mobile phone maker Nokia, which runs cell phone take-back programs in Asia, Middle East, and Africa ("Mayor Bloomberg and Nokia," 2007). The recycling and resale company ReCellular places about 70 percentage of recycled phones in the secondary market in Asia and Latin America.

The above examples all show that while global expansion of transnational corporations has negative implications for local cultures, it also has positive outcomes, especially in the areas such as workplace equality, diversity, and recycling. In the case study below, we ask whether it is possible to stir in local culture and mix it in a Hollywood film so that the hybrid product pleases both the American and Chinese audience.

Case Study: Marketing a Hollywood Movie in China

Hollywood's domination over other film industries is often explained by the universal appeal of its movies. Regardless of where the moviegoers come from, it is assumed that they will have no problem with

211

understanding the stories and enjoying the plots. In contrast, non-Hollywood movies are said to be too culturally specific and that the US, if not global, audiences would have a hard time understanding the stories, much less enjoying the plots. Political economists have critiqued this cultural perspective to understand the global popularity of Hollywood movies as inadequate. For example, Janet Wasko (2003) urged us to see the domination of the US film industry from a historical perspective; US films were exported to Europe when the domestic industries were crippled after WWII. Also, Hollywood studios are lavish spenders on advertising, marketing, and promotion domestically and internationally.

In this case study, we aim to demystify the assumed cultural appeal of Hollywood films by looking at how *Transformers: Age of Extinction* (director Michael Bay, 2014) was marketed in mainland China. We argue that while a film may have culturally specific elements, culture can be made relevant to any audience member through marketing and promotion, thus begging the question: can culture be authentic in a highly commercial product? *Transformers 4* was the highest grossing film in Chinese history by the time of release. Although Hollywood releases many films of the adventure/action genre, the exceptional success of *Transformers 4* in China should be explained by the studio's deliberative and calculative decisions to include Chinese culture. However, what is meant by Chinese culture? Can culture be reduced to adding in well-known Chinese actors and showing Chinese brands in the film?

Step 1: Culturally Universal or Specific Film?

While a film's popularity cannot be universally explained by its universal appeal, the most popular Hollywood films of all time—as measured by box office—all seem to share some common elements. We can consult the list of highest grossing films at Wikipedia or Box Office Mojo to deduce some common elements of universally appealing films. For example, the films with the highest box office figures tend to be limited to a few genres: action, animation, and fantasy. Most of the films are in a series, such as *Harry Potter*, *Star Wars*, and *Transformers*. Because of the genres, these films tend to rely on special effects, such as CGI technology. We can further deduce that these films tend to follow the classic three-act story structure with a happy conclusion. The messages of these films are easy to deduce, such as good trumps

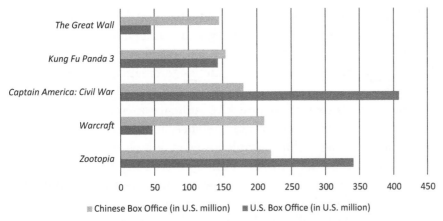

Figure 8.1 *Box offices of Hollywood films in the US and China, 2016*

Sources: *Forbes*, Boxofficemojo.com

bad, humans vs. nature, and the importance of friendship and family. Choosing any of the movies on the list will ensure that the film chosen for analysis has a universal appeal.

The second type of information required to analyze whether a film is universally appealing is the box office figure. Hollywood now makes films with the global audience in mind (Schuker, 2010). For some blockbusters, the overseas box office now accounts for a larger percentage of a film's total box office. Box office gross of Hollywood films in mainland China is predicted to surpass domestic box office gross. The website imdb.com provides data of overseas box office figures. From this site, we see *Transformers 4* grossed US$245 million domestically and US$1.1 billion internationally, of which the Chinese box office accounted for $300 million. In sum, more Chinese have seen the film in movie theaters than Americans have.

Step 2: Marketing Tactics: Positioning and Marketability

As suggested earlier, whether a US film has a successful box office overseas depends on more than the content, because it can be *made* relevant to audience members. Hollywood distributors use advertising, marketing, and promotion to tell the audience how a film can be interpreted. According to Miller, Govil, McMurria, and Maxwell (2004), Hollywood allocates a large budget for film marketing because filmmaking is seen as a risky business. Lavish spending on marketing is thus deemed necessary to ensure that a film has a decent box office. Miller et al. pointed out three tactics that Hollywood employs in marketing: positioning, playability, and marketability. In the following, we first define positioning and marketability. Then we illustrate how *Transformers 4* used the two tactics to create a "culture" for the audiences.

Positioning is defined as how the audience members are asked to relate to a film: "the mind of the audience, as a sales prospect, is conceived as an organ seeking simple answers in a cluttered information entertainment market" (Miller et al., 2004, p. 152). While some films do have different cuts to satisfy local regulators (for example, the European market allows for more explicit sex scenes but less violence than the US market allows), Hollywood studios usually distribute the same cut to different markets. Local distributors then play an important role in promoting the film to local audiences through marketing vehicles, such as movie posters and trailers.

The US and Chinese posters of *Transformers 4* are almost identical: both highlight the main robot character Optimus Prime and the film title "Transformers." The human characters only appear in one of the posters. The only two differences between the US and the Chinese posters are that the Chinese poster has the English text translated and the sequel number "4" is included in the film title. The robot character may be seen as universal enough for both the American and Chinese audience to know it is an action film. The American audience may already know it is the fourth installment in the series, so they need not to be reminded. In contrast, the Chinese audience may need to know that this film belongs to a series. The fact that it is already the fourth installment may imply the series is very good. Knowing the film belongs to a series may also attract viewers to watch the first three installments.

The trailers, however, are very different in both countries. The US trailer begins with a scene in an American small-town setting. The name "transformer" was announced by the narrator nearly a minute into the trailer before the director's name was shown. In the middle of the trailer, there are a few split-second images of the Hong Kong skyline and street scenes. No Chinese actors are included in the American trailer. In contrast, the trailer for the mainland Chinese market begins with a scene in a hi-tech laboratory in which inventors talk about a new type of metal. The trailer has more fight scenes, the Hong Kong skyline, and Chinese actors. The local distributor relates the film to the mainland Chinese audience by emphasizing technology—not only the technology of robots, but also that of Hollywood big-budget films. The highlights of the Hong Kong skyline and Chinese actors are unsurprising because the mainland Chinese audience can relate to them. In contrast, the audience may not relate to small-town life in Texas, so the trailer downplayed scenes that take place in the farmland.

Marketability is the second tactic that the local distributor uses to market the film. It is defined as the elements that can be commercialized through cross-promotions, such as retailers, fast food restaurants, and other entertainment media (Miller et al., 2004). For film series like *Transformers*, the studio would set up deals with manufacturers to produce toys, clothing, household items, and collectibles before the film went into production. *Transformers 4* has deals with 55 brands and was awarded the "film with the most product placement" in 2015. Some brands are American (such as Bud Light and General Motors) and others are Chinese (Shuhua milk, Pangu Plaza in Beijing, Chinese Construction Bank). The use of product placement in *Transformers 4* unfortunately also earned it the worst product placement award (Hawkes, 2015). Products are used illogically, such as a Texan withdrawing money from a Chinese bank ATM (Jenkins, 2014). The abundance of sponsors gave the director a difficult task to juggle all the brands; a Chinese state-owned resort was disappointed to not find the logo in the film and proceeded to sue the studio (Libbey, n/a). It is hard to argue that the placements of one or two Chinese brand logos show respect and appreciation of Chinese culture. It is more likely that Hollywood sees films as a platform on which brands pay to reach global and local audiences. Films are like billboards, only they are more mobile across national boundaries.

The studio also spent lavishly on advertising and promotion. Because one-third of the *Transformers 4* scenes took place in Hong Kong, the city was chosen to be the main Chinese city for promotion. A 20-foot-tall Optimus Prime model was erected by the waterfront in a popular spot with mainland Chinese tourists. In China, ads appeared on television, the Internet, and the exterior of trains. Cross-promotions were also used: the robots appear in Chinese advertisements to sell protein pills, milk, mobile phones, real estate, automobiles, energy drinks, and restaurants. Lastly, *Transformer* characters appeared in a popular mobile game *Angry Birds* with a Chinese New Year theme. Just as some Chinese critics argue that the Chinese elements in the movie are incoherent, the association between transformers with the wide array of products also appears to be rather random. The products do not seem to speak to the attributes of the robots. Even to devoted fans, it requires some imagination to find the relevance between protein pills, milk, and transformers.

Conclusion

We began this chapter by asking why we discuss the lens "cultures" in a book about the business of the media. The assumed boundary between culture and business leads to such economic discussion as whether the state should fund high culture institutions, such as ballet and opera. We show that although scholars were critical of how the industry produced mass culture, the state has been selling culture by promoting the cultural capital of the population. We then introduce the concept "the audience" by discussing how digital technology has changed its meaning: while the media audience is said to be more fragmented than before, fans are also more visible in social media. We further look at two types of culture that are related to the media: the first is production culture—how media practitioners learn about work culture; the second is global corporation culture—how global corporations bring practices to local branch offices. We conclude the chapter by looking at how Hollywood made a film relevant to the Chinese audience by incorporating Chinese elements and marketing.

References

Amrhein, S. (n/a). Quinceañera: Coming of age at Disney. *VisitFlorida*. Retrieved from www.visitflorida.com/en-us/articles/15/freelance/quince anera-coming-of-age-disney-Amrhein.html

Badenhausen, K. (2012, August 40). How Usain Bolt earns $20 million a year. *Forbes*. Retrieved from www.forbes.com/sites/kurtbadenhausen/ 2012/08/04/how-usain-bolt-earns-20-million-a-year/#389a82bafd48

Bourdieu, P. (1984). *Distinction: A social critique of the judgment of taste*. New York: Routledge.

Eng, L. (2012). Strategies of engagement: Discovering, defining, and describing Otaku culture in the United States. In O. Ito, D. Okabe, & I. Tsuji (Eds.), *Fandom unbound: Otaku culture in a connected world* (pp. 33–44). New Haven, CT: Yale University Press.

Forbes. (2016). *2016 celebrity 100 earnings*. Retrieved from: www.forbes.com/ profile/neymar/

Frank, T. (1997). *The conquest of cool: Business culture, counterculture, and the rise of hip consumerism*. Chicago: University of Chicago Press.

Friedman, T. L., Lewis, K., & Reverand, S. (2004). *Thomas L. Friedman's reporting: The other side of outsourcing* [DVD]. Silver Spring, MD: Discovery Communications.

Fung, A., & Lee, M. (2009). Localizing a global amusement park: Hong Kong's Disneyland. *Continuum: Journal of Media and Cultural Studies, 23*(2), 195–206.

Ganguly, D. (2016, July 4). Google, American Express are top workplaces in India: ET survey. *India Times*. Retrieved from http://economictimes.india times.com/jobs/google-american-express-are-top-workplaces-in-india-et-survey/articleshow/53037344.cms

Gerencer, T. (2016, August 4). Michael Phelps net worth. *MoneyNation*. Retrieved from http://moneynation.com/michael-phelps-net-worth/

Hagey, K., & Vranica, S. (December 19, 2014). Nielsen to measure Netflix viewing. *Wall Street Journal*. Retrieved from www.wsj.com/articles/nielsen-to-measure-netflix-viewing-1416357093

Havens, T., & Lotz, A. (2012). *Understanding media industries*. New York: Oxford University Press.

Hawkes, R. (2015, March 4). Transformers: Age of extinction wins "worst product placement" award. *The Telegraph*. Retrieved from www.telegraph.co.uk/culture/film/film-news/11449730/Transformers-Age-of-Extinction-wins-worst-product-placement-award.html

Illingworth, E. (2015, May 19). Cine de México: A new hope. *Council on Hemispheric Affairs*. Retrieved from www.coha.org/cine-de-mexico-a-new-hope/

The International Olympic Committee. *The organisation*. Retrieved from www.olympic.org/about-ioc-institution

Jenkins, H. (2006). *Fans, bloggers, and gamers: Exploring participatory culture*. New York: New York University Press.

Jenkins, N. (2014, July 8). How *Transformers 4* became the no. 1 film in Chinese history. *Time*. Retrieved from http://time.com/2965333/how-transformers-4-became-the-number-one-film-in-chinese-history/

Kellner, D. (2009). Media industries, political economy, and media/cultural studies: An articulation. In J. Holt & A. Perran (Eds.), *Media industries: History, theory, and method* (95–107). Malden, MA: Wiley-Blackwell.

Libbey, D. (n/a). How product placement went wrong for *Transformers 4*. *CinemaBlend*. Retrieved from www.cinemablend.com/new/How-Product-Placement-Went-Wrong-Transformers-4-127447.html

Macedo, P. (2015, November 17). Globo vende mais de R$ 3 bilhões de cotas comerciais para 2016. *Propmark*. Retrieved from http://propmark.com.br/midia/globo-vende-mais-de-r-3-bilhoes-de-cotas-comerciais-para-2016

Marling, K. A. (1992). Letter from Japan: Kenbei vs. All-American kawaii at Tokyo Disneyland. *American Art, 6*(2), 102–111.

Maxwell, R., & Miller, T. (2012). *Greening the media*. New York: Oxford University Press.

Mayer, V. (2011). *Below the line: Producers and production studies in the new television economy*. Durham, NC: Duke University Press.

Mayer, V., Banks, M. J., & Caldwell, J. T. (2009). *Production studies: Cultural studies of media industries*. New York: Routledge.

Mayor Bloomberg and Nokia to challenge New Yorkers to properly dispose of unwanted mobile phones. (2007, October 4). *PR Newswire*. Retrieved from www.prnewswire.com/news-releases/mayor-bloomberg-and-nokia-to-challenge-new-yorkers-to-properly-dispose-of-unwanted-mobile-phones-58463342.html

Meehan, E. (1993). Heads of household and ladies of the house: Gender, genre, and broadcast ratings, 1929–1990. In W. S. Solomon & R. W. McChesney (Eds.), *Ruthless criticism: New perspectives in US communication history* (pp. 204–221). Minneapolis, MN: University of Minnesota Press.

Meehan, E. (2005). *Why TV is not our fault: Television programming, viewers, and who's really in control*. Lanham, MD: Rowman and Littlefield.

Miller, T., Govil, N., McMurria, J., Maxwell, R., & Wang, T. (2004). *Global Hollywood 2*. London: BFI.

Mōri, Y. (2013). Winter Sonata and cultural practices of active fans in Japan: Considering middle aged women as cultural agents. In Y. Kim (Ed.), *The Korean Wave: Korean media go global* (pp. 127–141). Abingdon, Oxon: Routledge.

Morley, D. (1980). *The nationwide audience*. London: BFI.

Mosco, V. (2009). *The political economy of communication* (2nd ed.). New York: Sage.

Newman, D. (2008). In the service of the Empire: "Runaway" screen production in Aotearoa New Zealand and Canada, 1997–2006. In J. Wasko & M. Erickson (Eds.), *Cross-border cultural production: Economic runaway or globalization?* (pp. 217–250). Amherst, NY: Cambria Press.

Nichols, R. (2008). Ancillary markets: Merchandising and video game. In P. McDonald & J. Wasko (Eds.), *The contemporary Hollywood film industry* (pp. 133–142). Malden, MA: Blackwell.

Nye, J. S. (2009, July/August). Get smart: Combing hard and soft power. *Foreign Affairs*. Retrieved from www.foreignaffairs.com/articles/2009-07-01/get-smart

Olympic summer games total global TV audience in 2008 and 2012 (in billions). (2012). *Statista*. Retrieved from www.statista.com/statistics/280502/total-number-of-tv-viewers-of-olympic-summer-games-worldwide/

Ritzer, G. (2011). *The McDonaldization of society* (6th ed.). Thousand Oaks, CA: Pine Forge Press.

Sagir, E. (2016, June). Broadcasting the Olympics in Brazil and beyond. *Taylor Wessing*. Retrieved from https://united-kingdom.taylorwessing.com/download/article-broadcasting-the-olympics.html.

Schuker, L. A. (2010, August 2). Plot change: Foreign forces transform Hollywood films. *Wall Street Journal*. Retrieved from www.wsj.com/articles/SB10001424052748704913304575371394036766312

Schwartzel, E. (2016, July 29). At comic-con, writers tout their stocks. *Wall Street Journal*, p. B6.

Sharma, A., & Stewart C. R. S. (2014, February 13). Nielsen feels heat as rivals promote digital measure. *Wall Street Journal*, p. D1.

Stryker, M. (2015, October 1). Banksy mural from Detroit sells for $137,500. *Detroit Free Press*. Retrieved from www.freep.com/story/entertainment/arts/mark-stryker/2015/09/30/banksy-mural-detroit-sells-137500/73102246/

Tsuji, A. (2016, August). Serena Williams, Kevin Durant, Neymar challenge regular people in star-packed Nike ad. *USA Today Sports*. Retrieved from http://ftw.usatoday.com/2016/08/serena-williams-kevin-durant-neymar-nike-ad-video

UNESCO. (2016). *The globalization of cultural trade: A Shift in Consumption: International flows of cultural goods and services 2004–2013*. Paris: UNESCO.

Vascellaro, J. E., Marr, M., & Schechner, S. (2008, April 23). Editor out as Murdoch speeds change at WSJ. *Wall Street Journal*. Retrieved from www.wsj.com/articles/SB120887959358334849

Vranica, S., & Flint, J. (2016, August 7). NBC fails to score gold with Olympics open ceremony. *Wall Street Journal*. Retrieved from www.wsj.com/articles/nbc-fails-to-score-gold-with-olympics-opening-ceremony-1470576727

Wasko, J. (2001). *Understanding Disney*. Malden, MA: Polity.

Wasko, J. (2003). *How Hollywood works*. London: Sage.

Labor

9

At the end of the chapter, students will be able to:

- explain why labor is transnational and global in the digital age;
- suggest how the three approaches (media economics, political economy of communication, and production studies) conceptualize labor in the business of media;
- explain how labor is understood in both microeconomics and macroeconomics;
- explain why political economists think labor is objectified, exploited, and alienated;
- suggest how media workers are different kind of professionals, compared to such professionals as doctors, lawyers, and engineers;
- state how academics and the industry classify media workers;
- explain why labor can be subjective;
- define flexible labor, affective labor, and free labor. Give an example to illustrate each of them;
- suggest how flexible labor, affective labor, and free labor may be harmful to the livelihoods of media workers;
- define playbor and explain why it is a form of free labor;
- analyze the status of women's employment in the media industry.

Let's look at three job advertisements and consider the descriptions and required qualifications:

Job advertisement 1: "You'll drive new innovations and build beautiful user experiences"; "you'll work with world-class [people] and resources"; "we hire people with a broad set of skills who are ready to tackle some of the greatest challenges and make an impact on millions, if not billions, of [people]"; "working proficiency and communication skills in verbal and written English."

Job advertisement 2: "[Our organization] creates, distributes, and promotes free media resources to support innovative teaching and learning for all ages"; "we enable our audiences to expand their knowledge, improve their skills, and enrich their lives"; "candidates must be able to multitask, set priorities, and manage deadlines in a fast-paced environment. Strong organizational, written, and oral communication skills and a strict attention to detail are essential."

Job advertisement 3: "[Employees'] responsibilities require them to be on their feet working while clocked in, unless on break. If they are not busy, they are expected to take on tasks they see that need to get done, and pitch in to help their teammates"; "providing friendly, quality customer service"; "have the ability to speak clearly and listen attentively"; "have the ability to maintain a professional appearance at all times and display a positive and enthusiastic approach to all assignments"; "be able to exhibit a cheerful and helpful attitude"; "have the ability to be cross-trained in all areas"; "have the ability to communicate in the primary language(s) of the work location."

After looking at the job advertisements, let's ask ourselves some questions: which of the above jobs pays best? Which job is the most flexible in terms of work schedule? Which job allows employees to develop professionally? Which job allows employees to be creative?

The answer: the first job.

Addressing future employees as "you," aspiring workers are already charged with being the best at their work. The company in turn promises future employees that they will do things that profoundly impact many people and will work with the best minds. The second job may also allow employees to develop professionally, but it has an inflexible schedule because of the pressing deadlines. The third job requires the most physical stamina (standing on feet during work hours) and the best personal skills (pleasing the customers).

Besides the required technical skills for the jobs, the description for the first job does not tell future employees how they should appear and behave on the job, while the last one prescribes for future employees that they be cheerful, helpful, and pleasant. Ironically, the first job—that asks for the least social skills—is probably extremely competitive and the last one—that demands a lot of physical work and social skills—the least. If all three jobs require the same education level and technical qualifications, the first job is clearly the most attractive and the last one the least.

The first job is an entry-level engineering job at Google. Although they only ask applicants to have a university degree and one year of experience, applicants can expect to compete with other stellar candidates—some may have graduate degrees and years of experience. The second job is an entry-level job at PBS, a public television broadcaster in the US (see Chapter 7, "Civil Societies"). Applicants are required to have a university degree and relevant skill sets. They can expect to compete with equally qualified candidates, but it is a less competitive job than the one with Google. The last job is an entry-level job at Chipotle—an international fast food chain. Applicants can expect that the job will not be too competitive, because the employee turnover rate in the service industry is high.

Now that we know which companies advertised the jobs, we can make further assumptions about the lucky few who are hired by these three companies. Google employees may see their jobs as more than "clock in and clock out"; they are likely to develop their career within the company by networking with people inside and outside the company. They expect long work hours and tight deadlines but also lucrative compensation and upward mobility in the professional world. If they leave Google, they can expect to work for companies of the same prestige, attend elite graduate schools, or launch their own start-up companies. Google employees will learn skills and knowledge that can be transferred to many different fields, from academia to business to other technical fields. No wonder why Fuchs (2013) calls Google engineers "aristocratic workers": they enjoy good job benefits and have a career path that few workers could dream of.

In a nonprofit media organization like PBS, employees can also expect long work hours and tight deadlines, but they cannot expect a handsome compensation and benefits. In fact, because of the long work hours, the average hourly pay may be low. They may also develop their careers in the organization, but they may also hope to move laterally to a more financially endowed company, such as a major broadcaster, or move upward to a similar size organization. They may apply their experiences to postgraduate work or they may leave the media industry altogether.

Fast food restaurant employees can expect to work as quickly as they can, but working efficiently does not mean they can leave work earlier. Their work schedule is fixed and has little flexibility. They cannot bargain for their wage or work benefits. They are less likely to see their jobs as a career. If they stay with the company longer than most employees do, they may be promoted to store manager, then regional manager. But the skills learned on the job cannot be easily transferred to another industry. The employees may only move upward professionally if they earn a degree that enables them to work in other industries.

Labor is the last lens introduced in this book. We discuss labor last because we want to position readers as aspiring media workers and professionals in the field. After learning about how the business of media can be viewed from the lenses of economies, politics, technologies, civil societies, and cultures, we hope readers can now think about how their economic and symbolic values in the industry are created from an interplay between economies, political systems, and technologies in a multi-platform era. In particular, we want to frame media workers as transnational/global and digital. By saying that labor is transnational/global, it means that workers around the world are connected, however indirectly. The largest media, telecommunications, and hi-tech companies are global in nature; workers find themselves working with colleagues in local offices around the world. Even for companies that are local, the workers likely come from different cultures; the chain of supply is likely to be global as well. By saying that labor is digital, it means that digital technology connects the transnational labor through webs of content, technology, and communication. While engineers at Google invent and improve upon digital technology, manual and service workers are partially digital as well. Surveillance technology, such as sales records and production logs, keep track of how productive individual workers are.

Nonetheless, this last chapter does not give career advice to aspiring media professionals or provide industry insiders' stories: many popular books in the market have already promised such information. Instead, we aim to urge readers to think about "labor" from different approaches. The job descriptions at the beginning of the chapter have already given readers a number of labor-related key concepts; to name a few, "salary," "wage," "work hours," "career development," "transferable knowledge," and "upward mobility." These keywords cannot be seen as "natural," because workers in the past may not have been familiar with the meanings of these terms. Because these terms emerged in specific socioeconomic political arrangements, understanding them requires an understanding of broader socioeconomic contexts.

Why Work in the Media?

Many students whom we have taught choose to study the media because they identify themselves as creative and artistic people who may not be satisfied with a "nine-to-five" desk job. Undoubtedly, jobs in the media are known to be more flexible and creative than jobs in other industries, such as accounting. Also, the media industry has an aura not shared by most industries; the potential to be rich and famous (or at least to work for the rich and famous) in the industry is undeniably luring. However, aspiring media professionals must also know that in the name of flexibility, many media jobs are not salaried jobs, but freelance jobs. Curtin and Sanson (2016) use the word "precarious" to describe work conditions from low-wage labor to professional elites: "[workers] must ready themselves for iterative change and persistent contingency as standard employment and its associated entitlements become artifacts of a bygone industrial era" (p. 6). Also in the name of flexibility, media professionals are asked to learn different skills so that they can tell stories across platforms.

Given the above, the big questions asked in this chapter are:

- Are media workers professionals? Media workers are unlike some highly paid professionals such as doctors, lawyers, and engineers. Yet, success in the jobs also requires technical skills and professional networking. When, how, and why did media workers become professionals?

- Is labor objective or subjective? Labor may be measured in terms of number of hours spent on a job, but labor can also be subjective. We will explore concepts such as flexible, affective, and free labor and examine why we need to think of labor as both objective and subjective.
- Last, we discuss how we can examine women's work conditions in the industry. The media industry is fast-changing. All workers are impacted by neoliberalism and globalization, but women workers—newcomers or veterans—face structural differences from men in career advancement in the industry.

How the Three Approaches Conceptualize Labor

All three approaches pay adequate attention to labor. Media economists and political economists tend to see labor as an objective concept, whereas production studies scholars tend to see it as subjective. While media economists conceptualize labor as a variable in both macro-level and micro-level economies, political economists *problematize* the concept of labor because they believe labor was made objective by capitalists. Unlike both media economists and political economists, production studies scholars see labor as something subjective, because it constitutes a worker's identity and a person's lived experience more than as a variable or a class relation.

Media Economics

Labor, like raw resources and rent, is seen as a variable in media economics. Labor can be studied at both macro and micro levels. In macroeconomics, employment rate is the percentage of people in the job market in relation to those looking for a job. At a national level, a high employment rate means that an economy is in a good shape. Politicians usually highlight how their policies will reduce the unemployment rate. However, they usually do not mention that the employed population includes part-time workers, temporary workers, and unpaid workers in family businesses. Employment does not mean that workers earn enough to sustain their lives. Even among the full-time employed populations, some may earn less than they should because they are overqualified for a job (such as a university graduate working as a restaurant server) or they switch to a new career and start from a junior position. Unemployment rate also does not include those who have given up looking for jobs and those who cannot work due to illness and disabilities. What it means is that a high employment rate does not necessarily mean that all workers are making a decent living.

Another macroeconomic concept is GDP (gross domestic product) and consumer power. People who are not in the labor force (such as retirees and 16 year olds and below) are assumed to have no labor power to produce goods and services. Unemployed people, on the other hand, are assumed to have labor power to produce goods and services for the economy. Therefore, the labor power of the unemployed is seen as a waste because unused labor does not contribute to an economy. Unemployed people also bring home less money, so they and their families may only be able to consume the necessities to sustain life.

Other macroeconomic concepts related to labor are employment cost index (how labor cost changes), labor productivity (output of value of goods and services per worker per hour), and wages across occupations.

Media economists also study labor at the micro level. Labor is seen as a variable at the micro level because it involves individual markets, firms, and products. Firms would care about the supply and demand of labor because the economic well-being of firms relies on productivity. For example, hi-tech industries have long worried about the shortage of technical workers. Firms like Microsoft and Google have lobbied the US government to increase the number of visas for highly skilled workers. Firms with overseas branches also rely on an educated and skilled local workforce for success. In contrast to highly skilled, specialized technical workers, there is a steady supply of entry-level media workers, such as production assistants, editorial assistants, and junior reporters. Entry-level workers may find themselves working for long hours but receiving a low wage. If there is an oversupply of labor, firms are able to suppress wages. Any business has fixed and variable costs. Whereas fixed costs are more or less constant regardless of output volume, variable costs are adjustable based on output volumes. For example, fixed costs of a television studio include rent and equipment; variable costs include labor and travel. During an economic downturn, businesses would first reduce variable costs, because it is easier to lay off workers than break the rental lease or sell equipment.

A Political Economy of Communication

Political economists also pay attention to labor, because they care about working conditions in the media industry. Some explored labor topics are transnational Hollywood workers (Miller et al., 2005), runaway production (Wasko & Erickson, 2008), exploited factory workers (Maxwell & Miller, 2012), exploited Hollywood workers (Curtin & Sanson, 2016), free labor (such as internship) (Hesmondhalgh, 2010), digital labor (Fuchs, 2014), and work automation. Although workers' conditions in the developed world can hardly be compared to those of factory workers during the Industrial Revolution, Marx's writings on capitalist labor have informed political economists about class relations, in particular the concepts of exploitation and alienation. Therefore, it is worthwhile to briefly summarize some of Marx's ideas and to relate their relevance to contemporary media industries.

In the preindustrial economy, farmers and artisans used their own modes of production to produce goods (such as food, clothing, and household items)—for their families. The surplus would be sold in the markets or bartered with other goods. In this mode of production, the producers owned their labor, skills, and time. The Industrial Revolution, however, changed the relationship between producers and goods. Factory workers—who may have been migrated farm workers and artisans—sold their labor power to capitalists. Because modern machines were more expensive than simple farming tools, only the capitalists could afford the means of production. Capitalists pay workers by calculating the number of hours that they sell. Workers do not own their skills and time during those sold hours. This process of labor objectification has transformed the senses of value, time, and labor. In preindustrial times, farmers and artisans produced goods of "use value"—goods that are necessary to sustain life. Their sense of time and labor is subjective, and workers could work at their own pace. However, industrialization has objectified senses of value, time, and labor. Factory workers produced goods with exchange value. The goods are called commodities and are produced for the market. Workers' time and labor were measured by how much they produced. Along with the goods that workers produced, labor power is said to be "commodified." Their time and labor power, like the goods that they produce, is a commodity.

The commodification of labor power resulted in exploitation and alienation. Workers were exploited because they were asked to work more for less money. As mentioned earlier, workers' wages are a variable cost in production. This cost is more flexible than other variable costs (such as natural resources) and fixed costs (such as machines). Alienation occurred when workers could no longer identify with the goods that they made. Workers do not make goods for their own use and they may not find the goods meaningful, and—most importantly—they cannot afford what they produce. A good example is the Chinese factory workers who produce decorations for holidays that they don't celebrate, such as Thanksgiving and Hanukkah. Similarly, Mexican farmers who used to grow traditional foods, such as corn and beans, now grow expensive specialty foods, such as strawberries, for export. The farmers cannot afford to buy the produce that they cultivate (Kneidel & Kneidel, 2005). Although few readers of the book may readily identify with workers' conditions in the 19th century, political economists argue that class relations have hardly changed between the capitalists and the workers from the Industrial Revolution to globalization. One remarkable difference, however, is that the capitalists in the media industry are not only individual entrepreneurs, but also shareholder-owned giant corporations. The heartless capitalists have been replaced by faceless corporations whose owners are not known by workers.

Political economists pay attention to the question of flexible labor in a post-Fordist mode of production and a globalized world (see Chapter 3 for a definition). They study how labor facilitates the movement of capital beyond a national boundary. For example, Hollywood is more transnational than ever (Miller et al., 2005); well-known high-profile "above-the-line" talents from Europe, Asia, and Latin America move to Hollywood to work. Directors such as Ang Lee from Taiwan (*Crouching Tiger, Hidden Dragon*) and Alejandro Iñárritu from Mexico (*Birdman*) are non-US-born creators who found success in the US industry. On the other hand, technical (aka "below-the-line") jobs have been shipped elsewhere in search of lower labor cost. Hollywood is not the only media industry that benefits from cheap labor; Japanese animation work is shipped to South Korea, Taiwan, and India (Schilling, 2012), and backroom office tasks such as data entry are shipped to India. The educated workers in India and China only earn a fraction of what their counterparts earn in the developed world. The chase for cheap labor never stops: Latin American countries are becoming more popular for IT and business processing call centers for US companies. These workers have one skill that workers in India don't— they are fluent Spanish speakers (Sutter & Williams, 2014).

Political economists are also critical of the exploitation of cheap or free labor in the creative industry. Working in film and video, and fashion and design, is seen as glamorous, thus jobs in these industries are highly competitive even though the work is unstable and tends to be contract or project based. These industries also enjoy a steady supply of free labor, because aspiring workers are eager to work for free so that they can get their foot in the door. Political economists also renew theories of exploitation and alienation by looking at the demanding work conditions of factory workers who manufacture Apple products in China (Johnson, 2011) and television sets in Mexico (Ross, 2004); urban scavengers who extract metals from electronic waste in dumping sites (Maxwell & Miller, 2012); and African slaves who mine metals in war-torn countries (Fuchs, 2013). Political economists want to show that labor is more transnational than before—consumption habits in one part of the globe have impact on populations in other parts. Demands for consumer goods among the affluent global populations may increase risks among other populations, from hazardous work environments to bonded and slave labor.

Production Studies

Production studies has foregrounded labor issues in the business of media (Lobato & Thomas, 2015). However, scholars from this approach conceptualize labor differently than media economists and political economists do, because they see labor as something subjective, something experienced by those who work in the industry.

Table 9.1 *How the three approaches conceptualize labor*

	Media Economics	Political Economy of Communication	Production Studies
How labor is related to an economy	As a variable in both micro- and macroeconomics	As an objectified commodity in a capitalist market; as a resource at the worker's disposal in a noncapitalist market	As a subjective, lived experience
Concepts that are associated with the study of labor	Employment rate; unemployment rate; consumer power	Use/exchange value; labor/time as commodities	Producers; professionals; workers; amateurs; identity

Therefore, they do not just call workers "workers," but also producers and professionals. The variation shows that "worker" is not a monolithic concept, but a situational identity. Production studies scholars' emphasis on identity and self-identification means social beings are multifaceted. Workers are not just people who exchange their time for money, but are also media consumers and public advocates. In the next section, we discuss a central question asked by production studies scholars: when, how, and why do media workers become professionals?

Are Media Workers Professionals?

University programs train students to become promising professionals in the industry. Consider how two highly respected film and video programs in the US tell prospective students what they do: New York University (NYU) says, "our program mentors young artists in the traditions and innovations of an evolving media landscape that is deeply rooted in visual storytelling" (New York University, n/a). The University of Southern California (USC) says that it

> teaches students how to make compelling, in-demand content for screens of every size—whether it's IMAX or a hand-held device. At [the School of Cinematic Arts], students quickly become adept at the tools of the trade, from cameras, light kits, and editing software to the newest cutting-edge techniques and technologies that are changing the professional production process.
> (University of Southern California, n/a)

To fulfill the need of the media industry in Mexico, the Center for Cinematography of the National Autonomous University of Mexico (UNAM) offers an organized program that deepens students' technical and theoretical knowledge related to audiovisual expression (National Autonomous University of Mexico, n/a). Even though both programs in the US have different foci—the film program at NYU is known to train workers in the arthouse cinema tradition while USC trains workers for Hollywood, they do not call students "workers" but future artists and professionals in the trade.

If media jobs that require a college degree are professional jobs, how about those that do not, such as carpenters who construct the set and electricians who connect the wires? Is it more appropriate to call them workers than professionals? How about high-profile workers such as movie stars and famous directors? Is it more appropriate to call them performers than professionals? If the word "professional" is not an inclusive term for all people who work in the industry, then what terms would be more appropriate? Based on these questions, we will first explore when and how there was a rise of the professional class; then we compare two typologies of workers in the media industry; and last we look at how the film and television industries categorize workers. We argue that even though digital technology is said to disrupt the industry, the organization of labor has not been transformed overnight.

The Rise of the Professional Class and Where Media Workers Fit Into This Class

The professional class is a relatively modern concept that used to refer to learned *men* who were trained in specific fields, such as medicine, law, and engineering. This new professional class was different from other dominant classes in Europe—and arguably elsewhere—before the 18th century, because their social status and power did not come from religious institutions, as in the case of clergy members and aristocrats. In contemporary times, the scope of the professional class has expanded to include teachers, scientists, accountants, and so on; some may even call service industry workers (such as kitchen help and office cleaners) professionals. For our purpose, we use "profession" to refer to jobs that belong to "the knowledge-based category of service occupations" (Evetts, 2014, p. 33); therefore, manual workers in the service industry are not called professionals.

Professional knowledge may be acquired through a university education. To ensure that professionals have more or less the same knowledge base, national and international associations govern their respective professions by stipulating standards, certifying professionals, and enforcing codes of conduct. The professional class is a desirable social position, because it enjoys prestige, social status, career development, and a comfortable income. In some societies, being a professional is synonymous with being middle class.

The rise of the professional class and the emergence of modern cultural institutions are closely tied to the rise of capitalism. Critical communication scholar Raymond Williams (as discussed in Havens and Lotz, 2012) believed that capitalists—the new rich in the 19th century—wanted to show off their cultural taste by acquiring art and organizing cultural events (also see Chapter 8, "Cultures"). Artists at that time were both creative and business people, because they needed to sell their work while shaping the taste of the capitalist class. In the post–WWII era, cultural workers were employed by organizations (such as television and radio organizations, newspapers companies, and record labels) rather than self-employed artists. A Fordist production of work ensured each worker was specialized in a specific area: director, writer, marketer, and so on. The proliferation of media institutions meant the market catered to the masses, beyond the select few rich individuals in pre–WWII times. As such, cultural workers had to produce goods that responded to more popular taste.

Compared to many professions in the medical and legal fields, the media professions are relatively loosely structured and do not always require professional certification. There is no national board to certify workers, no examination to pass, and no standard curriculum. While a graduate from a reputable program may learn the skills necessary for the jobs, different programs may emphasize different skill sets for different media. Media workers are also drawn from graduates of different disciplines: media studies, film studies, creative arts, English, theater, and so on. Digital media also require workers with computer and quantitative skills. As shown in the above, NYU emphasizes that media workers are artists, while USC sees them as professionals in a trade. Moreover, job titles are relatively fluid in the industry; they may not correspond to the actual job duties. People who bear the same title differ in income, work experience, and job prospects. For example, directors can be extremely wealthy, powerful, and well-known individuals, such as George Lucas of *Star Wars*, but they can also be freelancers who need nonmedia-related part-time jobs to get by. But software developers can be movers and shakers in hi-tech firms. Their code may influence many users' experiences. But software developers may also be freelance app designers who sell their products in a crowded marketplace. The time spent on development may not even be rewarded by the few purchases. Moreover, self-employed professionals can give themselves whatever job titles they please. In addition, the industry has no prescribed career path: some with a few years of experience but a lot of talent (or sheer luck) may earn more than some others with decades of experience. The success stories of the former are more often told than the latter.

Experienced workers may also not have more advantages than inexperienced workers have. In fact, the industry is notoriously sexist and ageist: the preference for younger females is more pronounced with Hispanic female actresses. They are more likely than females from other races/ethnicities to be shown partially or fully naked on screen (Smith, Choueiti, & Piper, n/a). Female on-camera talents find it harder to find work once they reach their 40s. Experienced female workers have less negotiating power: the well-known actress Mila Kunis wrote an open letter regarding sexism in Hollywood. After refusing to pose semi-nude, her producer said she would "never work in this town again" (Gibson, 2016). Many actresses complain that older women have fewer roles to choose from and their roles are usually not sexual. At 37 years old, Maggie Gyllenhaal was considered too old to play a 55-year-old's love interest (So, 2016). In contrast, older male actors can still play a wide array of roles and they often play lovers of much younger women in films and television programs. Jake Gyllenhaal—three years younger than his sister—is still playing the lead roles with younger on-screen love interests. The youthful culture of hi-tech and social media firms such as Google and Facebook may also crowd out older workers. While older workers could bring in years of experience, their younger colleagues may consider someone who doesn't share their cultural codes to be less in tune with the company.

Typologies of Media Workers

In this section, we explore how workers can be categorized. We have reviewed in Chapter 4, "Economies," and Chapter 8, "Cultures," that international, regional, and national organizations develop their own categories for statistical purposes. There is no universal category of media worker. Adding to this complication is that scholars and industries have also developed different worker categories. In the following, we review one category that academics use. The category is based on the mode of production and the organization of productive forces.

Political economist Christian Fuchs (2013) has highlighted the transnational nature of digital labor; different types of labor from both developing and developed countries are needed for the global chain of production and distribution of digital products. Some countries (such as the Democratic Republic of Congo) are rich in natural resources but poor in technology know-how; some countries (such as China and Bangladesh) have a huge supply of manual workers; and yet other countries (such as Singapore) have knowledge workers but have little land. Fuchs's worker categories are based on specific modes of production and the organization of productive forces. (We will explore later how mode of production and productive forces are related.) For our current purpose, we define mode of production as how humans organize their labor in order to supply themselves with food and other necessities to sustain life. Mode of production is closely related to the type of society: slave, feudal, capitalist, and communist. In a slave society, slave owners control slaves' labor and reap the profits from their labor. In a capitalist society, workers sell their labor to capitalists in exchange for wages.

The work conditions of today's digital labor may appear to be less harsh than those experienced by slaves and factory workers, yet Fuchs pointed out how workers' conditions are drastically different in the global chain of digital production and distribution. On the one end, there are slave laborers in Africa who mine minerals for hi-tech products. These slave laborers work without pay and risk being killed by warlord-controlled armed forces. The profits made by the warlords are used to finance arms for civil wars.

In the middle of the digital labor spectrum, manual labor, such as factory and call center work, needs a large pool of cheap labor. China and India are two countries with a huge supply of manual labor. China has developed economic zones for foreign investment to materialize its Open Door Policy. Rural migrant workers move to newly industrial cities to manufacture hi-tech products, such as cell phones and laptop computers. The long work hours, low pay, and mundane lifestyle are likened to factory work during the Industrial Revolution. Labor is always gendered; women factory workers are always subject to more monitoring and harassment than men are. The documentary *Maquilapolis* (Funari & de la Torre, 2006) looks at factory work in Tijuana, Mexico, where labor is cheap and the work hours are long. Women workers become factory workers to afford a better lifestyle for themselves and their children. In the documentary, Carmen Duràn—a mother of three—worked long hours in a Sanyo factory and only earned US$6 a day, even though she was told she would earn US$11. In addition, Duràn faces health issues due to prolonged worktime.

Digital work also includes low-pay, high-pressure, and tedious digital work such as call center jobs, digital freelancers, and content farm workers. Call center workers are heavily monitored by supervisors: in addition to meeting a required quota, they also need to sound pleasant and nice all the time. Thus, not only are call center workers selling their time, but they also sell their affection to customers (we will explore the concept "affective labor" in the next section). Digital freelancers arise when companies, such as Amazon, become online brokers between those who need piecemeal work done and those who seek jobs. Freelancers are called "artificial artificial intelligence"; they are paid to perform tasks that have not been conquered by artificial intelligence. The freelancers earn as little as two US dollars an hour filling in surveys or identifying online products. Content farm workers are also a new class of digital workers. They are asked to write low-quality, unoriginal "journalistic" pieces for content farms, whose sole purpose is to attract clicks and hence advertising money (Scholz, 2017).

The other end of the digital labor spectrum has hi-tech workers, such as software engineers, in affluent cities. According to Fuchs (2013), they are also exploited. The booming Indian software industry is a partial result of cheaper labor costs of the educated workforce when compared to developed countries. Companies such as IBM moved their entire unit from the US to India (Bulkeley, 2009). US workers were allowed to keep their jobs only if they agreed to move to India and be paid the local wage. Even though it sounds like every worker in the digital workforce is losing out, Fuchs still thinks labor aristocrats, such as Google workers, are the winners of digital labor. They may be the envy of all workers because they earn more than most in the hi-tech industry, but they are also asked to put in extra time and effort in the job. As we saw at the beginning of the chapter, Google regularly boasts the "great" people who work for them and the immense global impact of the work. Words such as "the greatest" and "the smartest" foster a competitive workplace environment. Employees who clock in and out on time may be deemed not dedicated enough to their career. Six-figure hi-tech workers living in San Francisco complain about the high cost of living. Despite the fact that their income is the envy of low-income workers, they spend half or more of their salary on rent. Some of the young engineers are reportedly staying in a two-bedroom apartment with ten tenants (Solon, 2017). Women employees who have household duties need to be flexible to compete with their male counterparts. For example, workers with children would work in the evening after they put their children to bed.

Media industries also categorize workers in their own way. Here, we look at how the US film industry categorizes workers. Two categories of film workers are "above the line" and "below the line": the former are in charge of the creative side of filmmaking; the latter the technical side. Actors, directors, and writers belong to the former; cinematographers, costume designers, sound editors, and carpenters belong to the latter. Within both categories, different professions have their own unions that negotiate the work benefits and work conditions of their members with major Hollywood studios. It may be assumed that "above-the-line" workers have better income and work conditions than "below-the-line" workers have, but it is not strictly the case. Many scriptwriters earn very little because although Hollywood executives and producers buy many screenplays, very few of them are made into films. A screenplay that is not developed into a film means the creators cannot earn additional money after selling the rights to the studios. Writers now also have to prepare different scripts for transmedia storytelling.

Another way to think of the differences among film workers is their degree of mobility: those who are well known may move anywhere in the world and are still offered jobs; others are bounded by their locations. For example, A-list stars from most film industries can live anywhere. Film directors and executives are willing to travel anywhere to negotiate with them if their names sell tickets. However, less-well-known workers cannot expect work once they move out of a locally based network. Many have pointed out how runaway production has weakened Hollywood "below-the-line" workers. When a lot of film jobs have moved from California to Georgia, Louisiana, and New Mexico, workers with little job mobility have no choice but to see their income dwindling.

Digital technology may seem to have disrupted the industry: online streaming services such as Hulu, Amazon, and Netflix now produce their own shows and online news seems to have made print media obsolete. However, organization of labor is stubborn to change: one reason is that digital media workers still assume old titles such as reporters, directors, promoters, and so on. Another reason is that the more established industry has labor unions that protect workers from digital disruption. What is true, though, is that the divide between the best-paid media workers and the worst paid has widened. The most well-known artists earn much more than those in the 1960s did. At the same time, a huge reserve army of workers receive little to no pay. The next section will touch upon related concepts, such as flexible labor and free labor.

Flexible Labor, Affective Labor, and Free Labor

At the beginning of the chapter, we quoted from three job advertisements to show how hourly wageworkers are expected to behave in a certain way: being friendly, having good listening skills, and being helpful are some listed job requirements for a fast food restaurant job. These workers are explicitly asked to sell affects—emotions, feelings— to customers so that they feel valued and welcomed. This group of workers is also the most vulnerable in a bad economy. The workforce of low-level service jobs can be immediately shrunk if the company is not making money.

Entry-level jobs in a media organization are also flexible. The statement that "candidates must be able to multitask, set priorities, and manage deadlines in a fast-paced environment" means the ideal employees should make themselves available for a range of tasks that may or may not be directly related to the job title. Turnover rate for entry-level jobs is also high; some workers may move laterally to another job, and others may move upward to a junior management position. More likely than not, the ideal candidate should have had at least one internship at another media organization before being offered an entry-level job. What it means is that ideal employees should already have gained some on-job experience and have learned the culture of the trade. The industry is not interested in spending time to teach entry-level workers. The training responsibilities have been shifted to higher education institutions and the individual. This differs from media organizations that follow a Fordist mode of production. Promising graduates with no work experience are recruited for training. However, in countries where higher education is still a rarity, work experience may not matter to job prospects as much as the prestige of the university and students' grades in school.

The salary and benefits of Google software engineers may be the envy of both service workers and entry-level media workers, but their labor is also flexible. The competitive work environment at Google encourages employees to stay longer at the office or to bring work home. Google's "one day for research" policy allows employees to launch new projects that may become a company product (such as Google News) or the employees' own start-up companies. The one-day research policy is said to emulate the work life of professors at research institutions, but it may also ask employees to see their careers as a project that needs to be constantly improved. Michel Foucault coined the term "governmentality" to refer to modern individuals seeing themselves as projects that need to be constantly self-monitored and improved upon (see Li, 2007). In this way, Google workers are also flexible, because any job is only a phase in their career. The concept of "precarious labor" (Curtin & Sanson, 2016) points out the contingent nature of media work. Workers have to constantly develop two records: one to show their productivity to their organization and another to show other organizations how willing they are to develop their skills in case they lose their job.

Flexible workers contrast with the image of a breadwinner in the post–WWII era—an idealized male worker who puts in eight hours of work a day, five days a week in an office or a factory. This idealized male worker seems to belong to a bygone era, a character in 1960s television shows. Nowadays, putting in the hours and maintaining productivity are the minimum requirement for most jobs. In contrast, lifetime employment is much less common: workers not only work for more organizations in their lifetime, but they also change their career once or more. Even in Japan, the "salaryman" prototype (male workers who can expect a fixed career path in their lifelong employment) went away when the Japanese economy burst in the 1990s. With the growth of flexible labor, how can we understand labor in the so-called post-Fordist economy? In the following, we examine what is so "flexible" about labor by focusing on subjective labor, affective labor, and free labor.

Is Labor Objective or Subjective?

We argued in an earlier section that media economists see labor as something objective, because labor is a variable in both micro- and macroeconomic analysis. At a micro level, productive labor is essential to firms and industries. Industries that do not attract enough labor will shrink and labor cost will increase. In contrast, industries that attract too much labor will expand and labor costs will be driven down. In most advanced economies, there is less labor in the agricultural sector than in the service sector. At a macro level, the state has to ensure that the education system produces and trains appropriate labor so as to maintain a country's productivity. For example, countries with an aging population, such as Japan and China, will need to think about ways to maintain the same level of productivity. Some societies (such as Singapore) combat this problem by giving incentives to couples to have more children; others (Canada, US) have liberal immigration policies to attract young people from foreign countries to study there and work. In addition, some countries invest in training specific kinds of labor. As we covered in Chapter 5, "Politics," and Chapter 8, "Cultures," some governments (such as Ireland and Australia) highlight the economic importance of creative media industries and fund universities to train more workers for them. Other countries (such as the US) do not directly fund universities but prefer to have immigrant visas to attract educated workers to stay.

Unlike media economists, political economists do not accept that labor is *naturally* objective. Instead, they want to understand how labor was *made* objective. Marx wrote that wage is calculated from how much value of goods a worker produces. Because of this calculation, not only is labor power objectified, but time and value are objectified as well. During the Industrial Revolution, stories of exploited children and women were often used to illustrate the greed of capitalists. As a result, labor unions were later formed to fight for workers' rights, wages, and work conditions. Although unionized workers have been in decline since the 1970s, US media workers are more unionized than they are elsewhere. There are unions for both above-the-line workers (such as the Writers Guild of America, West; Directors Guild of America; and Producers Guild of America) and below-the-line workers (such as Motion Picture Sound Editors and Motion Picture Editors Guild). Labor unions carry out collective bargaining negotiations with major studios on behalf of members. For example, in 2007 and 2008, the Writers Guild of America (West and East) went on strike because major media companies did not pay writers residuals for DVD sales. Media companies argued that DVDs are just promotion for shows, so writers should not receive residuals for such sales. Writers went on strike to show the industry that if they stop working, there will not be any new shows. As a result, television stations had to rerun old television shows. Another issue that concerns labor unions is keeping jobs in a region. To labor unions, the worth of media workers can be reflected from the monetary value of media work in the local economy. In this way, labor unions reinforce the notion that labor is objective, because it is directly linked to the exchange value of media goods. Labor unions are suspicious of digital work, because it is almost impossible to organize freelance workers dispersed around the globe.

What is the problem of objectified labor? Marx (1844) believed that objectified labor stripped off workers' creativity. In addition, when the market privileges exchange value over use value, there would be commodity fetishism—that people would put more emphasis on how much something is worth rather than how useful something is (see Chapter 3 for the definition of "use value"). For example, media producers would focus on making shows with many viewers rather than shows that would make a positive social impact. Marx's (1844) view on objectified labor may not resonate with contemporary media workers for a few reasons: first, most media workers may identify themselves as creative workers rather than manual workers. Despite the pressure to produce goods that cater to consumers' tastes, most media workers would not think the production of media goods is as "soulless" as that of manufactured goods. Second, Marx may argue that media goods do not have any inherent use value because they do not sustain life. In fact, according to Marx, advertising and marketing workers are parasites who feed on the surplus value produced by productive labor. To this end, the concept of objective labor does not provide a full understanding of the complexities of media work in contemporary times, because labor and commodities are not qualitatively identical across industries. Therefore, we suggest in the following how the concepts of both subjective and objective labor are needed to understand flexible work, affective work, and free labor.

Global Free Agents

As we discussed in Chapter 2, the global production of media goods is characterized as post-Fordist. What this means is that the circulation of capital and labor is no longer localized; both now flow around the globe seeking maximum profits and minimum costs. Digitization enables media production to be done beyond a certain locale. While most print newspapers still occupy a production plant, many offices of online websites are actually done in the editors' homes. Similarly, media productions do not have to take place within a state or national boundary. They can be done anywhere in the world as long as there is a supply of appropriate labor: sometimes it is because labor cost is low, and sometimes it is because the labor force has specific skills.

What does flexible production mean to media workers? Media corporations do not seek long-term relationships with workers—they are ready to move productions to other places if labor is cheaper. In the same way, workers rarely pledge lifelong loyalty to one single company; they expect themselves to change jobs or even careers a few times. Shorter-term commitments to work have impacted workers' sense of agency as well: they are no longer employees for a company on a long-term basis, but free agents in a network of professionals. Some employers and employees foster an ideology of "free agents": that individuals can choose how to spend their time; that work autonomy is in the full control of the workers.

Students and graduates are asked to "network" because they may meet hiring managers (such as assistant directors on a film set or a human resource manager) in an informal setting. Being in a professional network also brings job opportunities, because media jobs are not always advertised in newspapers or online. Being a free agent has a price to pay, which is enduring unstable jobs and income. Recent graduates who work in the media industry have remarked how unstable work is: production assistants and game designers may work for 16 hours a day for two weeks before months of "in-between jobs"—a euphemism for unemployment. For jobs that offer a monthly salary, such as newscasters and advertising account executives, changing jobs is a better path to be promoted than waiting to be promoted in the same organization. For jobs such as newscasters and news producers, it may mean moving to another part of the country in order to be promoted.

Despite irregular work hours and unstable work, media programs across the globe are expanding and the number of enrolled students keeps rising. Why? When we ask our recent graduates why they are content with such work prospects, they cited some "magical" moments in their jobs: sometimes it is meeting a Hollywood star on a set, sometimes it is seeing their name online or in the credits, sometimes it is a dislike to wear suits. How do we understand these "incentives" in nonmonetary terms? On the one hand, scholars may criticize that media workers are under a false consciousness, that young people have been ideologically conditioned to self-exploit themselves. On the other hand, we should recognize workers' subjectivity, that they establish a sense of identity and social meaning through working in the media. "Incentives" such as self-affirmation and self-identification cannot be measured in monetary terms. While Marx suggested that workers could only have a sense of agency if they control the mode of production and labor, contemporary media workers may gain this sense of agency if they control how they make meaning in their lives, even if they do not control the mode of production.

Affective Labor

Another kind of labor that cannot be objectively measured is affective labor. Affective labor is defined as work that evokes feelings of emotions, care, and sentiment for others. Traditionally, women's work inside and outside the home involves affective labor: a mother is supposed to be caring and nurturing for family members; kindergarten teachers and caregivers are supposed to be understanding of children's needs and wants. Some media jobs also require affective labor. For example, production assistants and assistant directors have to deal with paperwork and scheduling, and women are perceived to be better at details and human relationships. Another affective labor example is "booth babe" (Huntemann, 2016)—promotional models at trade shows such as video game conventions. Apart from dressing in sexy outfits, they are also supposed to have a cheerful and sociable personality that is inviting to critics and other opinion makers.

Some forms of affective labor may have an anticapitalistic effect, because workers can exchange their time and labor with others' time and labor, thus bypassing capitalists as the middle person. For example, some co-ops in poor neighborhoods in both developed and developing countries facilitate labor exchange. Low-income immigrants from Central America who live in the San Fernando Valley in Los Angeles try to better their community by sharing skills (such as sewing, cooking, and teaching Spanish) in a barter economy (Perlman, 2010). For example, someone who knows how to do plumbing can fix others' sewage in exchange for a few hours of childcare. The emphasis on use value highlights how capitalist societies see money as a fetish, that money is the only reward for work. Another example of affective labor being anti-corporation is workers withholding their affective labor at strikes. For example, Cathay Pacific flight attendants refused to smile or serve alcohol to passengers to protest the company's refusal to raise pay ("Cathay Pacific crews," 2012). This case shows that affective labor is expected and taken for granted at some jobs, and women disproportionately provide affective labor for free.

However, Michael Hardt (1999) believes that most affective labor in capitalist societies does not liberate workers from a capitalist social relation. In fact, affective labor reinforces a capitalist class relation because affects are "manipulated" for exchange. This is the case of service work, where customers prefer a "personalized" and "customized" experience. For example, Disneyland policies stipulate how workers should provide a "friendly" and "helpful" experience for visitors. Disneyland employees wear nametags with only their first names; they are not allowed to say "no" to any questions or use "upsetting" words such as "vomit" and "death" in the park. Affective labor can also be found on digital sites that broker services. Sites such as TaskRabbit promote themselves as a digital neighborhood. Those who provide services such as assembling IKEA furniture or cleaning the house are like the neighbors whom one does not yet know. The sellers of services are not said to be freelance workers, but friendly people who love to help out.

Free Labor

Free labor is another kind of labor that cannot be objectively measured. Here we focus on three kinds of free labor: the first kind is unpaid internship at media organizations; the second kind is free labor spent on producing collective goods, such as free and open source software; the third kind is "playbor," free labor extracted from audience members when they watch advertisements on television and other media outlets. Unpaid work may challenge an economic assumption that individuals only work for concrete goals (such as money) and their own gains. However, the fact that people would work for free does not mean labor cannot be objectified. Political economists have effectively shown how capitalist media organizations exploit the labor of aspiring media professionals and media consumers.

Internship has become a popular type of learning in higher education. While some types of internship are paid, most in media organizations—especially the small ones—are not. Internship, along with fieldwork and service learning, is called "experiential learning" in which students learn through "reflection on doing." Some higher education institutions—particularly those in the US, Canada, and the Commonwealth system—give credits to students who undertake an internship. Why would universities be eager to provide free labor to media organizations? Why would students give their labor for free? As mentioned, higher education institutions are asked to train job-ready students. In order to attract high-quality students, higher education institutions need to advertise their internship programs. For example, the New England Center for Investigative Reporting at Boston University lists skills that interns learn, such as public records research, database analysis, and computer-assisted reporting. Undoubtedly, these skills are important to journalism students. However, why aren't students paid for their work? The supply-and-demand theory (see Chapter 3 for a definition) may explain this by an oversupply of labor in the journalism industry: when there are more workers to compete for fewer jobs, labor cost will be driven down. A survey conducted by the National Association of Colleges and Employers states that internships are imperative for a full-time job offer with higher compensation (National Association of College and Employers, 2014).

A flexible mode of production relies on low production cost, and free labor is a way to keep cost low. Therefore, interns are not necessarily students enrolled in a university program and internship duties are not necessarily conducive to learning. In 2012, two former interns who worked on the film *Black Swan* at Fox Searchlight (owned by the conglomerate News Corporation) successfully sued the company for exploiting their labor for free. Instead of gaining experience at film-making, they were asked to do clerical work, such as placing purchase orders and copying documents. One interesting thing about this lawsuit is that one of the interns was a 40-year-old insurance professional wishing for a career change. He testified in court that he was given the advice that an unpaid internship would help him get a foot in the door. However, after his internship, he said he:

> feels a big problem with unpaid internships is that they disrupt the labor market for entry-level workers by forcing people at the beginning of their careers to work for no pay and suppressing wages for people who have been on the job for several years.
>
> (Satran, 2012, para. 6)

This lawsuit shows that the film industry knowingly exploits free labor from workers—students or not—who have convinced themselves that they can work for no pay because they love the media. Whether this sense of love results in monetary gains or not, it is a form of subjective labor. Once again, internship is a less popular way to learn in countries where few attend university, because there is a supply shortage of specific types of workers.

Another kind of free labor that has attracted scholars' attention is free labor contributing towards collaborative online projects. The free and open source software movement is one of the most discussed cases among scholars. As we mentioned in Chapter 7, "Civil Societies," some founders of the free and open source movement have an anti-corporation mentality; they believe proprietary codes owned by corporations such as IBM and Apple stifle creativity. Privately owned codes can hardly be improved upon because the copyright owners are afraid that some would steal the code for their own gains. Linux, one of the most commonly used operating systems, is an open source code. Two implications of open source code are, first, anyone can download the source code and install it in a computer. Users can download updates of the code without having to pay for the upgrade. Second, anyone can write or edit the source code. Linux, then, is an ongoing collaborative online project that produces a common good. Surveys (Lakhani & Wolf, 2005) showed that participants are motivated by a few things to offer their labor for free: some are anti-corporation, and some believe in altruism; yet some want to establish a name in the community and see their work as a credential for career development. This form of labor is subjective because participants own their time, labor, and mode of production. They are likened to artisan producers, such as glass blowers and bakers in the preindustrial era. Unlike artisan producers of the old days, the collective outcome of this kind of free labor is a common good that is free to the community and the public. Online collaboration has attracted scholars' attention, and some (such as Benkler, 2006) claim that the Web has ushered in a new kind of economy: wealth is not about how much money and assets an individual owns, but how much knowledge the Web circulates. Although online collaborative projects seem to exemplify a different mode of economic production, free and open source participants tend to be educated men in developed countries. These participants may already have a source of income and have extra time and energy to spare on a collaborative project. For many workers, they are not able to participate in the community because their spare time and energy are spent on paid work that sustains life.

The last type of free labor is "playbor" (play and labor)—labor that is extracted from consumers when they watch advertisements on television or when they browse social media posts. Political economist Dallas Smythe wrote the provocative essay "Communications: Blindspot of Western Marxism" (1977) to argue that when television viewers watch advertisements, they are exchanging their time for free content. The workers sell their labor during the day to the owners of the mode of production and their time to advertisers by watching advertisements. Media economists call the media industry a dual product market: media organizations provide content to consumers, and they deliver consumers to advertisers. Smythe (1977) suggested that the content is nothing but "bait" to lure viewers to their television sets. In this argument, viewers' labor is seen as objective because their time spent on watching advertisements can be measured, and so is the amount of money advertisers spend on buying airtime.

In a digital media landscape, Smythe's argument has been revisited (see McGuigan & Manzerolle, 2014). How can we understand the behaviors of watching advertisements in a digital age? Viewers may be exposed to more advertisements, but they also have different ways to skip advertisements, such as prerecording shows and relying on on-demand media. Moreover, advertisements on Google and Facebook target a small segment of users, so there is hardly any mass audience on the search engine. Despite the new technologies, it does not mean "playbor" cannot be measured objectively; it only means the audience members cannot be sold as a "mass" from the media content providers to advertisers.

Terranova (2004) identified platform users as a new class. The analysis of Facebook users is not that simple, because advertisers and Facebook itself utilize users based not only on gender and age but also on class in the process of commodification (Jin, 2015). As Fuchs (2010) argues, "class relationships have become generalized. The production of surplus value and hence exploitation is not limited to wage-labor, but reaches society as a whole" (p. 188). In other words:

[P]lay labor (playbor) creates a data commodity that is sold to advertising clients as a commodity. They thereby obtain the possibility of presenting advertisements that are targeted to users' interests and online behavior. Targeted advertising is at the heart of the capital accumulation model of many corporate social media platforms.

(Fuchs & Sevignani, 2013, p. 237)

Case Study: Women Workers in the Industry

Media studies feminists such as Angela McRobbie (2004) and Rosalind Gill (2011) have pointed out the danger of post-feminist beliefs held by young women and the general population in some developed countries. Young women may convince themselves that academic attainments and career choices are results of individual excellence. Digital technology is also said to be a disruptive force in gender hierarchy. As the famous saying goes, "on the Internet, nobody knows you are a dog." Some expand the saying and argue that gender identity is irrelevant online. Post-feminist beliefs make women conveniently ignore the decades, if not centuries, of women's struggles for rights and gender equality. Post-feminist ideology is reinforced by the images of high-profile women executives in the technology sector, such as Sheryl Sandberg of Facebook and Marissa Mayer of Yahoo. These "poster girls" of the hi-tech industry tell young women that if they are smart and determined enough, they will be recognized in a male-dominated industry. What can aspiring female students expect as media workers? How can they know the status of women's employment in the industry? What resources and support can women workers expect in the industry?

Step 1: Gender Development Index

The first step for women students to know the work conditions of the industry is to investigate how women's lives differ from men's in their country. The United Nations Development Agency (UNDP) has published the Gender and Development Index (GDI) since 1995. The main three criteria to compare the lives of women and men are a long and healthy life, knowledge (average years of schooling and expected year of schooling), and standard of living (gross national income). While these three factors alone may not lead to a fulfilling and productive life, they may reflect a state's investment in girl children and how it values girl children in relation to boy children. The top 20 countries with "very high human development" index are, unsurprisingly, European and North American countries; the only exceptions are Japan, South Korea, and Hong Kong in Asia and Israel in the Middle East (Human Development Report Office, 2015). This may confirm a post-feminist belief that young women in some developed economies can fairly compete with their male counterparts in any industry.

In addition to GDI, data that give a holistic sense of gender equality are the ratio of female to male students in secondary and tertiary institutions; women's workplace participation; the age of women's first marriage; the age of women's first childbirth; the average number of children per woman; women's income in relation to men's; and women's poverty rate in relation to men's. It is assumed that if women receive more education, they are more likely to work outside home for pay. Also, if women are financially independent, they can have more decision-making power in the household, such as the number of children they wish to have. A country with a relatively high female workplace participation may mean female employment in the media industry is more or less accepted.

Step 2: Statistics on Employment in the Cultural and Media Sectors

Data that show men's and women's employment in the cultural and media sectors also reflect the work conditions of women media workers. In Chapter 4, "Economics," and Chapter 8, "Cultures," we review a number of regional and national agencies that collect such data. Some countries lump media sectors into the creative cultural sectors while some separate them. Big media, cultural, and technology companies also provide data on the gender ratios of female to male workers. However, one has to be cautious that these data may hide gender inequality, because women tend to occupy entry-level jobs, such as administrative assistant, rather than high-level executive positions. For example, Google stated that there are more than 10,000 women working in the company around the world (Google Diversity, n/a). However, it is unclear if women tend to work in more traditionally "feminine" positions, such as public relations, community relations, and marketing, rather than "masculine" ones, such as engineering and research and development.

One way to know what job titles women have in relation to men in a media organization is the list of credits. For example, print media such as newspapers and magazines usually have a page that lists the staff from the chief editor to editorial assistants. They are illustrative of gender equality in the newsroom: are all the senior positions occupied by one gender more than the other? Does one gender occupy certain desks? For example, men tend to work in hard news and investigative reporting while women tend to work in soft news and human interest stories. Credits of television shows and films are also sources that illustrate work distribution between the two genders.

It is of interest to know the ratio of women to men workers among above-the-line workers and below-the-line workers: do women tend to hold feminine positions, such as personal assistants, costume designers, and make-up artists? Do men tend to hold masculine positions, such as cinematographers, editors, electricians, and carpenters? One also has to bear in mind that the media and cultural industry encompasses many types of companies, from some that actively promote gender equality and inclusiveness (such as Google) to some that are known to be male-dominated and degrading to women (such as the pornographic media industry).

Step 3: Specific Gender Issues

Because of the large number of freelance, part-time, and temporary workers in the media industry, it is hard to know how women and men experience their work differently by merely looking at a media corporation's diversity policies. One can visit websites of workers' unions, professional groups, and trade groups to look at what issues are pertinent to women. As covered in earlier chapters, workers' unions negotiate with employers and trade groups about workers' rights and compensations. Professional groups aim to assist members with networking and professional development. Trade groups advocate for industry interests. Although they have different aims and serve different players in the industry, they may name gender equality and women's work conditions as an area of interest. More specifically, there are professional groups that are exclusively for women: not only do they provide mentorship to junior members, but they also have awards, competitions, and grants specifically for women in the field. One example is Women in Film and Video New England (WIFVNE) that "promotes positive images of women to the public, and works to empower women working in the industry to achieve their professional potential" (Women in Film & Video, n/a). Another one is the international nonprofit organization Women Who Code, which aims to inspire women, in particular young girls, to develop a technology career.

Conclusion

We began this chapter by looking at some job advertisements: the most desirable job claims to have the brightest people at the company, and the least desirable job looks for applicants with a pleasant manner and physical stamina. What should prospective media workers expect their profession to be? To answer this question, we first differentiate the term "professional" from "worker," then we look at how scholars and industries classify different types of media work. Like the concept of an economy, labor is both an objective and a subjective concept. Subjective labor includes flexible labor, affective labor, and free labor. We concluded the chapter by laying out how women workers can find out whether a media industry is women-friendly by looking at how the UN rates a country's gender development, how active the female workforce is in an industry, and how supportive professional women's groups are.

References

Benkler, Y. (2006). *The wealth of networks: How social production transforms markets and freedom.* New Haven, CT: Yale University Press.

Bulkeley, W. M. (2009, March 26). IBM to cut US jobs, expand in India. *Wall Street Journal.* Retrieved from www.wsj.com/articles/SB123799610 031239341

Cathay Pacific crews threaten "no-smile" strike. (2012, December 11). *The Telegraph.* Retrieved from www.telegraph.co.uk/finance/newsbysector/retailandconsumer/leisure/9737387/Cathay-Pacific-crews-threaten-no-smile-strike.html

Curtin, M., & Sanson, K. (Eds.). (2016) *Precarious creativity: Global media, local labor.* Berkeley, CA: University of California Press.

Evetts, J. (2014). The concept of professionalism: Professional work, professional practice and learning. In H. Gruber, S. Billett, & C. Harteis (Eds.), *International handbook of research in professional and practice-based learning* (pp. 29–56). Dordrecht, The Netherlands: Springer.

Fuchs, C. (2010). Labor in informational capitalism and on the Internet. *The Information Society, 26*(3), 179–196.

Fuchs, C. (2013). Theorising and analysing digital labor: From global value chains to modes of production. *The Political Economy of Communication, 2*(1), 3–27.

Fuchs, C. (2014). *Digital labor and Karl Marx.* New York: Routledge.

Fuchs, C., & Sevignani, S. (2013). What is digital labour? What is digital work? What's their difference? And why do these questions matter for understanding social media? *Triple C: Communication, Capitalism & Critique, 11*(2), 237–293.

Funari, V., & de la Torre, S. (Producers). (2006). *Maquilapolis.* San Francisco: Newsreel.

Gibson, C. (2016, November 4). Mila Kunis writes a livid letter about Hollywood sexism: "I'm done compromising." *Washington Post.* Retrieved from www.washingtonpost.com/news/arts-and-entertainment/wp/2016/11/04/mila-kunis-writes-a-livid-letter-about-hollywood-sexism-im-done-compromising/

Gill, R. (2011). Sexism reloaded, or it's time to get angry again! *Feminist Media Studies, 11*(1), 61–71.

Google Diversity. (n/a). *Fostering a fair and inclusive Google*. Retrieved from www.google.com/diversity/at-google.html

Hardt, M. (1999). Affective labour. *Boundary, 22*(2), 89–100.

Havens, T., & Lotz, A. (2012). *Understanding media industries*. New York: Oxford University Press.

Hesmondhalgh, D. (2010). User-generated content, free labour and the cultural industries. *Ephemera: Theory and Politics in Organization, 10*(3/4), 267–284.

Human Development Report Office. (2015). *Human development report 2015: Work for human development*. New York: UNDP.

Huntemann, N. (2016). Working the booth: Promotional models and the value of affective labor. In M. Banks, B. Conor & V. Mayer (Eds.), *Production studies, the sequel! Cultural studies of global media industries* (pp. 39–45). New York: Routledge.

Jin, D. Y. (2015). Critical analysis of user commodities as free labor in social networking sites: A case study of Cyworld. *Continuum, 29*(6), 938–950.

Johnson, J. (2011, February). 1 Million workers, 90 million iPhones. 17 suicides. *Wired*. Retrieved from www.wired.com/2011/02/ff_joelinchina/

Kneidel, S., & Kneidel, S. K. (2005). *Veggie revolution: Smart choices for a healthy body and a healthy planet*. Golden, Colorado: Fulcrum Publishing.

Lakhani, K. R., & Wolf, R. G. (2005). Why hackers do what they do: Understanding motivation and efforts in free/open source software projects. In J. Heller, B. Fitzgerald, S. A. Hissam & K. R. Lakhani (Eds.), *Perspectives on free and open source software* (pp. 279–296). Cambridge, MA: The MIT Press.

Li, T. M. (2007). *Governmentality. Anthropologica, 49*(2), 275–281.

Lobato, R., & Thomas, J. (2015). *The informal media economy*. Malden, MA: Polity.

Marx, K. (1844). *Economic and philosophic manuscripts of 1844*. Retrieved from https://www.marxists.org/archive/marx/works/download/pdf/Economic-Philosophic-Manuscripts-1844.pdf

Maxwell, R., & Miller, T. (2012). *Greening the media*. New York: Oxford University Press.

McGuigan, L. J., & Manzerolle, V. (Eds.). (2014). *The audience commodity in a digital era: Revisiting a critical theory of commercial media*. New York: Peter Lang.

McRobbie, A. (2004). Post-feminism and popular culture. *Feminist Media Studies, 4*(3), 255–264.

Miller, T., Govil, N., McMurria, J., Maxwell, R., & Wang, T. (2005). *Global Hollywood 2*. London: BFI.

National Association of Colleges and Employers. (2014, September). *The class of 2014 student survey*. Retrieved from http://career.sa.ucsb.edu/files/docs/handouts/2014-student-survey.pdf

New York University. (n/a). *Kanbar Institute of Film and Television: Undergraduate Film & Television*. Retrieved from http://tisch.nyu.edu/film-tv

Perlman, J. (2010). *Favela: Four decades of living on the edge in Rio de Janeiro*. New York: Oxford University Press.

Ross, A. (2004). *Low pay, high profile: The global push for fair labor*. New York: New Press.

Satran, J. (2012, August 24). "Black Swan" intern lawsuit proceeds, striking blow against unpaid labor in film. *Huffington Post*. Retrieved from www.huffingtonpost.com/2012/08/24/black-swan-intern-lawsuit_n_1828206.html

Schilling, M. (2012, January 28). Japanese companies outsourcing anime. *Variety*. Retrieved from http://variety.com/2012/digital/news/japanese-companies-outsourcing-anime-1118049388/

Scholz, T. (2017). *Uberworld and underpaid: How workers are disrupting the digital economy*. Cambridge: Polity.

Smith, S. L., Choueiti, M., & Pieper, K. (n/a). Race/ethnicity in 600 popular films: Examining on screen portrayals and behind the camera diversity. Retrieved from http://annenberg.usc.edu/sitecore/shell/Applications/Content%20Manager/~/media/MDSCI/Racial%20Inequality%20in%20Film%202007-2013%20Final.ashx?db=master&la=en&vs=1&ts=20140731T1347226383%20

Smythe, D. (1977). Communications: Blindspot of Western Marxism. *Canadian Journal of Political and Social Theory, 1*(3), 1–27.

So, G. (2016, August 14). Young actress benefit from ageism in the film industry, but it won't last forever. *Independent*. Retrieved from www.independent.co.uk/voices/ageism-sexism-film-industry-hollywood-anne-hathaway-maggie-gyllenhaal-a7189976.html

Solon, O. (2017, February 27). Scraping by on six figures? Tech workers feel poor in Silicon Valley's wealth bubble. *The Guardian*. Retrieved from www.theguardian.com/technology/2017/feb/27/silicon-aa-cost-of-living-crisis-has-americas-highest-paid-feeling-poor

Sutter, M., & Williams, A. (2014). Special report: Outsourcing 2.0. *Latin Trade*. Retrieved from http://latintrade.com/special-report-outsourcing-2-0/

Terranova, T. (2004). *Network culture: Politics for the information age*. New York: Pluto Press.

Universidad Nacional Autónoma de México. (n/a). *Centro Universitario de Estudio Cinematográficos*. Retrieved from www.cuec.unam.mx/

University of South California. (n/a). *USC cinematic arts*. Retrieved from http://cinema.usc.edu/production/index.cfm

Wasko, J., & Erickson, M. (Eds.). (2008) *Cross-border cultural production: Economic runaway or globalization?* Amherst, NY: Cambria.

Women in Film & Video New England. (n/a). Retrieved from http://womeninfilmvideo.org/

Conclusion

In the networked 21st century, media and culture—broadly encompassing newspaper, broadcasting, film, music, and gaming—as well as new media such as social networking sites and digital platforms—have substantially influenced people's daily activities. The media and cultural industries are able to have such an influence because they provide tools for users to enjoy. In addition, huge corporations in the industries also influence public opinion, because their CEOs and key personnel are seen as forward-thinking pioneers. In addition, these companies can use lobbying to influence policies. The media and cultural industries are no longer peripheral industries, as they were before. Economically, they are as important as energy and infrastructural industries that enhance national, and indeed, global economies.

As we have discussed throughout the book, the business of media has rapidly changed in the past two decades as a result of new media technologies and related media polices. This book has discussed the transformation of the business of media with the major characteristics mentioned above in mind. To begin with, we provide three different perspectives, namely, media economics, political economy, and production studies to study the industries by discussing the merits and shortcomings of each approach. Traditionally, media studies scholars have applied two approaches (media economics and political economy) to analyze the media industries. As Wasko and Meehan (2013) aptly put it:

> [T]he study of media industries has been relatively new; however, it has included research on the interconnected industries of telephony, radio, film, television, and journalism. Much of this work can be identified into two different perspectives: on the one hand, it celebrates the individuals, working cohorts, companies, and markets constituting the entertainment-information sector of the national and/or global economy; on the other hand, it contextualizes those individuals, working cohorts, companies, and markets within the ongoing development of capitalism. The celebratory approach has often been called media economics, whereas the contextual approach is generally called political economy of the media.
>
> (pp. 150–151)

Although these two approaches have been the most applied by scholars, several new approaches came out under diverse rubrics, including creative industries, convergence culture, production culture, production studies, cultural economy, and media industry studies. In other words, there are several emerging frameworks in analyzing the rapid and significant growth of the global media industries. Among these, we select one new approach—production studies—in order to provide diverse and different perspectives in understanding the media industries, and therefore, the business of media in the 21st century.

In our discussion of three major theoretical frameworks, none of them is privileged over the other two approaches, although we explained that the three approaches come from different traditions, and therefore, more advanced readers need to differentiate between them and explain the merits and shortcomings of each. We want readers to learn different approaches to understand the business of media. While some students prefer one approach to the other two, multiple perspectives certainly enable them to think about the business in a more complex way, which helps the innovative thinking essential for making better economic and business decisions. We are certain that understanding diverse perspectives will help students become critical content creators and well-informed consumers, because there is nothing absolute about how the business of media should be understood and run.

In Chapter 2, we cover the history of the study of media business; in Chapter 3, we cover theories and approaches to study the business of media. From Chapter 4 to Chapter 9, we introduce six lenses (economies, politics, technologies, civil societies, cultures, and labor) through which readers can understand the business of media. By developing issues related to the lenses, we explained what the lenses are and why they shed a new light on understanding the business of media. Unlike popular books about the media business that seem to emphasize money and fame, we explain that economic and business decisions are not always about money. Politics, technologies, and cultures affect economic and business decisions as well.

This book also presents case studies to conclude the six chapters on lenses. We show how the concepts and terms can be applied to real-world examples. We also incorporate examples outside the US and Europe, because we believe students learn best when they draw on their knowledge in the local context. Drawing on local examples aids in comprehending the complicated power relations between global and local forces, between the "West" and "rest." The influence from powerful corporations is uneven. In the realm of popular culture, for example, the American media industry has been powerful enough to export Hollywood films and popular music to East Asia since the 1960s. However, some American media and cultural products (such as magazines) remain obscure in the East Asian markets. In the business of technologies, such as mobile phones, East Asia was more advanced than the US before the launch of iPhone in 2007. In fact, the Japanese government intentionally developed itself to be the global mobile technology leader in the 1990s. Therefore, it is wrong to assume that the US industry overwhelmingly dominates the media industries of other countries.

Regardless of the fact that the US has continued to dominate the global cultural and media markets in general, some countries have strongly tried to protect their media and cultural markets. Unlike the laissez-faire market system in North America, governments such as South Korea and Japan often intervene in the markets. For example, after WWII, the Japanese government designated that the audiovisual equipment industry be bolstered. As a result, several corporations, such as Sony and Panasonic, became well-known brands beyond East Asia. The Korean government has also continued to support the cultural industries, and therefore the government has worked with the private cultural industries to create the Korean Wave phenomenon since the late 1990s. We illustrated these power relations by giving examples from North America, Africa, Europe, Latin America, and the Middle East, as well as Asia. As such, we emphasize that readers need to pay attention to the examples of media business from different regions of the world. Many students may plan to work in a specific region as an entry-level writer, producer, and creator; however, there are more opportunities for them to work overseas as they advance in their careers, and this is particularly the case if they work for any transnational media corporation.

Eventually, we hope that this book helps readers envision themselves to be entry-level media workers and later media leaders or scholars. Although this book does not provide insider tips on how to succeed in the industry, we believe that students could better position themselves in the job market by understanding how their future employment is contingent upon a number of factors, such as politics and technologies. Therefore, we ask readers to look at media and cultural industries as interlocking systems. While students may assume a particular title (such as movie director) in a media company, the company itself may have business interests in other media industries or even other sectors. A broader scope of knowledge enables workers to know how the company runs as a whole. Moreover, the digitization of production asks practitioners to pick up more roles than before. This means that the student readers of the book who plan to work in the media and cultural industries need to comprehend the convergence of old media and new media, which would be a critical asset for their future career, as well as studies.

More specifically, we focused on the transformation of the business of media as a result of the emergence of digital technologies. Digital technologies and/or platform technologies, including social media platforms, offer users more choices to consume cultural products. Because of the expansion of distribution options in the midst of the growth of digital platforms, traditional media companies such as broadcasting stations and film studios have been exploring different ways to deliver content. Consequently, people may not even go to the theater to watch films anymore, because they exclusively rely on user-generated content platforms like YouTube. Only a decade ago, people had to buy DVDs, CDs, and cassette tapes in order to enjoy popular culture. In the platform era, electronic hardware is less tied to software, thus allowing for consumers to choose how to enjoy popular culture (Jin & Yoon, 2016).

We have explained the massive influences of digital technologies on the transformation of the media industries. Before the media and technological convergence, media corporations had their own unique areas that tied to specific "media": Walt Disney focused on theme parks and movies, News Corporation was a newspaper company, and Time was a magazine company. As a result of deregulation, these companies developed into mega media giants that own companies across media.

However, new technologies did challenge media corporations to think differently about how to capture the Internet as a major engine for growth. Traditional media industry (like broadcasting and film) ventured into the Internet market because they believed the integration would aid the growth. The rapid growth of social media and smartphone technologies continue prodding media corporations to pursue an integration of content with digital media technologies (Jin, 2013).

The media industries have experienced a substantial transformation as a result of the emergence of digital and/or social media industries, as well as digital platform technologies. Since Google bought YouTube in 2006, several media corporations have pursued their media convergence by acquiring new media corporations. For example, Facebook bought WhatsApp—a free mobile messenger—and Instagram. However, not all acquisition was successful; News Corporation's deal with Myspace was soon proven unwise. The rapid growth of these new technologies and media convergence have changed the landscape of global media industries. According to *Forbes* (La, 2015), as of May of 2015, the world's largest ten media corporations were: Comcast (now ComcastUniversal), Walt Disney, 21st Century Fox, Time Warner, Time Warner Cable, DIRECTV, WPP, CBS, Viacom, and British Sky Broadcasting. Another list compiled by *Business Insider* also included platform companies such as Alphabet (the parent company of Google), Facebook, and Baidu of China (O'Reilly, 2016). Global media corporations have rapidly acquired other media corporations—this is true in both Western and non-Western countries. The media and cultural industries have been structurally altered in the 21st century as a result of major media and cultural industries corporations employing convergence or de-convergence business models (Jin, 2013).

While it is easy to use technology to explain the change in the industries, we also include several key issues to explain shifting cultural policies. Neoliberalism and globalization are two such issues.

Some scholars coined the term "neoliberal globalization" to emphasize the reduction of the public sector to guarantee maximum profits for the private sectors, which are controlled by global corporations and their local affiliates. When policy makers operate with a neoliberal globalization mentality, they develop business-friendly policies that emphasize deregulation and liberalization/privatization. Deregulation leads to policies that stipulate that one owner can own more companies within and across sectors. Liberalization/privatization means previously state-owned industries, such as telecommunications, have been sold to private business. Therefore, we examined in Chapter 5, "Politics," whether the nation-state in the neoliberal globalization era continues its role as a meaningful political body to deal with private industries.

Finally, we explore how digital technologies have brought along a different understanding of media labor. The concept of "prosumers" is introduced to describe the large-scale change as a result of technologies. In an analog era, only media workers employed by organizations produced media content (such as news, films, dramas, music, and games). Because different technologies required different training, media workers were highly specialized as well: those who wrote news stories did not typeset, and those who operated a camera did not promote the production. However, the emergence of new media, such as social media platforms, enables consumers to produce media content. Technologies blur the boundary between who produces the content, who invents the technologies, and who distributes the content. For example, many college students create their own short video clips and upload them on YouTube, so that they as producers are also consumers who enjoy this content. At the same time, new media technologies, such as robots and artificial intelligence (AI), gradually replace traditional media and media works. New media, in this regard, play as a double-edged sword. New media technologies have jeopardized the livelihood of media workers in a new media environment.

Producers and consumers are equally important in the media industries; therefore, it is critical for readers to understand their roles in the business of media. Media consumers are presented with choices: whether you should pay for the products; which platform you choose to enjoy the products; and what alternative products and platforms exist. Media producers have to know their consumers in order to identify which major messages to deliver, what subjects to include, and the most appropriate methods of presentation. As much as media consumers are making economic decisions, media producers make conscious business decisions of how their products can be distributed. Indeed, this book is written to help readers answer the set of questions about economic and business decisions. These questions help them move away from a media consumer to a media producer position by considering what questions media producers ask when they engage in the business. Students must understand this new milieu and properly prepare for the changing patterns in the media market.

In the near future, we may expect to see further developments in new media technologies. Several platform developers continue to create cutting-edge tools and platforms, such as using AI and algorithms to analyze big data. News agencies have also utilized robots to write stories. In some areas like baseball games and financial markets, robots are gradually replacing human reporters. While we do not expect to see the total replacement of human beings by robots and AI, these new phenomena certainly alert us to the future of the business. In other words, the milieu surrounding the business of media will rapidly change, and therefore, readers of the book may need to expect these changes by learning diverse perspectives. Understanding diverse perspectives would provide better positions for readers to prepare for their jobs (whether as future practitioners or scholars), and therefore, eventually, the shifting environment surrounding the business of media.

References

Jin, D. Y. (2013). *De-convergence of the global media industries*. London: Routledge.

Jin, D. Y., & Yoon, K. (2016). The social mediascape of transnational Korean pop culture: *Hallyu 2.0* as spreadable media practice. *New Media and Society*, *18*(7), 1277–1292.

La, V. (2015, May 22). The world's largest media companies of 2015. *Forbes*. Retrieved from www.forbes.com/sites/vannale/2015/05/22/the-worlds-largest-media-companies-of-2015/#246c9d994161

O'Reilly, L. (2016, May 31). The 30 biggest media companies in the world. *Business Insider*. Retrieved from www.businessinsider.com/the-30-biggest-media-owners-in-the-world-2016-5/#30-time-inc—287-billion-in-media-revenue-1

Wasko, J., & Meehan, E. R. (2013). Critical crossroads or parallel routes? Political economy and new approaches to studying media industries and cultural products. *Cinema Journal*, *52*(3), 150–157.

Index